Urban Planning in India

Urban Planning in India

AMIYA KUMAR DAS

RAWAT PUBLICATIONS

Jaipur • New Delhi • Bangalore • Mumbai • Hyderabad • Guwahati

ISBN 81-316-0094-7

Published by
Prem Rawat for **Rawat Publications**
Satyam Apts, Sector 3, Jawahar Nagar, Jaipur 302 004 (India)
Phone: 0141 265 1748 / 7006 Fax: 0141 265 1748
E-mail: info@rawatbooks.com
Website: www.rawatbooks.com

New Delhi Office
4858/24, Ansari Road, Daryaganj, New Delhi 110 002
Phone: 011 2326 3290

Also at Bangalore, Mumbai, Hyderabad and Guwahati

Typeset by Rawat Computers, Jaipur
Printed at Chaman Enterprises, New Delhi

Contents

Preface

I am an agitator, a minority. The failure of planning in Assam, where I worked for two years, has frustrated and haunted me. My personal conviction is that planning will improve with the understanding of city planning by the citizens, legislators, administrators, technocrats, and planners. This conviction is my driving force in writing this book.

My area of concern is urban planning. My efforts in this book are intended to motivate readers to create a better living environment for all – urban and rural, rich and poor. The purpose of this book is public education in city planning. After retirement I am indulging in my thoughts which have accumulated over the years on city planning.

In a small volume like this, it is an arduous task to explain the many dimensions of urban planning including historical background, the influence of inventions and the industrial revolution, urban sociology, environmental concerns, public health, philosophies, theories, principles, practices, urban planning laws, the future of urbanization, etc. This book is like an elephant in a vase. It is something like Shankardev's condensation of the *Bhagavad Gita* into *Gunamala* (*bhurukat hati bharowa*).

Urban planning is not a pure science like mathematics, physics, chemistry, or biology. It is a social science. There are many variable conditions such as economy, technology, environment, political idealisms, and human behavior which influence urban planning. These conditions are not predictable in the long term. Yet there are certain evolving facts, principles, theories, experiences, laws, and understandings on which urban planning is based.

This book is an invitation to the urban and rural planning universe, to those who develop cities and those who inhabit them. I hope that readers will become familiar with the basic thoughts of city and rural planning, emerge as active participants in the planning and implementation process, and evolve into activists for a better urban and rural development and environment. I will consider this book a partial success if it can provoke the thoughts and responses of citizens and their governments about the urban and rural environment they live in. Intelligent public participation is an obligatory civic duty. Readers can participate intelligently by keeping up with the current explosion of knowledge, which is happening in every field of knowledge, and in this case advancement in urban and rural planning thoughts.

In the race towards progress, the countries, states, and communities that react slowly or never react will fall behind. This book is to motivate better planning and plan execution such that we do not fall behind.

Acknowledgement

I am grateful to the persons who helped me during the preparation of this book and in publication.

Ananta Nath reviewed the chapters on drainage and flood control and suggested valuable input. Tejaswi Tharakabhushanam helped me in preparing graphics. Dr. Rathin Sarma and his associates provided the GIS maps for Guwahati as well as additional support. My wife Reeta and daughters Roopa and Smita reviewed the text, made graphics, and encouraged me. I am also thankful to Mr. Pranit Rawat of Rawat Publications for helpful suggestions in forming the book for publication.

Introduction

The purpose of this book is to impart basic information on urban planning to the citizens who are interested in a better community; legislators and administrators who make decisions on urban planning; technocrats who often perform technical tasks effecting urban planning; and planners and would be planners who pursue a career in urban planning. This book is intended to provide a total picture of major aspects in urban planning from beginning to end. However, it does not include technical materials such as analytical methods, statistical models, etc. I hope that the readers will be better acquainted with the process of urban planning, plan implementation and problems solving. Continuing education in the field is essential.

It is imperative that problems should be detected and remedial actions taken in the early stages of any problem. If urban planning problems are inadequately understood, the solutions may also turn out to be inadequate and possibly have unintended adverse effects. All good public policy decisions will come from good intentions and good understanding of the planning laws, solutions to problems, planning process, plan implementation, and financial mechanisms. Elected representatives and administrators have the power to make public decisions. A determined leadership is needed at both the government level and the administrative level. If these representatives and administrators are concerned with personal gain, or are prejudiced on issues, or are incompetent, no public good is done. The Government also ignores expert advice because of preoccupation with politics. A silent citizenry would not get what they want. "Elections are one alternative, but the damage is usually done by the time the incompetents and rascals are thrown out."[1] However, there is no assurance that a better governing body will be elected next time. Good governance is precious and lasting. Moreover the tenure of elected representatives is temporary. The administrators come and go – they are transferred or retire before or after they learn about planning of the community. As a result, the legislators and the administrators do not have long-term power and commitments. However, the citizens are permanent residents in the community. Therefore, interested and devoted citizens must continue the mission for a better community by pursuing the goals and objectives of growth and development in both urban and rural areas. Citizen participation is very important. The democratic process implies that citizens have a responsibility to advocate for improved living conditions made possible through urban planning. Expert help is available. When the citizens, municipal and state government are in unison, good things will happen.

The western world has gone through the process of urbanization, success and failure. From their experience we can learn and use the knowledge to our advantage. Therefore, many discussions in this book will be based on western urban planning. We also need to include Indian political process, social values, proven methods and planning process.

Now we move on to the contents of this book and give a summary. Chapters 1 through 9 impart an overall knowledge in urban planning. Chapters 10 through 13 are case studies on Assam, why planning failed in Assam and what can be done.

Chapter 1: A Brief History of City Building. This gives us an understanding of gradual development of cities and their planning. There are six periods of city development: ancient, classic, medieval, neo-classic, colonial and industrial, and modern. Ancient cities developed more than five thousand years ago in the great river valleys because of availability of water, fertile land, and water transportation. The cities were small and the buildings were built with reeds, wood, and sundry bricks. The village chiefs gained power and elevated themselves to rulers and kings. They fought for power, possessions and territory. Since then inventions, defense and warfare, economic needs, social and political process transformed civilization, architecture, and the cities to the current state.

In the classical period, which started in about 5th century B.C., Athens, Alexandria, and Roman cities were built. Fortresses and buildings inside were built with stones. The cities were small and could accommodate royal palaces, garrisons, a granary, and housing for the aristocrats. As the kings gained more power, fortresses were made bigger, civilization advanced; agoras, markets, religious buildings, amphitheaters, museums, opera halls, gardens, fountains etc were added. Architects designed ornate buildings for the glory of the rulers. The common people lived outside the fortresses. The classic period ended when the Roman Empire crumbled. Barbaric rulers started city-states and wars among feudal lords began. The Dark Ages continued for about five hundred years.

The Medieval period (6th to 14th century) overlapped with the Dark Ages. This period was dominated with warfare and strategic sites on hilltops with fortifications.

Gothic buildings with plazas were built and cities were very small. There were no water supply and sewage systems. Streets were narrow and made for pedestrians only.

Neo-classic cities started during the 14th century. Large wooden ships increased world travel and trade. Merchants gained economic power, power of feudal lords declined, military aggression diminished, and there was rise of nationalism. The invention of gunpowder in the 15th century made long-range artillery possible and the fortress became useless. Fortress walls came down and the cities expanded in unconfined space. An age of monument building and wide vistas started.

Colonial and industrial cities were built during 15th and 20th century. Mariner's compass aided explorers to find the Americas and new places in the old continents. Powerful nations started colonies. French and Italian architects and planners planned many cities for colonial powers. Gridiron street patterns were used. Industrial cities first started in England in the 18th century and spread throughout the world. There were mass migrations of people from rural areas to the industrial cities. They lacked adequate housing, water supply, sanitation, light, air and ventilation. They were overcrowded. Under such conditions, diseases such as typhus, cholera, yellow fever, tuberculosis, and plague flourished. The loss of life prompted urban planning, housing, distribution of purified water, sewer disposal, garbage collection, electricity, and communication. Sanitary reform and planning legislation began in Great Britain when the Public Health Act of 1848 was passed.

Many great cities were reconstructed after fire, earthquake, war, and for congestion. Fires in London and Chicago destroyed most of these cities; hundreds of people died, homes and businesses were destroyed. The cities were redesigned and stricter building codes were adopted. The great earthquake of 1906 destroyed San Francisco and earthquake resistant constructions were introduced. In the Second World War many cities in England, Germany, Poland, Russia, and Japan were destroyed. This created an opportunity to redesign and reconstruct the cities using modern planning concepts. Because of congestion and political reasons, most of Paris was reconstructed with wide boulevards in the 1850s.

In the later part of the 19th century, modern city developments started. William Lever built his industrial complex with the concept called "prosperity sharing" by building 1,000 housing units and community facilities for his workers in 1889. Patrick Geddes, in 1892, advocated integration of physical planning with social and economic improvements. Ebenezer Howard came up with the idea of Garden Cities in England in 1898. His concept was integration of urban development with rural settings. The concept of Garden City had widespread acceptance. Thirty-four new British towns were built using this concept. Garden City and greenbelt idea spread rapidly to Sweden, Finland, Germany, Russia, France, United States, Japan and other countries.

Great Britain was serious about improving housing and urban conditions, and passed a series of legislations. The Housing and Town Planning Act of 1909 authorized local jurisdictions to plan on their own. In 1927, the Greater London Regional Planning Committee was created. The Town and Country Planning Act of 1932 extended the responsibility of local authorities to include urban and rural land and preservation of historic buildings and natural landscape. The Ribbon Development Act of 1935 regulated space along highways. In 1940 the Barlow Commission Report recommended: restriction of industrial development in London, distribution of industry and population to regional centers, redevelopment of congested areas, and comprehensive legislation. The Green Belt Act of 1938 authorized money to local authorities to purchase land for greenbelt. The New Towns Act of 1946 gave authority to build new towns.

Capital cities that were built on virgin land in the 20th century include: New Delhi, Chandigarh, Islamabad, Canberra, and Brasilia. All these plans were conceived with space organization, functionality, and efficiency just like in architecture. Monumentality and gridiron pattern of streets did not dominate the designs. Each of them had some influence of the garden city in the organization of space.

Chapter 2: Development of Modern Urban Planning. Urban planning developed from the colonial and industrial ages to the modern age through scientific and technological inventions, art and architectural movements, social reforms, emergence of planning laws, urban growth management, ecological and environmental awareness, changing emphasis in planning, and development of new planning tools.

The scientific and technological inventions that influenced urban planning are: the steam engine for moving people and goods, mass production of steel, cement and concrete, and method of structural calculations. With lighter and stronger construction high rise buildings became possible and economical. Massive stone buildings became obsolete. If current research into the production of liquefied hydrogen gas from water is successful in the future, the global energy problem will be solved and it will have great impact on the economy, politics, and urbanization.

Impressionist paintings depicted openness, gardens and a romantic environment. Architecture rejected ornamentation; new forms emerged based on new materials; 'form follows function' dictum changed architectural space organization and new forms emerged. Architects started designing functional spaces in the buildings and the form of the buildings became secondary. Urban space design also changed under the influence of painting and architecture.

Public health, public safety, and public welfare are the purpose of planning. These words found new definitions and the purpose of planning also changed. Public health used to be defined as a medical model – absence of disease or infirmity. A social model defines health as a state of complete physical, mental, and social well-being and not merely the absence of disease and infirmity. This model also considers environmental pollution and the loss of trees which lead to a decrease in oxygen supply. Public safety means physical safety. It is now accepted that physical design affects behavior. The urban space can be made safer by physical design, lighting and clean environment. Public welfare means public well-being. Provisions for health services, schools, libraries, parks and recreational facilities, play fields, post offices, communities meeting spaces, shopping, etc. are for public welfare.

The Master Plan concept is outdated. The new concepts are comprehensive planning, urban growth management, and sustainable community planning. Plans in India tend to emphasize physical plans without policy plans. Policy plans emphasize policies or rules including goals and objectives to accomplish physical plans.

Land developments have environmental consequences such as destruction of forest, erosion, loss of animal habitat, drainage problems, air pollution, water contamination, etc. Therefore, probable environmental consequences must be addressed and remedial measures must be taken.

Politicians and administrators come and go, but residents do not go. Therefore, the citizens must participate in the planning and plan implementation process. It is after all their community. The planning process is complex. This book is intended to familiarise citizens with the planning process.

There are innovative planning tools such as: (a) Geographic Information System (GIS) – Aerial photos are taken from satellite of any geographic area required. From these maps location, size, and topological and contour data can be obtained and used very correctly in urban planning. This eliminates expensive and time consuming survey work. (b) Transfer of Development Rights (TDR) – Every land has a certain capacity to develop as per zoning and density restrictions. If a land owner decides not to develop the land to the fullest extent, the owner may sell the unused development portion of right. TDR is helpful in the preservation of historic and religious sites. (c) Planned Unit Development (PUD) – It is an alternative to traditional construction on individual lots. Several lots can be combined as one site and units can be constructed on zero lot line (removing the need for space between units) and the open space can be kept together and landscaped. It is economical since road length, water and sewer line lengths can be reduced. (d) Development of Regional Impact (DRI) – Large developments impact the surrounding areas, environment and infrastructure. Therefore DRI projects must mitigate the impact. (e) Public Land Banking – The city plan implementation authority may acquire all land for future development and have a land bank. This gives better opportunity for organized development and simpler than planning in private land. Inflation of land price can also be controlled. (f) Timing Development – All the land in the planning area cannot develop simultaneously and infrastructure cannot be provided for all land at the same time. Therefore, developments are done in phases. This also creates an opportunity to adjust to a long term development plan.

Chapter 3: The General Plan Preparation. First plan how to prepare the General Plan. Next follow planning analysis of current situations. Thereafter, prepare physical planning and community development elements and their vision, goals, objectives, and policies. Planning elements include: environmental protection, historic preservation, housing, office, wholesale and retail business, industrial and economic developments, and transportation. Municipal and other governmental service elements include: water supply, sewerage, solid disposal, stormwater and drainage, electricity, civic facilities, public health protection, public safety, post office, property identification and postal address. The plan also must address public participation, intra-governmental coordination, and inter-governmental coordination. A set of drawings must be prepared for future land use and transportation. Land use plans should not be confused with zoning plans and regulations. Land use needs may change in the future and must be monitored and revised every five years.

Chapter 4: The Planning Agency: Organization and Structure. City plan can be prepared by a state planning agency, by a local government planning agency, and in some cases by an independent planning commission. In the western world, state planning agency never plans but regulates state planning law, offers technical help to the local planning agencies, and recommends changes to the planning law. Functions of planning agencies are also discussed in this chapter. Leadership and perseverance are very important in planning.

Chapter 5: Plan Implementation. The success of building a beautiful and functional city depends on the formulation and implementation of major components: zoning ordinance, subdivision regulation, building codes, urban renewal, and infrastructure development. Zoning and subdivision regulation are the most misunderstood components. People confuse zoning with a land use map. A Land use map is a future land use idea. Zoning regulations create restrictions according to land use characteristics. There are innovative zoning techniques. Subdivision does not mean just dividing a parcel of land, but planning a large land area or a sector and dividing it into lots for different uses. Building codes include: building construction, plumbing, electrical, gas, and mechanical which includes air conditioning and household appliances. Building code is created for public safety.

Primary infrastructure includes roads, water supply, sewers, drainage, solid waste collection and disposal, and communication. Others include: facilities for employment, education, civic functions, and health. The city must maintain an inventory of infrastructure, monitor conditions for improvements, coordinate with providers, and look for financial resources. The city must have projects, planning, programming, and budgeting for a capital improvement program.

Chapter 6: Budgeting and Finance. The prospect of implementing plans increases with budgeting and financing of planning activities. Most plans fail for lack of budgeting and financing. Municipal revenue cannot support large scale improvements. There are international organizations such as USAID, World Bank, and Asia Development Bank. These organizations give long term loans at low interest rates to credit worthy municipalities. The state and national governments must give guarantees for repayment. The other option is privatization of projects. The private organizations must be able to recover their cost and make a profit by charging fees to the consumers. There are consultants who will prepare project plans, estimate costs, and write grant applications. The municipality must be fully committed and must have strict anti-corruption measures.

Chapter 7: Planning Law: Legal Basis of Planning. The Constitution of India provides power, authority, and responsibility of municipalities in Article 243W. The legislature of a state may endow such power to the municipalities. State planning laws must define planning functions, intent of planning, perimeters of planning, legal authority of planning agencies, and the constitution of planning agencies, and provide funding provisions.

If the planning law is inadequate, the planning approach will fail. It need to be reviewed periodically, say every five years, to adjust to the latest planning concepts and needs. There are issues such as property rights within the context of social planning, land use restrictions, taking land for public purpose, physical planning on developable land, and harmful laws that have encouraged slums or made plan implementation difficult.

Chapter 8: India's Housing Crisis. The housing crisis in India is frightening. In 2001, there was a housing shortage of 19.40 million units. In Greater Mumbai 54 percent of the population live in slums. In 27 cities of over one million population, 24.1 percent are slum dwellers.

The major obstacles in housing are: (1) Developed lots with infrastructure are in extremely short supply and very expensive. (2) Developable lands are in the hands of small landholders and therefore, difficult to acquire and plan. (3) India is not encouraging private large-scale developers. Only housing development authorities, with bureaucracies and without motivation for cost reduction and profit, are encouraged. (4) Long term home mortgage loans are not available at a fair interest rate. (5) Home construction for sale and rental apartment construction has not developed and been recognized as an industry. (6) Rental housing is in extremely short supply. Because of unfair rent control laws and tenant eviction difficulties, private landlords are hesitant to rent property. (7) Innovative technologies in construction methods and new building materials can reduce construction costs and construction time but have not been used or developed.

Chapter 9: The Future of Urbanization in India. According to the 2001 census, 30 percent of India's population lived in urban areas. This percentage is expected gradually to increase to 70 percent by the middle of the 21st century. The urban population growth will take place in existing urban areas, increasing the size of small cities or in new cities created for industrial and economic development. There should be deliberate decisions on where to direct the population in a planned manner.

Existing cities with populations over one million should be discouraged from further growth by denying further economic opportunities. Smaller cities should be planned to take additional economic opportunities and employments. New towns should be planned for economic growth and urbanization. Central place theory should be applied for balanced economic and urban development throughout the country. Regional planning and state land use planning must be encouraged. Mahatma Gandhi's desire to take employment to the people should be fulfilled. There will be fewer slums in our cities if cities are spread out and economic development is distributed. Big metropolitan areas are difficult and expensive to manage.

An economic boom in India has started and it will continue if the government improves infrastructure and decreases red tape. Global entrepreneurs are looking to use cheaper labor costs for manufacturing and to market consumer products in the vast Indian market.

The following four chapters are case studies in Assam. This will give an account of failures in planning and implementation. Some suggestions are made on drainage and flood control.

Chapter 10: An Evaluation of Guwahati Master Plan: A Sad Story of Missed Opportunities. The Assam Town and Country Planning Act were passed in 1959 when the population of Guwahati was just below 100,000. The Act was timely for a growing city but the plan and enforcement were poor. The Act is also poorly written and has not been amended within the main frame of the Act. Out of 90 Sections in the Act, only one section is devoted to the contents of the master plan and one section to the implementation of the plan. The guidelines are not specific. Implementation of the development scheme provision would have given some orderly development in Guwahati, but the development authority totally ignored this provision. There was no oversight by the state government. It also overlooked this provision and other aspects of planning and implementation. The development authority gave building permits to build 12' wide roads, which lack the space necessary for two cars to pass. The authority also permitted building on any land irrespective of zoning regulations, just by taking thousands of affidavits agreeing to break down the buildings when asked by the authority. The planning result is dismal. The population of the Guwahati Metropolitan Area increased to 890,773 in 2001. The city has become extremely congested and dysfunctional.

Chapter 11: Urban Renewal and Infrastructure Improvement. Urban renewal is important because cities develop, mature, and decay over years. Certain land uses and buildings are no longer suitable and must be demolished and rebuilt. Sometimes the existing land use is no longer appropriate. The buildings may be dilapidated or the building floor space is small in a high land value location. By relocating government offices and living quarters and factories, these sites may become available for urban renewal.

For example, the old jail is in the center of Guwahati. It is obsolete and occupying a large piece of valuable land. This site is fit for urban renewal. Ideas for urban renewal on this site are discussed here.

Chapter 12: Solutions to Drainage Problems in Guwahati. Drainage problems pose serious health risks in Guwahati. Rainwater runoff mixed with contaminated water from drains and septic tank effluents, flood homes and streets during monsoon. This spreads waterborne diseases and damages property.

There are many reasons for flooding. Natural drains and wetlands are no more. Those are land filled for construction. The little drains are filled with silts from the hills. There are no stormwater retention ponds. About nine square miles of Guwahati is below the highest flood level of the river Brahmaputra. The Bahini River and the Bharalu River also pass through Guwahati. These rivers bring more water in addition to rainwater to Guwahati.

A comprehensive stormwater management plan is required. Regulatory control is required to stop construction on wetlands, to reduce lot coverage, and to create water holding ponds. It is necessary to follow the principle that the volume and rate of post land development runoff from a site should not exceed the site's pre-development volume and rate of runoff. The wetlands must be preserved. Stormwater from the hills should be contained in artificial lakes. Large underground drains must be constructed.

Chapter 13: Managing Flood with Conservation of Flood Water in Lakes and Wetlands. Assam has attempted to control flood water since the 1950s without success. The current strategy has been to drain flood water by building embankments along all tributaries and the Brahmaputra River. It is not working. Environmental consequences are disastrous. Silt is deposited in river bottoms and river beds have become shallow and lost water carrying capacity. Water overflows over the embankments and create havoc. This strategy dried out the natural lakes and wetlands. The fish and bird population diminished. The farm land is no longer made fertile by silt. There is loss of cultural heritage, ecological disaster, and economic loss to the rural population. The solution is to cooperate with nature. Flood water must be conserved in natural lakes and wetlands. Humans must recognize that we have limited control over nature.

Note

1. E.S. Quade, *Analysis for Public Decisions*, American Elsevier Publishing Co., New York, 1976.

1

A Brief History of City Building

City developments may be divided into six periods: ancient, classic, medieval, neo-classic, colonial and industrial, and modern. There are overlaps or transition years between periods. The development process of city planning is same as in other fields of discipline: progressive thinking, advancements in science and technology, social reforms, understanding of ecology, political process, economics, and justice. City planning is an interdisciplinary field and hence very complex.

ANCIENT CITIES

Early civilizations developed in the great river valleys: the Nile, the Tigris-Euphrates, the Indus, and the Hwang Ho. The ancient towns developed in more than five thousand years ago at Ur, Harappa, Mohenjo-Daro, Thebes, Uaxactrun, Nippur, Uruk, Heliopolis, Babylon, Jerusalem, Assur, and Nineveh. Not more than 25,000 people inhabited each town. Houses were built with reeds, wood or sundry bricks. All cities had compact homes with a courtyard in the middle for light and ventilation. They were built with common property walls. Harappa only had detached homes. In early civilizations, the chiefs protected people and domesticated animals from wild beasts and invaders. As the chiefs gained power, they elevated themselves to the status of rulers and kings. The kings often fought for power, possessions and territory. Since then successive small and big inventions, economic needs, defense and warfare, social and political process transformed civilization, architecture, and the cities to the current state.

Figure 1.1
Ancient Cities

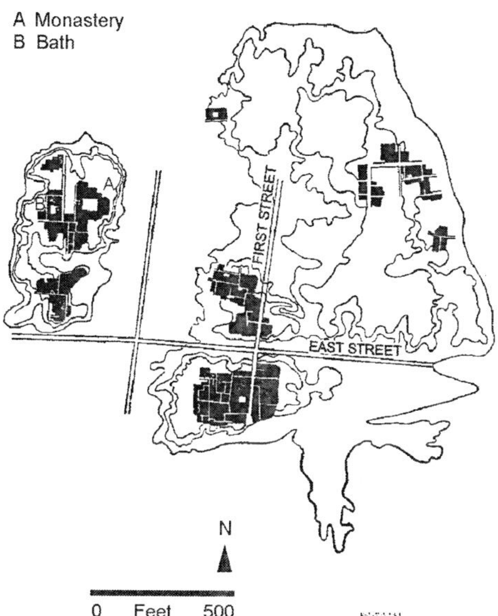

MOHENJO-DARO

Excavations at Mohenjo-Daro in the Indus Valley have revealed the remains of a large city built about 3000 B.C. It is apparent that a relatively advanced civilization flourished in this city. Houses ranged in size from two rooms to mansions with numerous rooms. The map shows the archeologists' assumption that a major street ran in the north-south (First Street) and east-west (East Street) directions. Areas shown in black have been excavated and indicate the intricate plan of narrow roads. Buildings were of masonry, streets were paved, and considerable evidence of sewer drainage from dwellings has been uncovered. The principal buildings excavated are a public bath and a monastery.

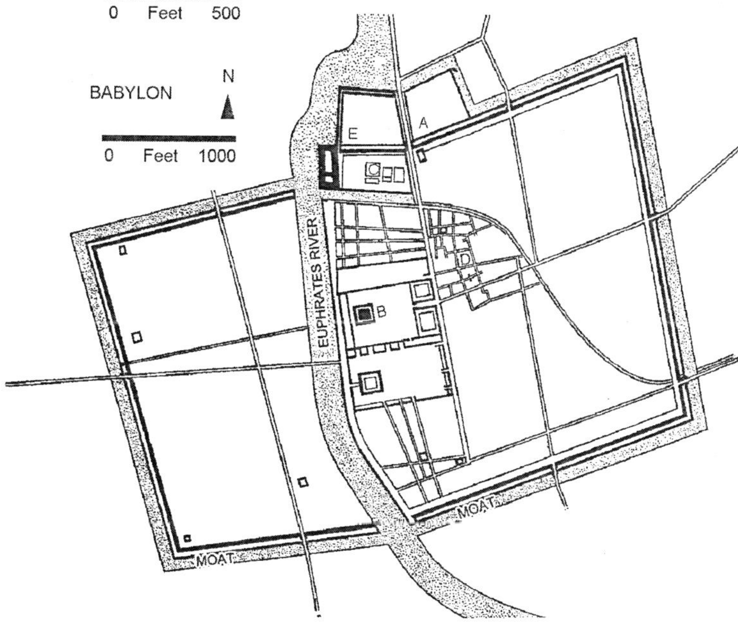

A Ishtar Gate
B Temple
C Hanging Gardens
D Ancient Street System
E Fortress

In the sixth century B.C. Babylon was a large city spanning the Euphrates River. Surrounded by great walls and a moat, it was a monumental city of kings – the processional avenue leading to the magnificent Ishtar Gate, the Temple, and the Hanging Gardens of Nebuchadnezzar's Palace. When Babylon was but a village, the streets were probably irregular; as it grew into a flourishing city, the avenues were laid with a more regular form as described by Herodotus. At that time the palatial monuments were built and the dwellings increased in height and crowding.

Source: Gallion and Eisner, *The Urban Pattern*.

CLASSIC CITIES

In the classical period Athens, Greece was the best known city. Athens has its roots from the bronze ages, but gradually gained prominence from the 5th century B.C. Its influence extended to Rome and other cities in Europe. Alexandria, Egypt was planned around 331 B.C. Roman Empire started in the 1st century B.C. For protection, they built stronger buildings and fortresses with stones. Townships were built containing royal palaces, garrisons, granary, stables, burial places, and housing for the aristocrats, wealthy and privileged. As civilization advanced agoras, markets, religious buildings, libraries, amphitheaters, museums, opera halls, etc. were added. Common people lived mostly outside the city. Architects designed ornate buildings, for the glory of the rulers. It contained gardens, sculptures, fountains and paintings and the related professions flourished. Finest arts and architectures were produced. However, the building material was stone. Since there was no scientific method of calculating tension and compression in structural members, designs were based on experience. The buildings turned out to be massive. Windows were small and high due to the necessity of protection from invaders but did not have adequate light and ventilation. Dwelling for the common people had no consideration. They could not afford stone buildings. This was the trend in the classical cities and medieval towns. Outside the western world, Baghdad was built in the 8th century A.D. and was known as paradise on earth. Chinese cities were built on cosmological considerations in the 6th century A.D. or earlier.

Geometrical streets patterns existed in early towns of Egypt, Mesopotamia, and the Indus Valley. In the latter part of 5th century, Hippodamus, a Greek architect, advanced theories about art and science of city planning. He introduced gridiron pattern of roads, rational arrangement of buildings and circulation. He designed cities to serve people and individual dwelling was the common denominator in his designs. Aristotle credited Hippodamus with the invention of gridiron, but recent archeological findings have proved Greek colonies in southern Italy and Sicily used grid type layout in the 7th century B.C.

Gridiron pattern of streets is simple to layout on land, easier for land surveyors, look organized, easy to lay water, sewer, and electric lines, easier to locate and identify a property. But the pattern is monotonous, closely spaced streets takes too much land, and slows down traffic movement because of closely spaced stop signs and traffic lights. Streets became canyons under tall buildings deprived of sunlight.

The classic period ended with the dark-ages. Roman Empire crumbled due to luxury, ceremonies, and corruption. Barbaric rulers established city-states, feudal system started, wars between feudal lords were frequent, and western civilization started declining by the end of fifth century. Dark-ages continued for about five hundreds years.

Figure 1.2
Classic Cities

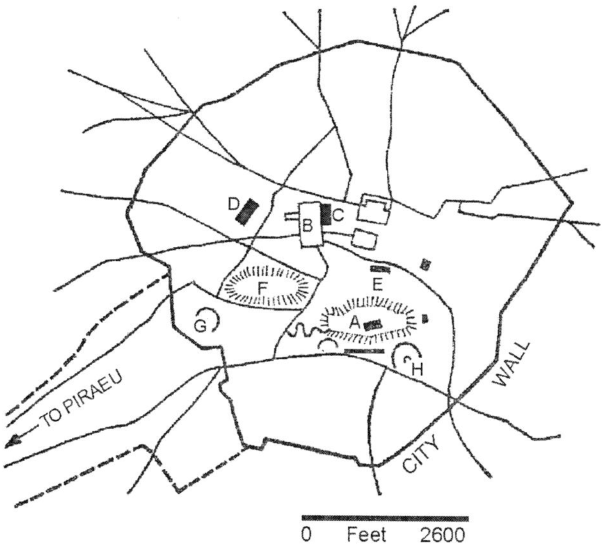

The temple rather than the palace of rulers dominated the ancient Hellenic city and a meeting place for political assembly of the people – the *pnyx*—was added to the urban pattern. As the power of kings diminished and democracy expanded, the houses of the people and the community facilities established for their use assumed greater importance in the city plan.

ANCIENT ATHENS

A Acropolis
B Agora
C Stoa
D Theseum
E Prytaneum
F Areopagus
G Pnyx
H Theater of Dionysus

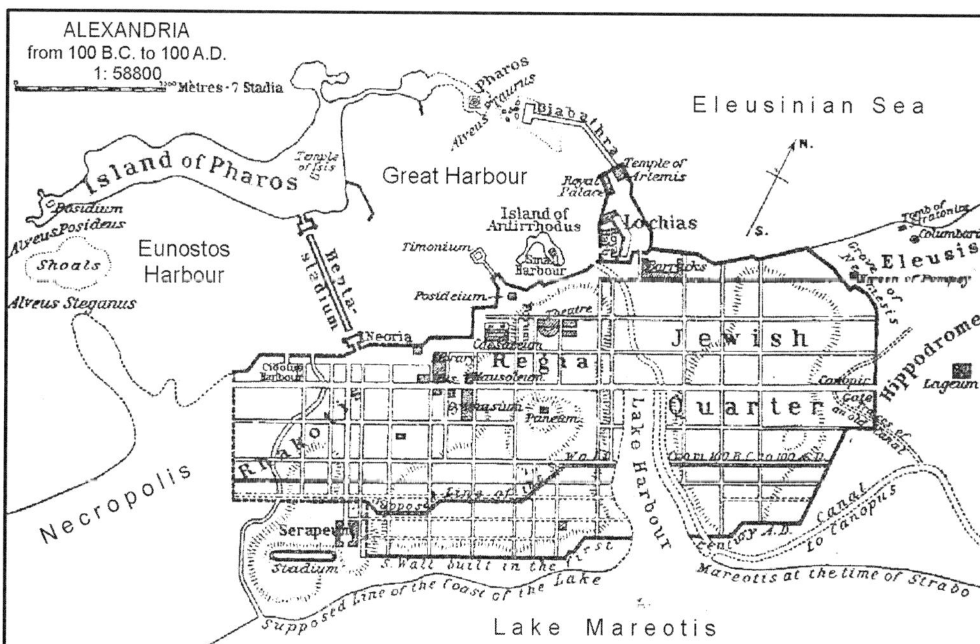

Reconstructed plan of Alexandria, capital of Ptolemaic Egypt, 100 B.C.—100 A.D., after Wagner and Debes. Perimeter wall is Roman.

Source: Gallion and Eisner, *The Urban Pattern*.

Figure 1.3
Classic Cities – Hellenic Period

PRIENE

A Agora
B Temple of Athene Polias
C Theater
D Stadium

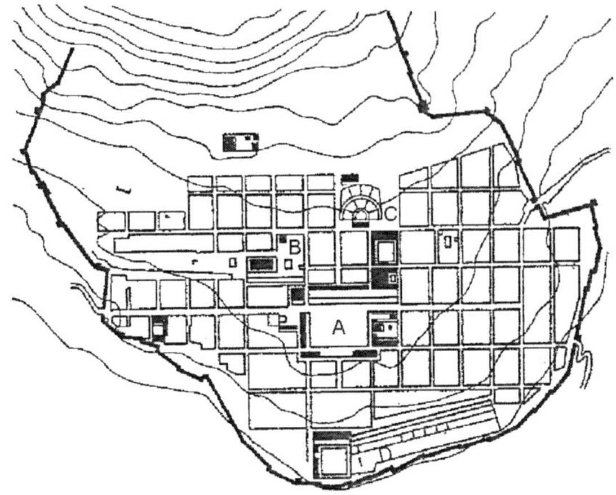

These cities demonstrate the Hippodamian plan as it developed toward the end of the Hellenic Period. The agora occupies the approximate geographical center of the town. Around it are the temple shrines, public buildings, and shops. The dwelling blocks are planned to provide the appropriate orientation of houses in a manner similar to that shown at Olynthus. Recreation and entertainment facilities are provided in the gymnasium, stadium, and theater. The contours of the site indicate that some of the streets were very steep, steps being frequently required, but the main streets connecting the gates and the agora were generally placed so that beasts of burden and carts could traverse them readily.

MILETUS

A Agora
B Theater
C Stadium
D Port

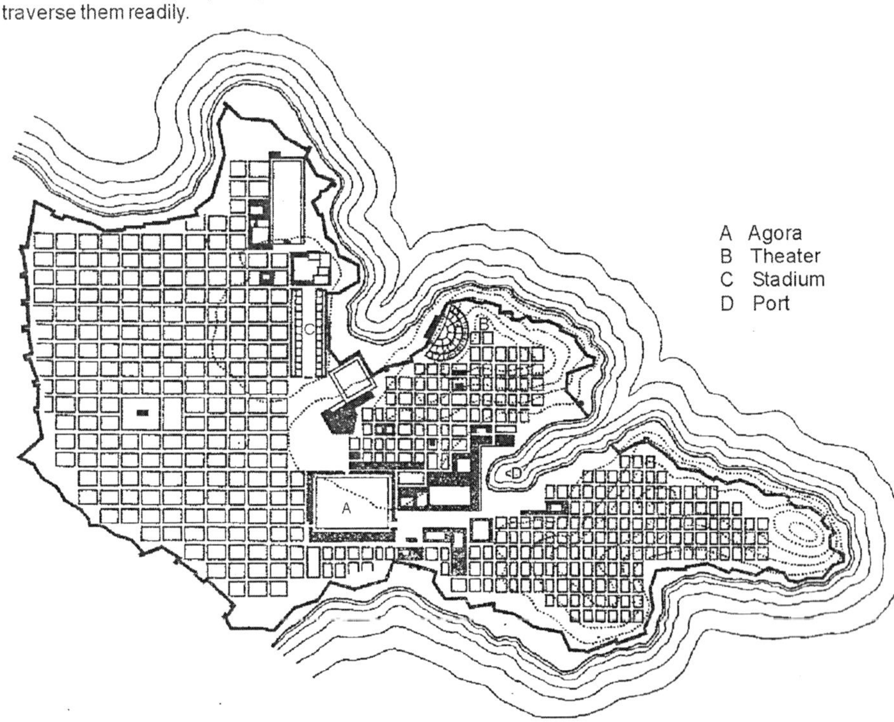

Source: Gallion and Eisner, *The Urban Pattern*.

MEDIEVAL CITIES

The medieval period (6th to 15th century), which overlapped with the dark-ages, was dominated by warfare and strategic sites were sought for fortification on hilltops. In early medieval towns churches and monasteries served as refuge for the oppressed. So churches became the dominating buildings in towns. Gothic buildings, plazas, streets, were integrated with irregular sites on hills. There was a revival of trades with the formation guilds among craftsmen and traders. Universities were founded in Bologna and Paris in 12th century and Cambridge and Salamanca in the 13th century. In India universities at Nalanda and Taxila existed before this period. Cities grew in numbers within the confines of fortresses and therefore, were small in size and congested. There were no water supply and sewage systems. Drains were on the roadsides. Roads were made for pedestrians only (see Figure 1.4).

NEO-CLASSIC CITIES

Neo-classic cities started during the 14th century. Large ships built with wood made world travel easier. Trade increased the economic power of merchants. London, Paris, Venice and Florence grew as mercantile economy expanded. Power of feudal lords declined, military aggression diminished, and there was rise of nationalism. In the 15th century gunpowder was invented. Long-range artillery made the fortress useless. Cities expanded beyond the ramparts and became bigger. Leonardo da Vinci was an artist, military engineer, architect and a planner. Monarchs wanted monuments. Artists, sculptors, architects and planners were in high demand and rewarded handsomely. The renaissance and baroque cities did not change much in planning but turned to architecture and elements of the classical period. St. Peter's Cathedral and Piazza, the Piazza di San Marco, Piazza del Popolo, and many other fine monuments were built. Gardens of Versailles, Karlsruhe, London, Place de La Concorde, Bloomsbury, etc were built or expanded. Fortress walls were torn down in Vienna, Tournay and many other cities to make room for wide roads and opening up to the country side with unconfined space. The monarchs wanted monumental vistas, royal gardens, palaces, and dwellings for the upper class and wealthy merchants. Behind the facades dwelt the congested urban population. After the Black Death in the 14th century the first sewer was installed in London. Water was connected to dwellings in the early 17th century.

In India, *Silpasastra*, a rich literature on cosmological and practical rule of layout of cities developed in the first millennium B.C., but there is no evidence of any city being built on these principles. Fatehpur-Sikri is the most splendid city, which was built by Akbar as his capital around 1573 A.D., only 24 miles west of Agra. This city exceeded London both in population and in grandeur. Buildings were built to human

Figure 1.4
Medieval Cities (12th and 13th Century)

Medieval cities of the twelfth and thirteenth centuries usually had irregular street patterns and heavy walls. Carcassonne was restored by Viollet-le-duc in the nineteenth century. In it we see the castle (B) with its own moat and walls, the market place (A), and the Church of St. Nazaire (C). The plan of Noerdlingen shows the radial and lateral pattern of irregular roadways with the church plaza as the principal focal point of the town. The city of the Middle Ages grew within the confines of the walls. While the population was small, there was space in the town, but when it increased the buildings were packed more closely and the open spaces filled. Sanitation and water supply remained the same. The result was intolerable congestion, lack of hygiene, and pestilence.

MONT ST. MICHEL

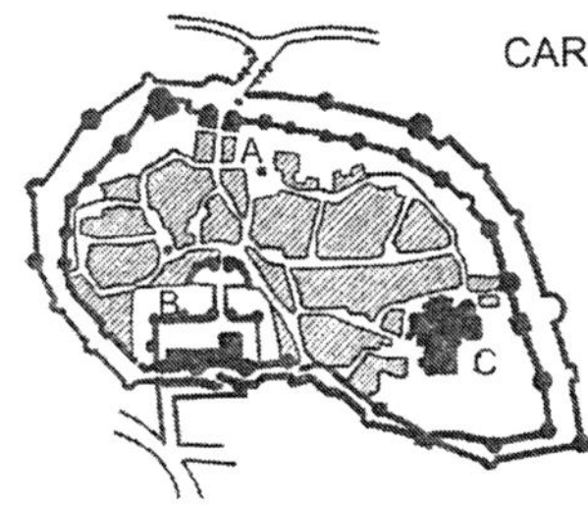

CARCASSONNE

A Market Square
B Castle
C Church of St. Nazaire

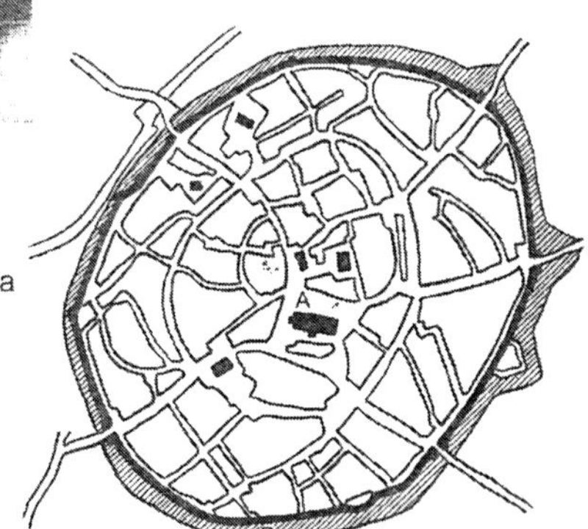

NOERDLINGEN

A Cathedral Plaza
B Mast

It was the church rather than the palace that dominated the medieval town. Encircled by its protective walls, the town was small, In later days the battlements were elaborately engineered, as in Naarden, and the populace was further separated from the open spaces about the town.

NAARDEN

Source: Gallion and Eisner, *The Urban Pattern*.

Figure 1.5
Neoclassic Cities

WASHINGTON, D.C.

The plan by Pierre L'Enfant, approved by Washington and Jefferson, began a series of city planning projects in which diagonal and radial streets were superimposed upon the typical gridiron layout. The city was designed as a huge monumental setting for the Federal government of a new nation.

L'ENFANT'S PLAN OF WASHINGTON, D.C.

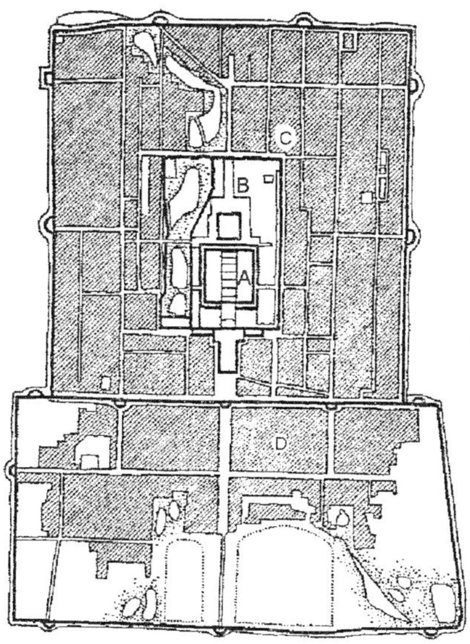

PEKING, China

A Forbidden City
B Imperial City
C Tartar City
D Chinese City

Within each of the cells surrounded by streets in the sketch is a maze of narrow minor roads, also laid out in rectilinear form.

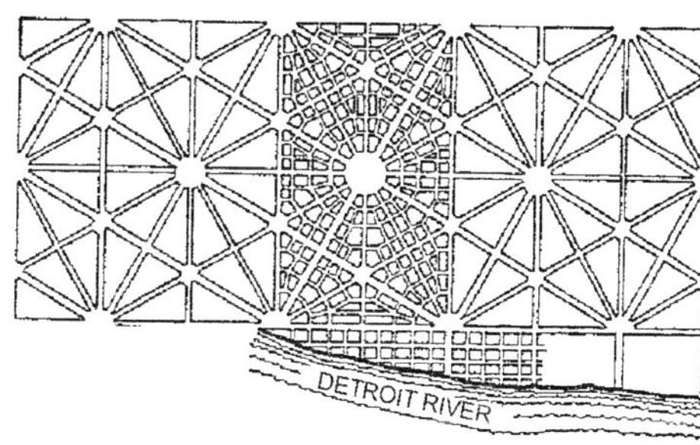

DETROIT

Judges' and Governor's Plan for Detroit, 1807

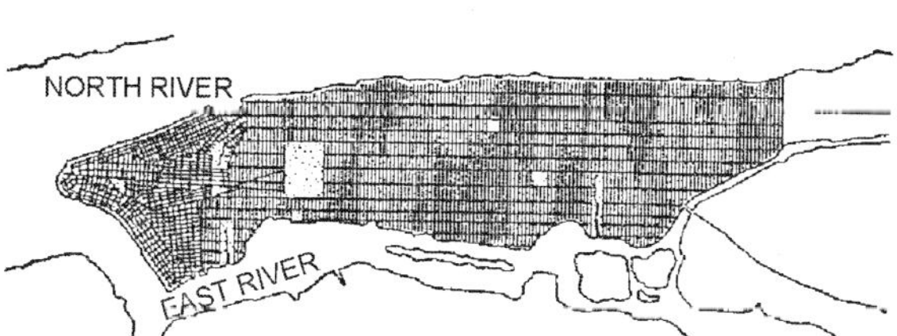

NEW YORK CITY

After turning down a proposal of the city surveyor and architect, Joseph Mangin, in 1800, a commission was appointed to arrive at a plan in 1811. Their plan was a rigid gridiron street pattern laid upon the irregular topography of the city. Open space was not generously allocated. A military parade ground of 69 acres, 55 acres for a public market, and 5 small parks were the only open areas provided in the plan. Despite the "uncommonly great" price of land, explained as the reason for the economy of open space, the layout of streets can hardly be construed as economical; they occupy some 30 per cent of the land area. This harsh and uncompromising plan is reflected in the city of today in which open space has all but completely vanished. It was not until the middle of the nineteenth century that the great Central Park was definitely established in the plan.

Source: Gallion and Eisner, *The Urban Pattern*.

scale, not dwarfing and overpowering people with height and massive walls. Spacious public halls, private palaces for Jodha Bai and Birbal, Panchmahal, pavilion, courtyards, mosque, library, treasury, etc. were delicately laid out with architectural unity. Shaikh Salim Chisti's tomb was adorned with marvelous marble grills. Roads were laid taking advantage of the hilly site. Unfortunately due to scarcity of water, this dream city was abandoned after 15 years.

COLONIAL AND INDUSTRIAL CITIES

Mariner's compass aided the courageous explorers to find Americas and new places in other continents during the 15th and 16th century. With the expansion of colonialism, a new generation of well-planned cities were built but the classical characters of the buildings still dominated. New cities such as Havana, San Juan, St. Augustine, Boston, Manhattan, Williamsburg, Annapolis, Philadelphia etc. were built in the 17th century and Washington D.C. in the 18th century in America.

In Russia, Czar Peter I, known as Peter the Great, obsessed with a glittering imperial city, decided to transfer the capital from Moscow to St. Petersburg. It is interesting to note several exemplary ideas and comprehensiveness of city planning thoughts. He wanted to transfer the government to westward thrust of the empire; make a maritime port city, modern and innovative city; a diversified employment base besides government such as industry, educational and cultural institutions; and introduction of settlement districts for each social class. He recruited French and Italian architect planners to design the city, like a planning competition. Peter, at the advice of his new building director, opted to develop the main land instead of an island suggested by the planners. Construction of the city started on an obscure place 200 miles northwest of Moscow in circa 1718 on a marshy land on the Gulf of Finland. It took countless loads of fill dart, pilling, and suffering of hundreds of thousands of workers to raise the swamp. Peter and his successor's unlimited power helped to overcome all obstacles in the development phase of St. Petersburg. Peter turned his vision into reality with an iron will.

The city of Jaipur built around year circa 1728, has *silpasastra* and European influence. The Pink City is laid out with Hawa-Mahal, palace, gardens, and artificial lakes.

The most significant plan in the colonial period was for Washington, D.C. Major Pierre Charles L'Enfant conceived the classic plan with diagonal streets overlaid on a gridiron pattern of streets. The U.S. congress approved this plan in 1791. The significance of this city was that it was a major non-mercantile city planned for national administration. It kept sufficient open land for expansion of the capital, monuments, and gardens. New York developed as a trade center on the southern tip of Manhattan Island. In circa 1800 the city was extended to the north with a gridiron street pattern and the Central Park.

Figure 1.6
Industrial Cities

STOKE-ON-TRENT, England *British Information Service*

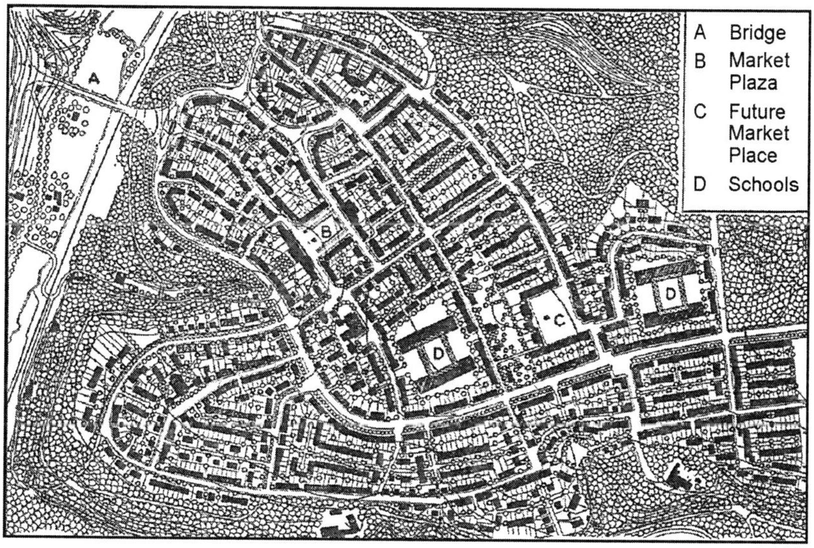

MARGARETHEN-HOHE, Essen *George Metzendori, Architect*

Emerging from the Garden City movement, this village was developed in 1912 by Krupp family for workers in the industrial steel plants in Essen. The community was planned for 2,000-2,500 dwellings (12,000-16,000 population) and the first stage is shown in black.

Source: Gallion and Eisner, *The Urban Pattern.*

Industrial developments and industrial cities first started in England in the 18th century. This phenomenon had spread to other countries and accelerated through the 19th century and first half of the 20th century. During industrial revolution, there was mass migration of people from rural areas to industrial cities. Industrial workers in the 19th century had no adequate housing. They lived in overcrowded conditions with no exposure to daylight, ventilation, open space, and without pure water. Under such conditions, diseases such as typhus, cholera, yellow fever and tuberculosis flourished. Loss of human life and economic wellbeing was deplorable. The ill effects of industrial cities and need for better living conditions gave rise to urban planning movements, philosophy, and planning legislations in the western world. Also adoption of new technologies such as purification and distribution of potable water, sewer disposal, electricity, communication system, etc. became essential.

Sanitary reform started in Great Britain. Chadwick Report "On the sanitary condition of the labouring population of Great Britain" had a tremendous impact. The Miasma theory that foul air indicates pathogen also influenced sanitary reform. Public Health Act of 1848 was passed. Urban planning initiatives such as sewerage, garbage collection, rodent control and mosquito abatement were taken.

RECONSTRUCTION OF CITIES

London and Chicago had great fire, San Francisco had earthquake and fire, Paris had Haussmann, and Germany had Second World War to reconstruct the cities. May be it is a desirable evil to have major disaster like fire and earthquake, or a Haussmann to reconstruct our congested cities.

In 1664-65 plague in London killed 75,000 people. Soon after the plague, on September 2, 1666 the Great Fire of London started in the house of the king's baker on Pudding Lane and continued through September 6th. The fire consumed four-fifths of medieval London, which was built with wood. The fire destroyed 13,200 houses, 80,000 persons became homeless, and total damage was £10 million. People fled to cities around London. England was also at war with France and Holland at the time. It was a critical time for London financially, manpower and building material for reconstruction. On September 13, a royal proclamation declared that the new city would be built of brick and stone, streets would be widened, and no building would be allowed that was not according to plan. Wider and straighter roads were planned. The reconstruction plan laid the foundation of modern London. Reconstruction of London started in 1668 and almost completed in 1672. Merchants and traders moved and settled permanently in suburbs after the fire, where the taxes were lower. Over 40 percent of the newly built houses remained vacant for sometime. Sir Christopher Wren, an engineer, astronomer, mathematician, and physicist was given the task of designing and supervision of rebuilding London including more than 50 churches in classical style.[1]

The 1871 fire transformed Chicago to the most modern city overnight. There was a long dry spell between July and October 1871. The story goes that Ms. Katherine O'Leary's cow kicked a kerosene lantern in the burn and fire started at 9 p.m. on Sunday, October 8, 1871. The fire burned an area one mile wide and four miles long. Nearly 300 persons died; 18,000 buildings were destroyed; 100,000 people became homeless; and $200 million in property damage; and thousands became unemployed. The infrastructure of Chicago such as water supply, sewage, and transportation, however remained intact after the fire. During reconstruction, the road system remained about the same, may be little wider. Along Lake Shore Drive, on the shore of Lake Michigan, Grant Park was developed; in many areas of the city, parks and playgrounds were landscaped; high class neighborhoods, business district, industrial areas, transportation routes, etc. were developed; and building code and fire code was made stringent. Reconstruction of Chicago started with enthusiasm. On the fourth day after the fire, when the burnt buildings were still smoking, ground had been broken for a new office block. No longer will buildings be built on external load bearing walls, but by a skeleton of steel structure and light-weight wall panels. This revolutionary construction method was economical both in use of material and construction time. Chicago became the birthplace of steel-framed skyscrapers.

The great earthquake and fire of April 18 to 21, 1906 destroyed the central business district of San Francisco. The 8.3 magnitude earthquake tremor lasted 40 seconds. After the collapse of buildings, fire started and continued for five days. The entire railway system was destroyed; twisted streetcar rails; ripped open roads; water mains ruptured at more than 300 locations; more than 3,000 persons died; and total damage was over $500 million. (Source: Museum of the City of San Francisco). Reconstruction of San Francisco was slow. The buildings, which were standing but damaged were torn down. San Francisco started reconstruction from rubbles. Large open spaces were left un-built for future use. The buildings in the Financial District were made of fireproof steel framed skyscrapers clad in historic imagery. Residential and commercial buildings were 3 to 6 stories and most of them were made of steel frames. Facades were decorated with Spanish colonial and Mediterranean Revival designs. (Source: S.E. Archaeological Center).

Baron Georges-Eugene Haussmann is the most fascinating person in reconstruction of a city in the entire world. Emperor Napoleon III of France faced with restlessness of the working class for poor housing. He thought demolition of slums and creation of open spaces would provide his soldiers advantage in controlling mob violence. He appointed Haussmann, a bureaucrat in the city administration, to take charge of the project in 1853. The project turned out to be more ambitious than the

Figure 1.7

Reconstruction of Cities (Neo-classic Cities)

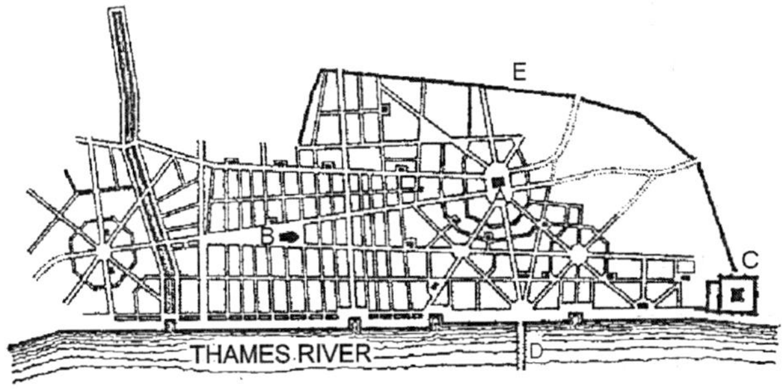

A Stock Exchange
B St. Paul's Cathedral
C Tower of London
D London Bridge
E Old Walls

LONDON (Christopher Wren's Plan)

PARIS

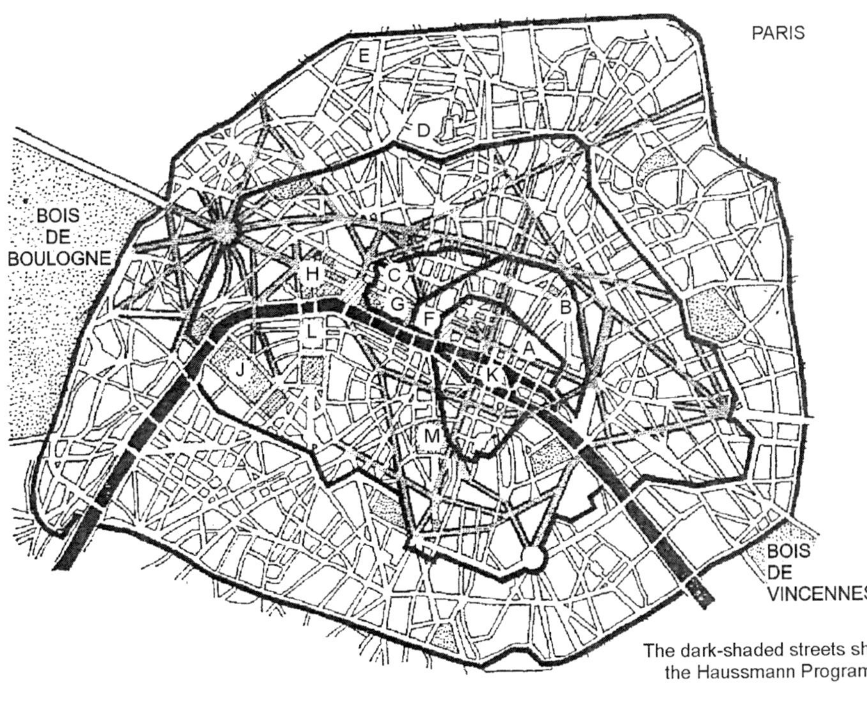

The dark-shaded streets show the Haussmann Program

Wall A Built by Philip Augustus, Twelfth century
Wall B Built by Charles V, Fourteenth century
Wall C Built by Louis XIII, Seventeenth century
Wall D Built by Louis XV, Eighteenth century
Wall E Built by Napoleon III, Nineteenth century

F The Louvre
G The Tuilleries
H The Champs Elysees
J The Champs de Mars
K The Ile de la Cite

L The Invalides
M The Luxembourg

Source: Gallion and Eisner, *The Urban Pattern*.

emperor envisioned. Haussmann's plan included the grand boulevard system cutting through winding medieval lanes and slums, design for traffic of a new industrial age, creation of chestnut-lined monumental avenues, improvement of existing plazas, creation of new plazas, extension of Louvre Museum, parks and gardens, and many impressive buildings in the tradition of monuments, and laying out sewers. He had opposition from the city council, which was reluctant to appropriate funds. Landlords were affected by the plan. With full support of the emperor, he completed the project in 1869 in seventeen years. Haussmann was criticized as arrogant, ruthless, authoritarian, opportunist and uncaring for the poor. He destroyed portions of medieval Paris and many slums. The criticisms may have been true, but the critics are long gone and the effects of the project have been positive and long lasting. It has been the greatest urban renewal project in history. He transformed Paris to one of the most magnificent cities in the world. Demolition of urban areas for reconstruction is now termed as Haussmannization by some planners.

Most cities in Germany, some cities in England, France, Poland and Japan were destroyed in the World War II. This gave an opportunity to modernize these cities. New cities were also built, which were influenced by the garden city movement started by Ebenezer Howard.

DEVELOPMENT OF MODERN CITIES

Development of New Towns as Solutions to Congestions and Urban Ills

Since the beginning of the industrial revolution poor housing, inadequate sanitation, industrial pollution, haphazard growth, suburban sprawl, transportation problems, and unhealthy living environment became a part of metropolitan urban living. Existing amenities became old and inadequate, industries needed bigger lots to expand and modernize, and demand for better housing kept increasing. In the later part of the 19th century there were some efforts to alleviate these problems. In England, about the beginning of the 20th century, some concrete thoughts and ideas crystallized, initiative by planners, citizens, and politicians increased, and the governments became supportive. The effort can be called a planning intervention. The solutions were construction of (a) alternate growth-poles such as industrial towns and capital cities to attract population from existing cities, (b) satellite towns around existing central cities, (c) independent and self-sufficient cities outside commuting distance to any existing metropolis, and (d) physically separate parallel or twin cities. (Source: Ervin Galantay) The construction of new towns in England is the biggest town building experiment in human history. In a short time of 27 years 32 new towns started between 1946 and 1973 and constructions completed by 1991. These are in addition to Letchworth and Welwyn garden cities.

The Garden City Movement

There were preludes to Ebenezer Howard's famous Garden City movement. In 1882, Arturo Soria, a Spaniard, launched the idea of *Ciudad Lineal* or linear city. He proposed a linear city around Madrid, a ring of about 50 km. long and at a distance 7 km. from the center. He proposed mass communication with highways and subway. Soviet planners and Le Corbusier later developed the same idea. Haphazard growth, inadequate housing and unhealthy condition of cities were depressing those days. Patrick Geddes, in 1892 advocated integration of physical planning with social and economic improvements. William Lever had built Port Sunlight in Cheshire, England from 1889. His concept was 'prosperity sharing' by producing over 1,000 houses and community facilities for workers from his factory. The development was visually appealing overlooking landscaped areas and served social purpose. This was an ideal plan and proved to be successful and inspiring.

Ebenezer Howard, a contemporary of Soria, came up with the idea of garden cities in England. It is interesting to note that Howard was a city clerk attending city commission meetings. After listening to commissioners deliberating the problems of London, he developed an insight and came up with the idea. In his little book entitled *Tomorrow*, Howard published the garden city idea in 1898. The garden city was defined as "town designed for healthy living and industry, of a size that makes possible the full measure of social life but no larger, surrounded by a rural belt, all of the land being in public ownership or held in trust for the community." The city was to have sufficient employment to reduce the journey-to-work and it was to be limited to its optimum size of 30,000 people on an area of 1,000 acres. The city would be located on cheap country land; the increment in real estate values would defray the cost of development and ultimately yield a handsome profit for the investment. Howard suggested a density of 12 families per acre. Planners uphold this density standard as appropriate even today. To quote Howard:

"Town and Country must be married, and out of this joyous union will spring a new hope, a new life, a new civilization."

"Two alternatives – town life and country life – but a third alternative, in which all the advantages of the most energetic and active town life, with all the beauty and delight of country, may be secured."

The Garden City Association was formed in 1899 and in 1903 the First Garden City, Limited, a limited dividend society, started Letchworth on 3,922 acres of land, 34 miles from London. This town was planned for 30,000 people to build on 1300 acre and a permanent greenbelt around. Villages were planned around a civic center, with a separate factory district, and a business district on the edge of the city. Houses were designed simple with harmonious building materials. The 2nd garden city Welwyn started in 1919 in the outer ring of London. Both the cities were built with private capitals, connected to London by railroads and roads, were designed as small towns, and many types of industry were to be prohibited. Both the towns were relatively successful in integrating town and country as intended by Howard. Population and industrial growth in both the cities were slow. Welwyn was more successful attracting population because of nearness to London. Both failed to develop into self-contained cities, and later on realized, a city has to be much larger to become self-contained.

Howard's Garden Cities were criticized by Soria's disciples as static and rejecting dynamic growth. Le Corbusier criticized it as inefficient and wasteful of the land; fostering individualism and downfall of collective forces. Infrastructure development is very expensive and therefore very low density is not financially practical. However, the garden city ideas stimulated many architects and planners all over the world. The British citizens held strong appeal, because they were desperate for better living. After the death of Howard in 1928, the Garden City Association, which was renamed Town and Country Planning Association, continued to influence British town planning and regional planning.

Planning Legislations

Great Britain was serious to improve housing and urban condition, and passed a series of legislations. The Housing and Town Planning Act of 1909 granted power to local authorities to prepare plans for their jurisdictions. In 1919 this Act introduced the policy of joint planning action among several local authorities to encourage building after World War I. In 1923 this Act empowered local authorities to plan for built-up and undeveloped areas. In 1925 this Act separated planning functions from housing. In 1927 Greater London Regional Planning Committee was created. The Town and Country Planning Act of 1932 extended the responsibility of local authorities to both urban and rural land, preservation of historic buildings and natural landscape. The Ribbon Development Act of 1935 regulated space along the highways.

In 1937 a Royal Commissions under the chairmanship of Sir Montague Barlow was established to inquire into the strategic advantages of distribution of industrial population, social, and economic improvements. The commission report published in 1940 recommended: further growth of industry in London must be restricted, industrial population must be distributed based on a new town policy, redevelopment of congested areas, creation of balanced industrial development, a comprehensive planning legislation be enacted, and to create a national authority to deal with these matters.

The Green Belt Act of 1938 was passed and the government granted 2 million pounds to local authorities to purchase land for the greenbelt.

In 1941 two new committees were created to study the recommendations of the Barlow Commission: The Scott Committee on Land Utilization in Rural Areas, and Uthwatt Committee on Compensation and Betterment. These committees recommended: creation of a central planning authority, insure state control of developments, increase power of local planning authorities for acquisition of land for open space and balanced development. The subsequent Acts of 1943, 1944, 1945, and 1946 provided necessary legal tools.

British New Towns

In 1944, Patrick Abercrombie prepared the *Greater London Plan,* in which he recommended to stop suburban sprawl, maximum density of 100 people per acre, and a permanent greenbelt around London. This implied that over a million people would need relocation from the inner ring of London. This called for immediate creation of ten new towns beyond the greenbelt.

Figure 1.8
British New Towns

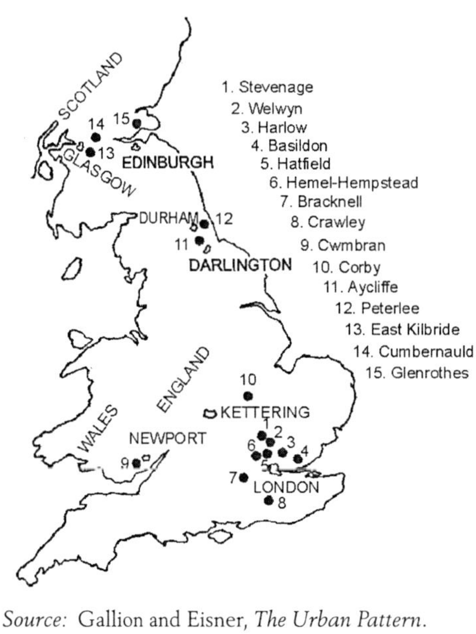

THE NEW TOWNS

Locations of the 15 New Towns in the initial program are shown on the map of England, Wales and Scotland. The towns are experiments in the design of an environment in which the human scale predominates. They are self-contained communities seeking a balance between sources of employment, business enterprise, shopping, education and recreation for those who live in them. They are, however, significant for another important reason: they are essentially an organic element in a broad program of decentralization of the congested urban centres, the London region having received the principal attention.

Source: Gallion and Eisner, *The Urban Pattern.*

Figure 1.9
London

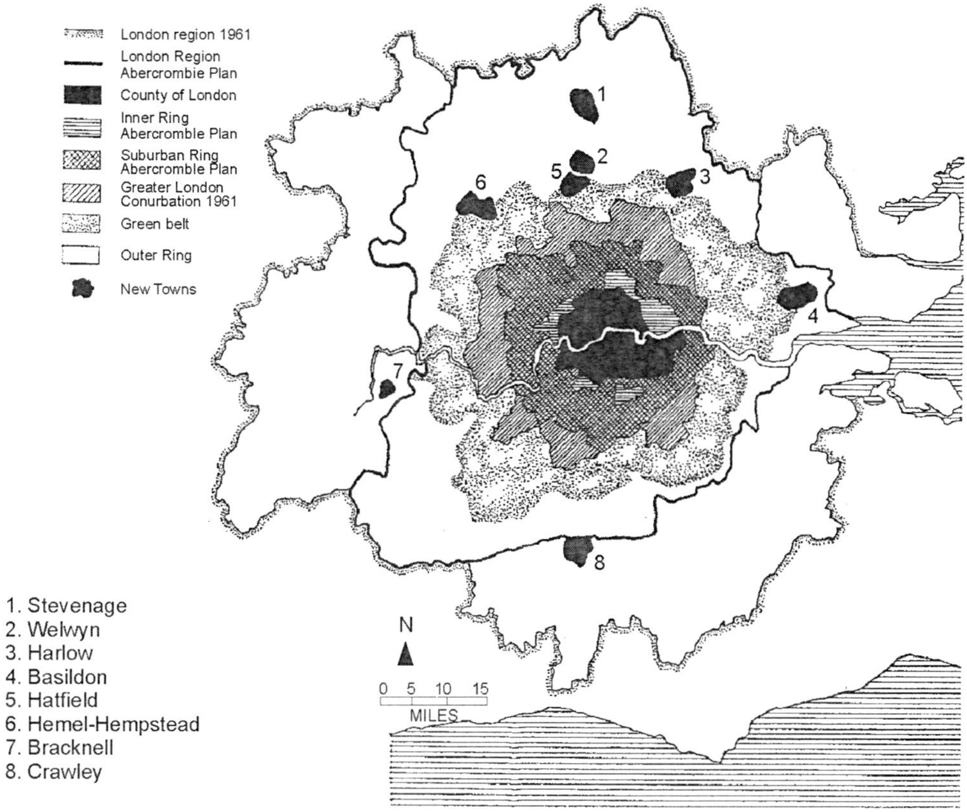

THE LONDON REGION

The Greater London Plan of 1944, by Patrick J. Abercrombie and F.J. Forshaw, embraced a region of 2,600 square miles. A series of four rings surrounded the county of London. The population within the heavily urbanized areas of the County and the Inner Ring was to be reduced by some 1,000,000 people by dispersal within the Suburban and Outer Rings. The urban conurbation (concentration) of the region has extended the boundaries of the Suburban Ring beyond the limits of the plan and has forced attention to the preservation and expansion of the greenbelt.

Source: Gallion and Eisner, *The Urban Pattern.*

In July of 1945 elections Labour Party replaced Conservative Party. Clement Attlee became the Prime Minister in place of Winston Churchill. The Labour Party took socialist programs such as National Health Service, nationalization of many industries, and new towns and housing. At the end of World War II 475,000 dwellings were destroyed or damaged. There was a housing crisis. Therefore, rebuilding of the war-torn cities and relieving the intolerable overcrowding was the highest priority to the Labour Party Government. The people living in Letchworth and Welwyn were happier than living in big cities and a dissipation of population would be least costly both emotionally and economically. Therefore, construction of new garden cities was the best solution. The British New Towns is one of the boldest and largest experiments in city building.

In 1945 the government appointed a new committee, with Lord Reith as chairman to elaborate proposals for the new towns. The Reith Committee suggested self-contained new towns to be located 40 to 50 km. from London, and the government should appoint development corporations to build the towns. Once completed, the towns would become self-governing. *The New Town Act of 1946* gave the authority to build new towns. The British New Towns may be divided into three generations corresponding to three distinct stages of the development of the Garden City theory.

The first generations of new towns are: Letchworth and Welwyn Garden City, which began before Howard's death and before the New Towns Act of 1946 was enacted. The concept of garden city was further refined, as more cities were built.

The second generation of 14 new towns in Great Britain started between 1946 and 1950 but construction continued to later years. Eight of them (including Welwyn Garden City) are located just outside the greenbelt of London, intended to draw industry and population from London. These are Stevenage (1946), Harlow (1949), Sasildon, Hatfield, Hemel-Hemsstead, Bracknell, and Crawley. Other seven new towns are located in Northern England, Wales and Scotland. It was a mammoth task but built with incredible speed and enthusiasms. The cities had good environment for living. In the formative stage social opportunities were less. These cities were designed for population 20,000 to 70,000. The small cities could not attract industries and became dormitory towns to London workers. The cities built farther from London, like Peterborough, Milton Keynes, and Telford were large enough to attract industries and were most successful as self-contained cities. The designers did not anticipate explosion of private automobile ownership. Therefore, plans had to be modified to accommodate more cars and parking. These cities depended on few large industries for generating employment and attracting other business and industries. But when any of these large industries fail, unemployment increase. Therefore, these cities are not sustainable.

The third generation of 18 new towns started between 1956 and 1972. Those are Cumbernauld (1956), Runcorn, Milton Keynes, Peterborough, Telford and 13 other cities. The third generation new towns worked on six principles: opportunity and freedom of choice, easy movement and access, balance and variety, creation of an attractive city, public awareness and involvement, and efficient use of resources. Great importance was given on parks and open space (22% of total city land), and zoning residential and commercial areas to avoid rush hour congestion. Pedestrian routes were separated from automobile. The Development Corporations were loaned huge amount of money by the government, had few restrictions on development, industries were built close to the main transportation routes, the infrastructure was completed before any building started, and rented building space cheaply to allow rapid growth. Therefore, the third generation of new towns was very successful. (Source: Fujita Research Report)

New towns were intended to alleviate the growth problems of London, Manchester, and other cities; to stimulate economic growth; to provide housing and community services; or to decentralize population. In all these accounts new towns were successful. By 1991 five new towns grew to over 100,000 populations: Redditch (814,000), Peterborough (266,000), Northampton (239,000), Milton Keynes (167,000) and Telford (125,000).

Influence of the Garden City Movement

The garden city and greenbelt idea had spread to Sweden, Finland, Germany, Russia, France, United States, Japan, and many other countries rapidly. The garden city movement brought the latest thoughts about city building and still the idea is going through further refinement and adjustments according to situations in different countries. It stimulated planners, architects, citizens, and politicians to think further.

Raymond Unwin, architect of Letchworth, suggested dormitory satellite towns surrounding an industrial center in 1922. In 1923 Ernst Gloeden, a German, proposed decentralized regional pattern in his nuclear towns concept with interrelated urban cells. Le Corbusier preferred his own concept of 'vertical garden cities' with high-rise buildings and lots of open spaces around to maximize air, space and greenery. Clarence Perry advocated self-contained neighborhoods of 5,000 people with a community center, schools, shopping, and other institutions in the center. This concept of neighborhood became an acceptable standard in planning.

In the United States, Clarence Stein, Henry Wright, and Lewis Mumford were in favor of garden city ideas. Clarence Stein and Henry Wright designed Radburn, New Jersey, the first American garden city, in 1928 for 25,000 people. In this plan, horizontal separation of vehicles and pedestrian was achieved by use of cul-de-sac. Green spaces were provided in the middle of the super blocks. Henry Wright prepared the 1926 regional plan for New York State and suggested a balanced distribution of population and industry by the creation of new towns. In 1935 the U.S. Congress created Resettlement Administration towards the end of great depression. This administration planned four cities: Greenbelt, Maryland; Greenhills, Ohio; Greendale, Wisconsin; and Greenbrook, New Jersey. The designs were inspired by Howard's Garden City ideas, but were not designed as self-contained city. These are

Figure 1.10
Garden Cities

THE GARDEN CITY AND THE SATELLITE TOWN

Reflecting the ideas of Ebenezer Howard, the Garden City of Letchworth was begun near London in 1903 and Welwyn soon followed. Limited in their initial planning to an ultimate maximum population, the garden cities were surrounded by agricultural fields similar to the original proposal by Robert Owen. The satellite towns of Wythenshawe and Becontree are similar to the garden cities with the primary exception that the latter are self-contained, each having its own industry, whereas the former are dependent upon the larger industrial cities, to which they are attached, for industrial employment.

Source: Gallion and Eisner, *The Urban Pattern*.

Figure 1.11
Garden Cities

THE GREENBELT TOWNS

As a component part of the Federal government's search for ways and means to cope with the modern city and its living environment, the Resettlement Administration planned four "greenbelt towns" beginning in 1935. They were satellite communities near large cities. The designs were inspired by Howard's Garden City idea, but they were not planned as self-contained towns; they were more like dormitory villages, the sources of employment for the residents being in the near-by cities. Each was surrounded by a belt of permanent open space, part of which could be farmed or gardened. A full complement of community facilities was included in each town – shopping, schools, and recreation space.

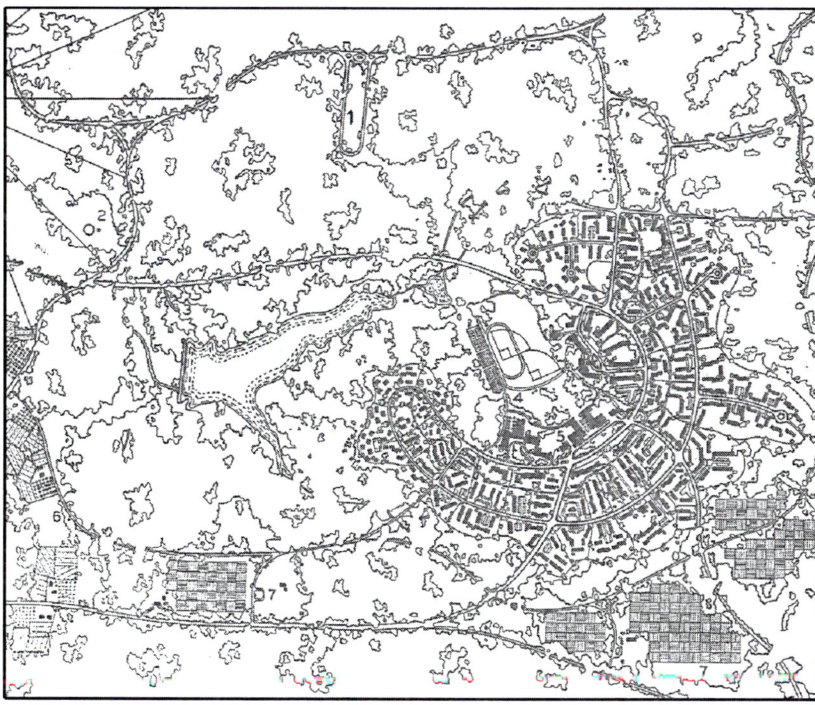

GREENBELT, Maryland

1 Water Tower
2 Disposal Plant and Incinerator
3. Picnic Center and Lake
4. Community Center
5. Store Group
6. Rural Homesteads
7. Allotment Gardens

This development is on a 2,100-acre site about 25 minutes' drive by automobile from Washington, D.C., and includes 712 dwellings in group houses and 288 in apartments, a total of 1,000 units occupying an area of 250 acres. There are 500 garages. The sixteen-room elementary school is jointly used as community center, and the shopping center includes space for a post office, food stores, a drug store, a dentist's and a doctor's offices, a 600-seat theater, and such service shops as shoe repair, laundry, tailor, barber, and beauty shops. There are a bus terminal, a garage and repair shop, a fire station, and a gas station. The recreation facilities include an athletic field, picnic grounds, and an artificial lake. The super-block is used, each block containing about 120 dwellings with interior play areas. Underpasses provide continuous pedestrian circulation without crossing main roads. The commercial and community center, in the approximate center of the plan, reduces to a minimum the walking distance from all dwellings.

Source: Gallion and Eisner, *The Urban Pattern*.

residential cities near big cities surrounded by greenbelts. Community facilities included shopping, schools, and recreation space.

In 1969 the National Committee on Urban Growth proposed 100 new towns averaging 100,000 people. The Housing and Urban Development Act of 1970 offered federal direct assistance to new communities. In 1968 the State of New York created an Urban Development Corporation giving power and authorized to float one billion dollars in tax-exempt bonds to finance its projects. The corporation proposed to channel one-third of the anticipated population growth of the state to the new communities. An American model of Garden City emerged about 1970, which is predominantly tertiary employment base in offices, education and research, resort and gambling, retirement towns, and leisure and tourist towns. All of these cities are planned for low density.

Reston, Virginia, 23 km. west of Washington D. C., was planned in 1961 for 75,000 people. The Reston plan integrates physical aspects of roads, utilities, housing; economic provisions for office and research facilities, industry, and commercial centers; and social opportunities including education, health care, recreation, religion, and civic organizations. The town is structured creating seven villages. It has a miniature urban center. It is considered the most successful planned community in the United States. Some of the new communities in the United States are: Columbia, Maryland (1972); Irvine, California (1973); Audobon, New York (1972); and Park Forest, Illinois; Anaheim, Culver City, Foster City, in California; Lake Havasu, Arizona; Richland, Washington; and Woodland, Texas.

After the World War II, housing crisis became serious. But France was engaged in rebuilding within the existing urban areas. When this did not solve the overcrowding, France opted for new towns. The 1960 Master Plan of the Paris region proposed eight provincial cities away from Paris to halt the physical growth of Paris. But people wanted further growth of Paris and this plan was rejected. The 1969 Paris Regional Master Plan proposed five satellite towns around Paris: Marne-la-Vallee, Melun, Cergy, St. Quentin, and Evry. Several satellite cities were built near other large cities of France. Emphasis was given to development of leisure areas in the satellite towns. The British experiment proved that industries can be enticed to relocate to new towns and France followed the same path later.

In 1950 Sweden proposed satellite towns of 50,000 people outside Stockholm along a new subway system. Each new town shall have neighborhoods of population 7,000 to 15,000. These towns are in a commuting distance of 30 minutes from the center of Stockholm, were not designed as self-sufficient employment, but schools, shopping, community facilities are provided. Seventy percent of the dwellings are rental apartments. Stockholm had a planning commission since 1637 for systematic growth. The commission has the tradition of acquiring land before development. The

same tradition continued after the 1950 plan was proposed, and 70 percent of the land belonged to public ownership in 1964. The cities that were built with the ideas of garden city are: Vallingby, Tensta-Rinkeby, Jarvafaltet, Jarva, and Norra Jarvafaltet.

In Finland, Tapiola the first satellite town of Helsinki was planned in 1951. A single person, Heikki von Hertzen, convinced a number of trade unions and welfare organizations to finance the construction of Tapiola. So it was built by a private, nonprofit organization without government support. It became an inspiration to new community developers in the United States. Seven more cities were planned in 1960's.

In Japan, the Greater Tokyo Plan had greenbelt around Tokyo like London and planned new towns following the Swedish model. In 1963 and 1970 Senri and Senboku were built as a joint venture of the government and the Japanese Housing Corporation. Several other new towns were built since.

Planning in Soviet Russia was a scheme of social and economic consideration without public participation. Planning became associated with communism, which was incompatible with the spirit of free enterprise. The population of Moscow reached six million in 1960. The 1960 Moscow and regional plan proposed decentralization of people by building satellite towns beyond a proposed greenbelt around Moscow. Afitchenko, a geographer, identified three types of satellites based on employment and dependence to the central city: dormitory suburbs, self-contained satellites and independent cities. Dormitory suburbs depend on the central city for employment, utilities, shopping, entertainment, and sports events. Self-contained satellites have some employment, can commute to the central city for employment, and enjoy most of urban facilities. Independent cities are far for commuting daily to the central city (distance ranging from 40 to 80 km.) but may take trips to the central city for cultural and sports events. The Russians learned from the British experience and proposed at least twenty new cities. Many of them were designed for teaching and research facilities.

Since 1950 the Government of India emphasized construction of new towns for heavy industry and steel plant such as Bhilai, Durgapur, and Rourkela. The Rurkela Plan designed by Konrad Seiler, a German planner, is the most interesting. It was designed for 100,000 people. The steel plant was separated from the town by a low range hills at a distance of 5 km. such that steel workers could commute to the plant by bicycle. The town consists of twenty villages, each with 5,000 people. A major collector loop road, passing through a continuous green strip, connects the town with the industries. A gross density of the town was proposed to 60 persons per ha. Each village is separated by green space.

CAPITAL CITIES OF THE 20TH CENTURY

Capital cities that were built on virgin land in the 20th century include: New Delhi, Chandigarh, Islamabad, Canberra, and Brasilia. All these plans were conceived with space organization just like in architecture. Monumentality and gridiron pattern of streets did not dominate the design. Each one of them had some influence of the garden city in the organization of spaces. Except Delhi all other cities introduced super blocks, large sectors with wide roads.

New Delhi

In India, colonial rulers laid out many cities with wide roads and administrative buildings such as Mumbai, Kolkata, Chennai, district head quarters, including Guwahati. The capital of India was moved from Calcutta to Delhi in 1911. New Delhi master plan was prepared by Sir Edward Lutyens but altered by Lord Hardinge and later expanded when a greater population was anticipated. New Delhi was formally inaugurated in 1929. The buildings are a compromise between European Renaissance and Indian style. New Delhi is a new city built to the south of Old Delhi and west of Yamuna River. Old monuments like Humayun's tomb, Lodi tomb, Safdarjang tomb, Purana Quila were integrated in the city plan. The plan had two prominent axis: Rajpath in east-west direction along Rashtrapati Bhavan, India Gate and Purana Quila, and Janpath in north-south direction from Connaught Place to Aurangzeb Road. There are three nodes: Connaught Place, India Gate, and the government complex in a triangle from which roads radiate. The street system is very complex. The most spectacular part of New Delhi is the Rajpath, a boulevard for parades, beautiful parks, and government buildings. New Delhi has lot of green spaces and a beautiful city.

New Delhi is a city where sense of direction is difficult to comprehend. This problem is farther compounded by lack of road signs.

Chandigarh

After partition of India, Chandigarh was built as the capital of Punjab State, and Islamabad as the capital of Pakistan. Prime Minister Jawaharlal Nehru took great interest in the construction of Chandigarh. In 1950 the Government of India gave the project to American planner Albert Mayer, and architect Mathew Novicki. Mayer proposed the capital to the north on the foothill of Sevalik hills, large neighborhoods, and a city for 500,000 people. In 1951 Novicki died in a plane accident. The government gave the project to architect planner Le Corbusier, and English architects

Figure 1.12
Capital Cities

NEW DELHI

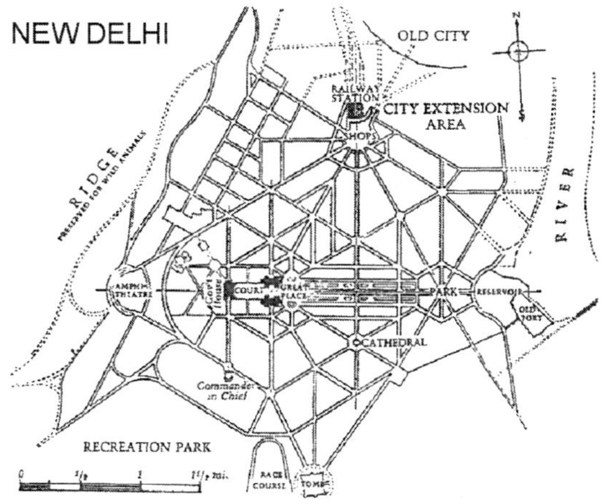

Plan of New Delhi by
Sir Edwin Lutyens, 1911

CHANDIGARH

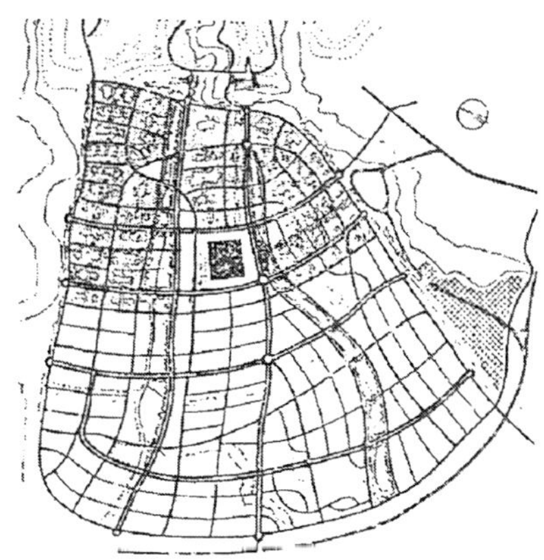

Chandigarh, India, original
Master Plan by Albert Mayer, 1950

Chandigarh: the Le Corbusier plan.
Actual layout, 1970

Source: Ervin Y. Galantay, *New Towns: Antiquity to the Present*.

Maxwell Fry and Jane Drew. Nehru instructed Le Corbusier to design the city as an expression of the nation's future and not as tradition of the past.

Le Corbusier did not alter Mayer's plan but rectified. He designed the city with rectangular super blocks of about a square kilometer as neighborhoods called sectors. Each residential sector was designed for 5,000 to 10,000 persons, containing a primary and a secondary school, a convenient small shopping center and a green space running through them. Lots were segregated by income level. Sector number 17 is the town center with town hall, shopping, movies, banks and library in a vast open plaza. Corbusier himself designed the capital with massive sculptural buildings on the foothill of the Sevalik with a man-made lake. Chandigarh turned out to be a dignified city and got worldwide attention. It became a pilgrimage of architects and urban planners. But the city has little to do with the Indian traditional living. The inhabitants had to adapt to the new way of living. In 1960 major constructions were complete.

Canberra

In 1912 an ambitious plan by the Chicago architect Walter Burley Griffin was selected, but actual construction started in 1957. The main features of the plan were damming the flood plain of the Monongolo River to create series of lakes; and a triangle formed by two miles long avenues connecting the capital, the city hall, and the railway station, very similar to New Delhi plan. It was designed as the national capital of Australia, educational center, cultural center, research center, and for light industries. Its population is homogenous and of high income. The national park in the vicinity and good environmental quality makes the city very livable. There is also plenty of area around for future expansion.

Brasilia

The first republican constitution of 1891 foresaw the need for a growth pole of development in the interior of Brazil and reserved a 14,400 sq. km. area for the future capital. In 1956 President Kubitschek created a development corporation for the new capital. In a national design competition, twenty-five projects were submitted and Lucio Costa's plan was accepted in 1957. Architect Oscar Niemeyer was given the charge of designing all public buildings. The capital city was built with unprecedented speed in three years. In April 1960 the city was officially opened and by 1970 it had a population of 500,000.

The city was planned on a lakeside. Costa's famous plan is bow-shaped with a string and an arrow. The monumental government buildings are located on the

Figure 1.13
Capital Cities

Plan of Canberra by Walter Burley Griffin, 1911

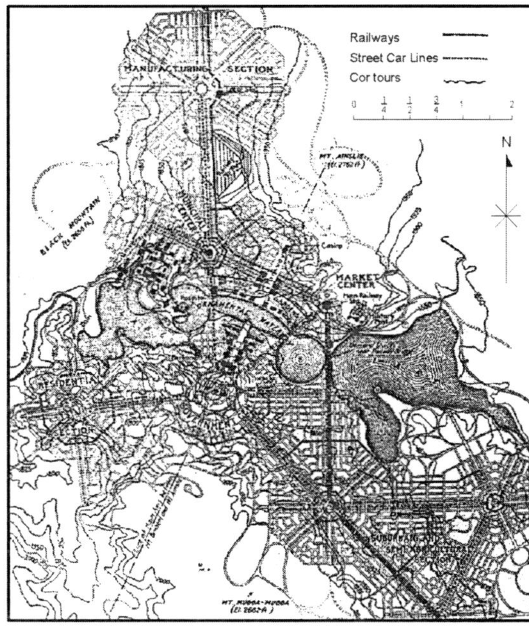

Canberra: Master Plan of center area, 1970.

1 War memorial and parade
3 City center
6 Executive offices
13 Parliamentary zones
15 Conference zone
16 Cultural zone

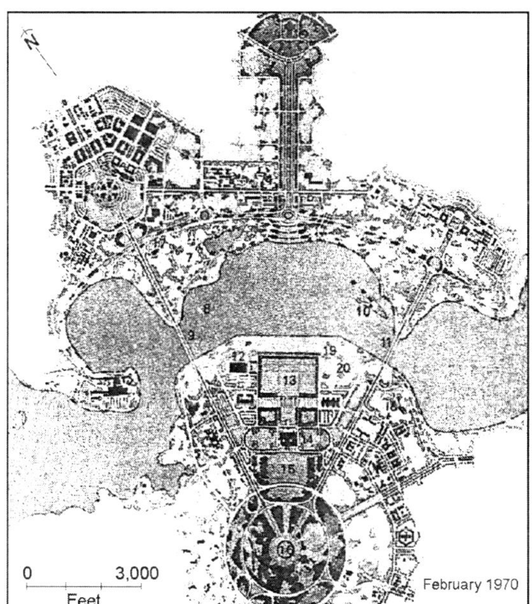

Source: Ervin Y. Galantay, *New Towns: Antiquity to the Present.*

Figure 1.14
Capital Cities

Islamabad, Pakistan: Master Plan of metropolitan area by C. Doxiades Associates, 1960.

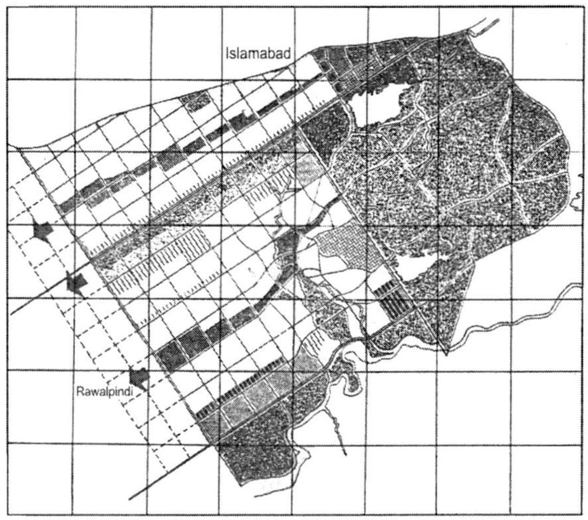

Source: Ervin Y. Galantay, *New Towns: Antiquity to the Present.*

BRASILIA

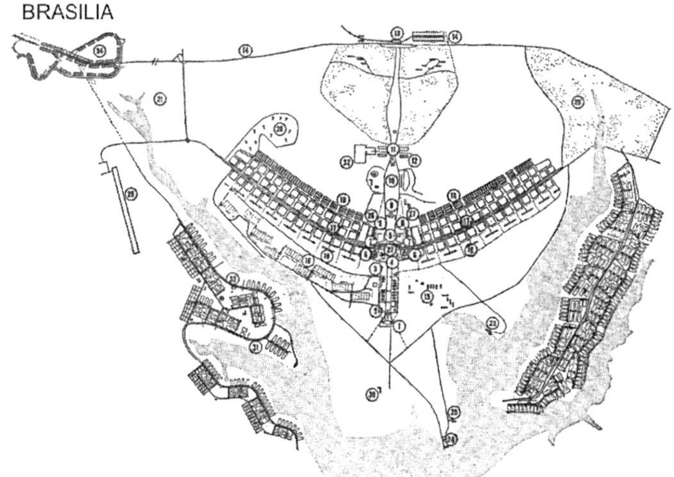

BRASILIA—General Plan

1. Plaza of the Three Powers
2. Esplanade of the Ministries
3. Cathèdral
4. Cultural Area
5. Amusement Section
6. Books and Offices
7. Commercial Area
8. Hotels
9. Radio and Television Towers
10. Sports Area
11. Municipal Plaza
12. Sentry Outpost
13. Railroad Station
14. Warehouses, Small Industries
15. The University
16. Embassies and Legations
17. Residential Zone
18. Twin Houses
19. Twin Super-Blocks
20. Botanical Gardens
21. The Zoo
22. Highway Terminal
23. Yacht Club
24. Residential Palace
25. Tourists' Hotel
26. Exhibition Grounds
27. Horse Club
28. The Cemetery
29. Airport
30. Golf Club
31. Individual Residences (So.)
32. Printing Facilities
33. Individual Residences (No.)
34. Suburban Residences (Pky.)

Source: Gallion and Eisner, *The Urban Pattern.*

arrowhead overlooking the lake. Separate areas were planned along the bow and string for residential villas for high officials, apartment buildings for middle class officials, low class workers and so on. It was a highly segregated plan by income classes. The intersection of the bow and arrow was the center for buses and urban transit. Satellite towns were planned for low income and migrant families at a distance 25 to 70 km. from Brasilia. This distance is not convenient for low-income commuters. The city was planned for speed of the automobile.

Islamabad

In 1959 Pakistan decided to build a new national capital, since Lahore was too close to the Indian boarder. Site selection was assigned to regional planner Sir Robert Matthew. He selected the site of Islamabad on the following justifications. The site to the north of Rawalpindi on the foothills of Murgala Hills has cool climate, plenty of water, and Rawalpindi nearby as a source of labor during construction. Rawalpindi and Islamabad was thought out as a twin city metropolitan area. Islamabad's function is to be an administrative and cultural center and Rawalpindi's function is to be a regional industrial and commercial center for North Pakistan and yet complementing each other. The twin-city planning district was designated with 64,000 hectors.

Preparation of the master plan was assigned to Constantinos Doxiades, a Greek architect and planner. Careful evaluation of Chandigarh and Brasilia plans, which were artistically inspired and just built, led Doxiades to a far more rational plan for Islamabad. In the plan, which he submitted in 1962, the city took the form of a triangle waged between Murgala Hills and Rawalpindi. The tip of the triangle to the northeast was planned for the capital and housing for the members of the parliament and diplomats. The city plan has a grid of four highways and arterial roads, rectangular sectors twice as large of Chandigarh sectors, each sector is a self contained town with residences, city center, business, and light industries. Each sector is again divided into three or four sub-sectors. The southwest areas of both the cities were reserved for future growth. In 1963 a Capital Development Authority was formed.

Dwarka

It is a sub-city of Delhi designed by Delhi Development Authority, construction of which started in mid-1990s. It has some interesting and new features. It has an area of 5648 Hectors. This residential city will have one million population when completed. Gross land uses includes residences 48.54 percent, recreational 20 percent, and transportation 14.33 percent. Most of the area as planed has 29 sectors. The sectors are smaller than in Chandigarh plan. The residential sectors are divided into very large plots (say 300'x1500') for flats, group housing societies with large open spaces, instead of small lots for individual homes. Such large lots are also allocated for institutional uses such as hospitals, schools, colleges, etc. Roads between sectors are three lanes each direction, with service roads on each sides. Few negative design flaws are observed. Shopping centers are placed on service roads at certain intersections of main roads, instead of large malls in those large plots. This gives the feeling of traditional street shopping, which turned out to be crowded, dirty looks, and shoppers crossing the main streets to the shops on the other on service roads. This has become a traffic hazard. Trashes on roadsides remain uncollected. Street hawkers are still there. Street signs are non-existent and therefore very difficult to get directions. Only sector numbers are posted.

Note

1. Reddaway, T. F., *The Rebuilding of London after the Great Fire*. London: Arnold.

2

Development of Modern Urban Planning

Urban planning has developed from the colonial and industrial age to the modern age through scientific and technological inventions, art and architectural movements, social reforms, emergence of planning laws, urban growth management, ecological and environmental awareness, changing emphasis in planning and development of new planning tools.

INFLUENCE OF SCIENTIFIC AND TECHNOLOGICAL INVENTIONS

There were numerous scientific and technological inventions, social and art movements in the 18th, 19th and 20th centuries, which influenced architecture, movement and agglomeration of people, and therefore urban planning. The inventions related to construction materials, economical methods of construction, and movement of people and goods influenced the growth and development of cities. These inventions made very high population densities possible. Therefore, urban planning had to adjust to these technological challenges and accomplish desired urban character. The process of adjustment to new technologies and new ideas keeps on going. A reasonably good urban plan becomes outdated over time and urban renewal becomes necessary. Hence urban planning becomes a continuous process.

Movement of People and Goods

In 1814 George Stevenson built the first steam engine railroad locomotive. This provided a cheaper way of transporting industrial products and people. Later local trains, airplanes, automobiles, subways, and monorails were invented. The invention of the automobile has a long history but in 1903, Ford Motor Company manufactured 1700 cars and the automobile age started. Later trucks and buses were built. Wider and longer roads and railroad tracks became essential parts of cities. Trains, buses and private automobiles made people mobile and able to access urban centers daily for work from considerable distances. Because of this convenience, urban centers grew bigger and encouraged urban sprawl to the nightmare of urban planners and city authorities.

Mass Production of Steel

In 1855 Englishman Sir Henry Bessemer invented a decarbonization process using a blast of air, the first process for mass-producing steel inexpensively. Mass production of steel led to wide use in bridge and skyscraper constructions. Though the first steel bridge was completed in Shropshire, England in 1779, it was only 100 ft. long. Almost a century later steel bridge construction was revolutionized with steel cable suspension bridges. Among the most famous are: End Bridge, St. Louis, 1,550 ft. long, completed in 1874; Brooklyn Bridge, New York, 3,460 ft. long, completed in 1883; First of Forth Bridge, Scotland, 8,276 ft. long, completed in 1890; Golden Gate Bridge, San Francisco, 8,981 ft. long, completed in 1937; and Akashi Kaikyo Bridge, Kobe, Japan, 12,828 ft. long, completed in 1998. Steel made construction of bridges economical and urban centers accessible over bodies of water.

Steel became the skeleton for modern skyscrapers. Home Insurance Building, Chicago, 138 ft. high, completed in 1885 was the first skyscraper built with a steel skeleton. Since then all skyscrapers, including world's tallest buildings, have been built with steel skeletons. The latest proposed tallest is World Trade Center Memorial, 1,775 ft. tall.

Cement and Concrete

In 1824 Joseph Aspdin, a British stonemason, invented cement. It resembled high quality stone quarried from the Isle of Portland off the British coast. Hence, it was called portland cement. It provided a durable mortar and plastering material and it became the main ingredient for concrete.

In 1849 Joseph Monir, a Parisian gardener, invented reinforced concrete, also called ferroconcrete. First he made garden posts and tubs with an iron mesh and concrete. Reinforced concrete combined the tensile or bendable strength of iron and the compressive strength of concrete to withstand heavy loads. He received a patent in 1867 and promoted reinforced concrete in railway ties, pipes, floors, arches, and bridges. This was a demonstration of the many uses of concrete. Concrete provided a strong and monolithic material for construction.

Figure 2.1

Alternate Subdivision Designs

DENSITY CONTROL

With the minimum prevailing lot area as the unit of measurement for the overall "gross density" in this illustration, the site would accommodate as many as 200 dwellings. Adjusting the internal street system to the topography in a typical subdivision plan, with the usual odd lot sizes which result, would produce only 137 individual lots in conformance with the standard regulations (Fig. 1). With the principle of density control applied, permitting 200 dwellings, an arrangement of clusters of row (alias "town," "group," "garden," or "Patio") houses about cul-de-sac roads results in the allocation of about one-fifth of the site for park development (Fig. 2).

This is the primary community interest served by density control. Other advantages may accrue in the planing of individual dwellings (Fig. 3), cul-de-sac roads (Fig. 4) (see next page), attractive planting along the main circulation roads, and economy in site improvement costs. These costs may be reduced to as much as one-half those of the conventional subdivision because of economy in grading, paving, drainage and utilities. The degree to which the consumer of housing shares in these economies will extend the broad social advantages which may also accrue.

Plans by courtesy of Richard Leitch, Architect

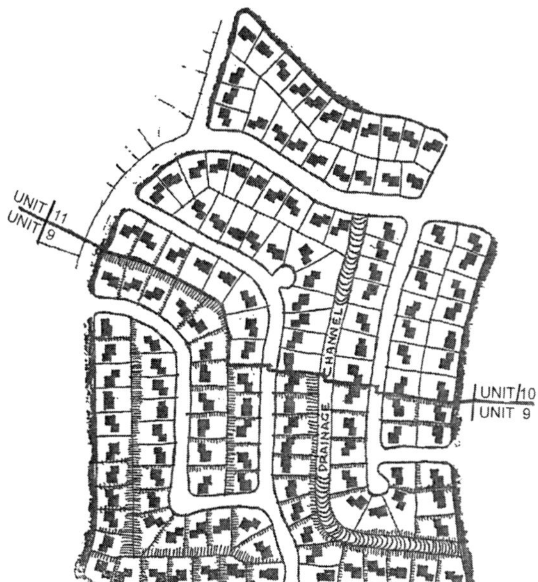

Fig. 1
CONVENTIONAL SUBDIVISION

Fig. 2
DENSITY CONTROL with CLUSTERS

Source: Gallion and Eisner, *The Urban Pattern.*

Figure 2.2

Cluster Development-Details

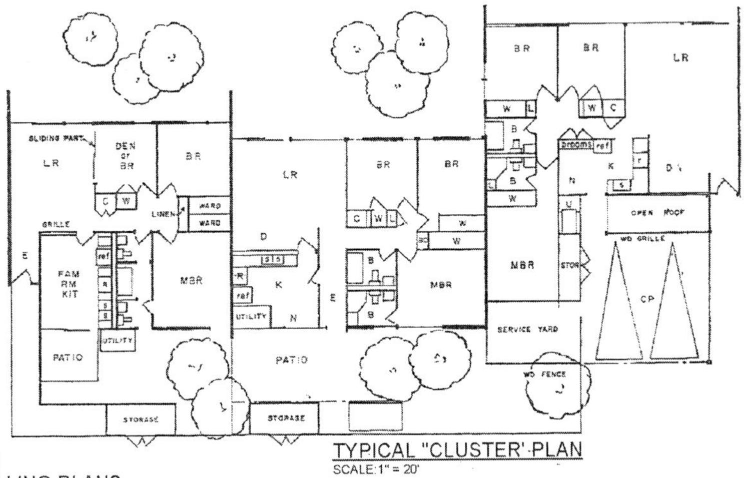

Fig. 3
DWELLING PLANS

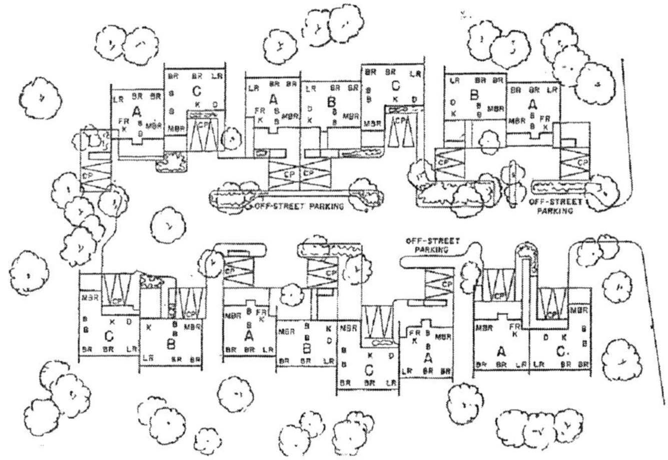

Fig. 4
DWELLING
CLUSTER
ON
CUL-DE-SAC
ROAD

VIEW
OF
CLUSTER

Source: Gallion and Eisner, *The Urban Pattern*.

In 1879, a concrete road was built in Scotland using portland cement. In 1880 the first reinforced concrete bridge was built. In 1894 Anatole de Baudot designed and built a church with slender reinforced concrete columns and vaults. This is probably the first building built with reinforced concrete. August Perret designed and built an apartment building using reinforced concrete in Paris in 1902. This influenced architecture and concrete construction. In 1908 Thomas Edition built 11 cheap, cast in place concrete houses in New Ville, New Jersey. In 1911 Rosorgime concrete bridge, spanning 328 feet, was built in Rome. In 1914 the Panama Canal dams and walls were built with reinforced steel and concrete. In 1927 Eugene Freyssinet, a French engineer, developed pre-stressed concrete. Concrete provided a very strong, rigid, durable, fireproof, and monolithic construction material for multiple uses.

Method of Structural Calculations

Steel and concrete became the new materials, replacing stone, for building and bridge construction. Acceptance of these materials was slow but certain. In 1836, the first systematic test of tensile and compressive strength was conducted in Germany. This became the basis for precise structural calculation of strength and size of steel and concrete structural members. Steel and concrete promised economy in material use; slender columns took the place of load bearing walls; extended limit of taller structures; more openness for air, ventilations and view; and faster construction time than stone. Since they are less expensive, they provided affordable and yet very good dwellings for the common people. Skyscrapers became a reality with scientific confidence.

Influence on Planning

Steel and concrete are lighter and stronger than stone, so less time is needed to erect a building than with stone. These projects are more economical due to less use of materials and reduced project financing time. The tall buildings with the aid of elevators (lifts) made urban density very high. High-rise buildings created the need for wider roads, more parking, public transportation, and urban services, which must be dealt with by planning at a very high cost. These tall office buildings bring a very high daytime population to the city centers creating a nightmare for transportation planners, utility companies, and city authorities. But the glamour of tall buildings has continued to attract people.

Energy Development

The world is waiting for liquid hydrogen gas to be invented. Fossil fuel is becoming very expensive and becoming depleted. When scientists can develop an inexpensive method of making liquid hydrogen gas from water, the energy problem will be solved forever. Water is inexhaustible and hydrogen gas is pollution free. Researchers in many countries are investigating this solution.

Once developed, it will be the greatest invention of the century. It will have tremendous positive impact on economy, political power, and urban development throughout the world.

INFLUENCE OF ART AND ARCHITECTURE MOVEMENTS ON PLANNING

Impressionist Paintings

Beginning about 1860 impressionist paintings by Claude Monet, William Turner, Francisco Goya, Edouard Manet, Paul Cezanne, Pierre Auguste Renoir, Paul Gauguin and Vincent van Gogh influenced architecture and urban planning. There is a freshness of open air, sunlight, garden and romantic environment in impressionist paintings, which was in contrast to the real living environment at the time, which was suffocating in the load of ornamentation and deprivation of air and nature. This appreciation of air, sunlight and nature gradually influenced architecture and urban planning.

Revolutionary Architectural Thoughts

Architecture is the closest profession to urban planning. Many architects are also urban planners. Hence, influence of architectural works on urban planning is undeniable.

William Morris created the famous Red House in 1851. He rejected architectural ornamentation and adopted essential building materials such as plain brick walls, a roof of heavy slates, and straightforward and sensible details. This house was a point of departure from ornamental design to a new movement in architecture. His architecture moved toward humanization, welfare and service. Lewis Mumford, a famous urban sociologist, called this a concept of new social order. Mumford quoted Morris: "Believe me, if we want art to begin at home, as it must, we must clear our houses of troublesome superfluities that are forever in our way; conventional comforts that are no real comforts, and do but make work for servants and doctors; if you want the golden rule that will fit everybody, this is it: have nothing in your house that you do not know to be useful or believe to be beautiful."

H. H. Richardson, an American master builder, turned to new forms based on new material and technology in the later part of 19th century. Until then, architectural forms were symmetrical. His works influenced Louis Sullivan and Frank Lloyd Wright, who worked for Sullivan several years.

Carlo Lodoli, who lived in Venice around 1750, first introduced the notion of function into architecture. He also introduced the notion of organic architecture. Horatio Greenough, an American neo-classicist sculptor, lived in Florence for most of his adult life. He learned Lodoli's philosophy from a book by Francisco Milizia, written in the late 18th century. Greenough wrote articles in 1840s on architecture and design in which the notion of function was emphasized. He idealized forms found in the nature. He wrote: "God's world has a distinct formula for every function, and we seek in vain to borrow shapes; we must make shapes and can only affect this by mastering the principles."

Sullivan summarized this philosophy in three words: 'Form Follows Function' in an article "The Tall Office Building Artistically Considered" published in 1896. This dictum fundamentally changed the architectural approach to design. Now architects pay more attention to functionality of a building, furniture, kitchen utensils, etc. and the form or shape follows the functionality of each object. In furniture design, a chair that fits the contours of the body is more comfortable and desirable than an elegantly decorated chair that is not functionally comfortable. Morris, Richardson and Sullivan understood the failure and paralysis of imagination of the architects of their age, who copied old architectural styles. With new materials of steel and concrete they found a new medium for architectural expression in a new social attitude. The urban planners also started following the same dictum in organization of space. Wright carried Sullivan's theme further. Some later architects believe that form and function are complementary to each other.

The Bauhaus was the most famous, inspiring, radical, visionary, and brilliant period of art, architecture, and craftsman as school or workshop of the 20th century founded by Walter Gropius (1883-1969) in 1919. It was based in Weimar then moved to Dessau in Germany in 1925. Gropius resigned as director in 1929 and moved to the United States and became Chairman of the Harvard Architecture School. Hannes Meyer, then Ludwig Mies Van der Rohe (1880 1969) became directors of the Bauhaus. The German word *'bau'* approximately means construction and building and Bauhaus means 'house of building'. The Bauhaus included architecture, carpentry, metal, pottery, stained glass, wall painting, weaving, graphics, typography, and stagecraft. The faculty included the most creative and famous people in each field. It was a community of visionaries, a spiritual center.

William Morris' theme "have nothing in your home that you do not know to be useful or believe to be beautiful" echoed in Bauhaus. Charles Rennie Mackintosh's conviction "construction should be decorated, and not decoration constructed ... the salient and most requisite features should be selected for ornamentation" found resonance in Bauhaus. The machine age arrived. The radical iron and glass pre-fabricated structure, called Crystal Palace, housed the Great Exhibition of industrial works in London in 1851. All these thoughts influenced Gropius. Gropius wanted his school to act as a catalyst of social change through design just like Expressionist Artists believed that art could change society. He believed architecture, painting, sculptors must all return to the craft. There is no difference between artist and craftsman and a foundation of craft-discipline is essential. Bauhaus incorporated technology, simplicity, and rational use of materials. In other words, it sought a new unity of art, architecture and technology. The Bauhaus was for beautiful forms, utility, honest use of materials, and efficiency of technology. Modern houses and buildings with glass and steel came into being – the modern architecture. Mies' dictum 'less is more' perfectly described his elegant architectural works of glass and steel buildings. The movement in new architecture had spread to other countries. Hitler and the Nazis called the Bauhaus a Jewish-Marxist manifestation and closed the Bauhaus on September 30, 1932. Mies immigrated to the Unites States in 1938 and became Head of the Architecture Department at the Illinois Institute of Technology, Chicago. Loszlo Moholy-Nagy also immigrated to Chicago. Other famous associates and students also took exile in U.S.A. and European countries. Bauhaus was gone but its ideas had spread.

SOCIAL REFORMS

The royalty, nobles, landlords, and merchants always had a place in city planning in history, but slaves and commoners did not. During the industrial revolution, there was no housing consideration for the workers in planning the cities. The slaves and commoners in Europe, Negroes and low-income people in the United States, and the *Harijans* and the poor in India all lived in isolated slums or ghettos in cities. Their services were required but they did not exist as human beings, living without healthy housing, infrastructures for health, recreational, educational, and social needs. Because of unhygienic conditions, plague and other epidemics broke out in many countries killing millions of people including the privileged. The conditions of unprivileged people and the effects of their bad living conditions on the privileged became an issue and gained consideration in planning.

Many industrialists took initiative to provide better living conditions for their workers such that they could be healthy and more productive. Subsidized housing, low-income housing, slum clearance, etc. became public policies of the governments. The planners were required to plan for the unprivileged. Lewis Mumford (1895-1990), an urban sociologist, is probably the most prolific writer of the century on urban sociology and on the conditions of the poor. He greatly influenced planning for the unprivileged.

CHANGING EMPHASIS IN PLANNING: PURPOSES OF PLANNING

The planning laws and urban planners universally agree the purpose of urban planning is to plan for public health, public safety and public welfare. In reality, all three purposes blend together and are hard to distinguish one from another. Let us discus these terms as applicable.

Public Health

Webster's dictionary defines health as: the condition of being sound in body, mind, or soul; freedom from physical disease or pain.

Public health engineering became the response to this problem. The medical approach to the public health issue was prevention of disease, which is now termed as the 'medical model'. The medical model defined health narrowly as absence of disease or infirmity. This model later recognized germ theory, control of pathogens, and public vaccination. Since then, the concept of health changed tremendously and so did the urban planning approach.

A 'social model' of public health is taking shape since 1980 or so. Public health professionals, urban planners, and city leaders recognize environmental effects on the physical and mental health of the public. There are two major environmental effects. (1) Environmental pollution of air and industrial pollution. The 'car-centric' society release carbon monoxide and lead from petroleum, and industrial pollutants like toxins and asbestoses cause asthma, allergic disorders, respiratory diseases and cancer. (2) Loss of trees and green spaces reduced oxygen supply; loss of open spaces and playgrounds reduced exercise and physical rejuvenation; lack of community meeting facilities reduced social contact. These two environmental outcomes have effected vitality (physical and mental) of the people in congested urban spaces. The social isolation caused loneliness, mental depression, distress, and deterioration of social ties increased alcohol consumption and violence. This effected the children and the elderly population the most.

The World Health Organization, Regional Office for Europe published a report *Healthy Cities and the City Planning Process* in 1999, written by L. J. Duhl and A. K. Sanchez of the University of California, Berkeley. This report suggests developing health as a key principle in urban planning. The Constitution of the World Health Organization defined health as:

"Health is a state of complete physical, mental and social well-being and not merely the absence of disease and infirmity. The enjoyment of the highest attainable standard of health is one of the fundamental rights of every human being without distinction of race, religion, political belief or economic and social condition."

In 1986, the First International Conference on Health Promotion, held in Ottawa declared: "the fundamental conditions and resources for health are peace, shelter, education, food, income, a stable ecosystem, sustainable resources, social justice and equity. Improvement in health requires a secure foundation in these requirements."

The new public health paradigm has six major guiding tenets or principles:

1. Health is not merely the absence of disease or disability.
2. Health problems are defined at the policy level.
3. Health is a social issue.
4. Improving health status requires a long-term focus on policy development.
5. Improving health status requires a primary focus on changing basic conditions.
6. Improving health status requires involving natural leaders in the process of change.

The public health is shifting its focus to this social model. In addition to the medical model, physical environment and social organizations are gaining attention.

India recognizes the severity of the environmental problems of public health, air and water pollution, wildlife, deforestation, and soil erosion. India adopted the 42nd Amendment to the Constitution in 1976 addressing the environment. India also passed the Environment Protection Act of 1986.

Public Safety

Webster's dictionary defines safety as: the condition of being safe from undergoing or causing hurt, injury, or loss. The word 'safe' also means free from threat of danger, harm, or loss. In urban planning and architectural design, safety will mean physical safety.

The urban space should be safe from any physical danger, harm, or injury. Urban planners are concerned about road accidents, fatalities and injuries. Blame for accidents cannot be placed on human error alone. Proper design of wide roads, traffic control, pedestrian crossing, wide and leveled sidewalks, safe playground and equipment standards, fire stations, etc. can reduce accidents.

Law enforcement is necessary to stop or reduce crime but crime cannot be completely resolved by the police force. Thomas McKeown's research supports the notion that physical design effects behavior. The city management can make the space safer by maintaining a well-lighted and clean environment. The urban planners, urban designers, and architects can make the urban space safer by thoughtful design of the urban space. Defensible space must be designed. Public use areas should be visible from long distances, design should not create hiding space, and a variety of activities should be planned such that there are people present through the end of operating hours.

Oscar Newman suggested some techniques in his book *Defensible Space* for residential neighborhoods. His techniques were based on surveillance of the intruders by the residents. He considered hierarchy of spaces: public space, semi-public space and private spaces. The main road in the neighborhood is a public space. Cul-de-sac, dead end roads, other limited access roads, and entrances to groups of homes are semi-public space. The space within the parcel of land is a private space. The residents in a semi-public space know each other. If a stranger enters this space, he may be detected by someone, which is a deterrent. He suggests group homes defined by street blocks. Vehicles are not restricted but discourage easy vehicular access. Real barriers such as U-shaped building, high walls or fences, locked gates and doors; and symbolic barriers such as open gateways, light standards, planting, and change of texture of the walking surface restrict the behavior of the intruder.

Residential neighborhoods are made safe by not allowing: through traffic, business that attracts strangers, and harmful industries. Gated residential communities, which prevent entering the community without a gate opening code, have been growing in number since 1975 or so in the United States.

Public Welfare

Webster's dictionary defines welfare as the state of doing well especially in respect to good fortune, happiness, well-being, or prosperity. This definition includes everything that a person would desire. A planner is limited in scope to facilitating the designation of space for development and growth of employment. He shall provide space for: health services, schools, libraries, parks and recreational facilities, fire stations, post offices, neighborhood shopping centers, community activities and meeting places for meaningful social contact, etc. to create an environment of community well-being. Community needs should be emphasized over individual needs, for a better society.

CHANGING URBAN PLANNING CONCEPTS

A Master Plan was thought to be the answer to ill-planning or an absence of planning in the industrial cities. Master plans were primarily an engineering blueprint for streets, transportation system, public buildings, parks, housing and other physical facilities for urban services. The blueprint was viewed as the end product. The company towns like a railway colony, oil refinery township, steel plant township, university campus are examples of master plans. This master plan concept was extended to cover the whole city (existing and future developments) with a fixed land use pattern and a finite city size. When planning a city, it involves much more than the requirements of a township in bigger scale such as varieties of land use, ecological and environmental issues, land conservation, recreational and open spaces, traffic circulation, mass transit, parking, airport, housing, sewer, drainage, water supply, electricity, historical and scenic preservation, intergovernmental coordination, etc. Some master plans started incorporating these planning elements. However, due to rigidity and lack of comprehensiveness, the master plan concept of urban planning was no longer considered a viable solution and it was totally abandoned around 1960 in the western world.

City Plans by Other Names

The comprehensive planning concept started incorporating planning elements mentioned above in 1938 and many cities started calling their plans Comprehensive Plans in mid-1960s. In 1964, T.J. Kent, Professor of City Planning, University of California, Berkeley called the city plan 'The Urban General Plan' in his book of the same name. The city of Orlando calls its plan Growth Management Plan. Some other cities call their plan Strategic Plan since they include strategies to implement their plan. A recent name is Sustainable Community Plan.

No matter what name is used, the objectives remain the same: to develop the city to a desired physical development, only the emphasis is changing.

Two Sides of the Coin

The purpose of urban planning is to accomplish a desirable physical environment. In India, physical planning is emphasized with little or no emphasis on policy planning. In the United States policy planning is first and physical planning follows. Both of these doctrines have pitfalls and need a hybrid or equal emphasis.

In physical planning doctrine, physical development decisions are made based on certain assumptions, and therefore are rigid and predictable but without any policy criteria. In policy planning doctrine, physical planning development decisions are made based on certain prewritten goals, objectives and policies, called the policy plan, and therefore fluid and uncertain until the land development takes place. What is needed is physical planning decisions based on goals, objectives and policies before the land development takes place on major projects like highway development, office park, residential subdivisions, commercial developments, civic center, etc.

URBAN GROWTH MANAGEMENT

What do we do when we suddenly experience vast urban growth? Can traditional planning or established land uses, zoning, or subdivision regulations help? The answer is no. The planners and city authorities in the United States could not figure out until the 1970s how to deal with the situation. India has had tremendous urban growth and will see even more with the spurring economy and after the completion of east-west and north-south corridors and many more and better roads. We can learn from the experiences of the United States and be prepared.

Many urban areas in the United States grew very fast post World War II. Three major factors contributed to this unprecedented urban growth: (a) a booming economy attracted people from rural areas, (b) construction of more, bigger and better roads increased mobility – construction of Interstate Freeways started in 1956 and completed in mid-70s, and (c) heavy immigration from war torn countries in Europe.

There were negative effects such as: fiscal inefficiency, social injustice, and environmental degradation. To relieve the pressure of overcrowding, urban sprawl and leapfrog developments took place. Some communities set standards for big lots and large homes, which were meant to exclude low and moderate income residents. This exclusionary zoning practice and unaffordable home prices drove them farther away, to developments in farmlands. Small communities in suburban areas and further out continued to develop. Compared to property tax earned, it was more expensive to provide electricity, water, sewer, drainage, and school buses to spread out communities. It encouraged segregation of families based on income and race. The tide of suburban low-density housing developments in the urban sprawl created environmental problems such as: replacement of scenic landscapes, forestlands, and farmland; flooding; and destruction of habitats for birds, fish, wild animals and plants which are part of the ecological system.

Growth management addresses six broad goals[1]:

(1) Protect lands that provide public and quasi-public goods – Public goods are clean air, flood and erosion control, recharged watersheds, protection of landscape, and habitats for threatened and endangered species. This can be done by regulation, land acquisition, subsidies for those complying with public policies, zoning restrictions, buffer requirements, pollution control, and targeting planning areas.

(2) Accommodate development needs – Contain urban development within certain designated geographic areas which are called urban growth boundaries (UGD). Assurance should be given that within 15 or 20 years urban services will be provided to certain areas within UGD, which will be called urban service areas (USAs). Flexible development regulations should be used such as planned unit development, zero lot line, high density but low land coverage, and single family homes.

(3) Provide adequate public facilities and services at minimal cost and distribute costs equitably – Adequate public facilities and services must be provided before building construction begins. The costs of public facilities and services must be distributed to other development projects that use them.

(4) Distribute the burdens and benefits of growth fairly – The whole community shares facilities such as a sanitary landfill, a water treatment plant, and a sewage treatment plant, and civic amenities and expenses should be shared equitably.

(5) Prevent or mitigate negative and foster positive externalities – Land development can have positive or negative effects or externalities. If the municipality builds a road, the property value will increase. When a sanitary landfill is created, land value will decrease. A noisy industry is not desirable near residences, and therefore has to mitigate the problem by solid boundary walls, using less noisy machinery or by some other means. Negative effects must be avoided or mitigated.

(6) Provide administrative efficiency – The growth management system must have long range planning, impact analysis, permitting process and negotiations with the developer, provide clear and objective standards for development, set deadlines for review, and involve elected officers, the developer and citizens.

ENVIRONMENTAL CONSCIOUSNESS

Environmental consciousness and issues began about 1970, about the same time as urban growth management became important. In the past development decisions were made on cost benefit analysis. Later on environmental impact analysis became a part of development decisions. It is now recognized that any land use will effect the earth and the ecosystem. Land developments impact the environment in many different ways: (a) destruction of forest, wetland, rivers, hills, trees and vegetation; (b) loss of environmentally sensitive areas cause loss of habitats for birds, plants, fish, and wildlife; (c) disturbing the natural drainage system causes flooding and soil erosion; and (d) air, water and noise pollution. The instances of cancer, lung diseases etc. of people due to industrial waste dumps polluting underground water and automobile pollution in the air are well documented. All these are happening due to ruinous exploitation of nature, which must be avoided.

A site development analysis includes environmental factors: earth (seismic hazard, soil condition, topography, unique features, wind erosion, water erosion, geologic hazards); air (quality, odors, climate); water (surface flow, absorption rates, drainage pattern, flood water, surface water, flow of ground water, ground water quality); plants and animals (diversity of species, rare species, new species, habitat areas); noise (noise level, exposure to noise); natural resources (use of natural resources, deplete resources); hazardous waste (toxic substances, emergency plan); housing development (existing housing, housing factors); transportation (vehicle movement, parking, transportation systems, circulation pattern, rail traffic, air traffic, traffic hazards); public services (fire protection, police protection, schools, park facilities, public facilities, other government services); energy (fuel, demand on energy); Utilities (power, natural gas, communication, water, sewer, storm drains, solid waste); and cultural (archeology, historic, paleontology, unique cultural values). (Source: *The Practice of Local Government Planning*, p. 94)

The United States passed the 1969 National Environmental Policy Act and established the Environmental Protection Agency (EPA). In 1970 Clean Air Act was passed and created national ambient air quality standards. Many states passed environmental laws since then. The State of Florida passed Florida Environmental Land and Water Management Act of 1972. Every major project is required to prepare and submit an Environmental Impact Report/Statement for review and approval to the State Planning Agency. Environmental analysis has become a very specialized subject.

India passed the 42nd Amendment to the Constitution in 1976, allowing for the state to intervene and to protect public health, forests and wildlife. But a clause stated "shall not be enforceable by any court". A more effective legislation, the Environmental Protection Act of 1986 was passed. The Ministry of Environment and Forests has overall responsibility for administering and enforcing environmental laws and policies.

SUSTAINABLE COMMUNITY

To sustain means to withstand, to prolong, to endure, or to survive well. The word sustainability is used frequently such as sustainable industry, sustainable agriculture, sustainable community, etc. As far as a community (city, town, village, and district) is concerned, it is the overall well-being of the community. The United Nations' World Commission on Environment and Development (The Bruntdland Commission) 1987 report, *Our Common Future*, defined sustainable development as "development that meets the need of the present without compromising the ability of future generations to meet their own needs." From the summer of 1994 to the spring of 1995, the U. S. National Science and Technology Council sponsored a series of policy workshops to develop the *Bridge to a Sustainable Future: National Environmental Technology Strategy*, published in April 1995. This may have been the beginning of the Sustainable Community Movement in the United States.

Sustainable community focuses on a long-term integrated systems approach, healthy communities, and quality-of-life issues by addressing economic, environmental, and social issues. These three issues are interconnected, interdependent, integrated, and in balance, analogous to a three-legged stool. The legs represent economic, social, and environmental components and the seat represents the sustainable community.

Economic issues include stable employment opportunities, good wages, technology development, and matching jobs with the skills and education of the available work force. If a community does not have a strong economy, it cannot sustain the community.

Environmental issues include protecting human and environmental health; healthy ecosystems and habitat; elimination of pollution in water, air, and land; green spaces and parks for wildlife and recreation; and protection of biodiversity. Life will be sustained in good environment.

Social issues include education level of the people in the community, educational opportunities, social organizations and opportunities, cultural activities, incidence of respiratory disease, persons below poverty level, and violent crime. If a community has significant social problems, it cannot be stable in the long term.

Maureen Hart in her book *Guide to Sustainable Community Indicators*, discussed sustainability indicators, community capital, and carrying capacity, which are briefly discussed below. What measures can be taken at the community level to make them sustainable is the focus of this discussion. The indicators must be identified and measured, and solutions must be found.

Economic Indicators: How is your town or city doing economically? What can be done to improve the economy? Examine these indicators: Can the wage earned support basic needs; diversity and vitality of local job base; number of large employers; available skill levels in the community; are the wages paid in the local economy spent in the local economy; local financial resilience.

Environmental Indicators: They are ambient levels of pollution in air and water; use and generation of toxic materials; tons of solid waste generated and recycled or composted; total energy used from all sources and cost of energy.

Social Indicators: Matching education and skills to the need of local economy by residents of the community; participation of the people in making democratic decisions for the community; social and cultural opportunities.

It is difficult to categorize a particular indicator in one of the above three categories. Therefore, the following list may be considered: economy, environment, society and culture, education, health, population, government/politics, housing, recreation, energy, land use, public safety, resource use, and transportation.

Community Capital

Capital refers to money and material goods. Community capital for sustainability refers to the following:

Built and financial capital: Manufactured goods, equipment, buildings, roads, water supply system, jobs, information resources, and the credit and debt of a community. A community that allows its buildings, roads, parks, power facilities, water facilities, and waste processing capability to decay is eroding its built capital.

Human and social capital: The people in a society, their skills, education, health, and ability to cooperate and work together. A community that allows its children to be poorly educated, under-nourished, and poorly housed is eroding its human capital. A community that allows its social interactions to decline through lack of trust, respect, and tolerance is eroding its social capital.

Natural capital: The natural environment, natural resources, the services that the ecosystem provides, and the life-enhancing qualities of nature. A community that allows wetland development, destroys hills, uses up water resources, pollutes the water, and removes forest is plundering the natural capital.

All three types of capital are necessary for communities and need to be improved over time.

Carrying Capacity

The ecosystem can support a community within certain limits before degradation. The carrying capacity is the number of people an ecosystem can support indefinitely. The limit is defined by the following three factors: (a) the amount of resources available in the ecosystem, (b) the size of population, and (c) the amount of resources each individual is consuming. We cannot use up the natural capital.

A simple example of carrying capacity for a farmer is: how many animals he could feed on his land. But if he brings fodder from outside the question of carrying capacity may be moot. Yet there is wide range of risks with erodible soil, poorly drained soil, floods, landslides, high water tables, and fragile flora and fauna. Therefore, the percentage of land that can be developed without environmental damage is limited. There are other factors which may limit natural carrying capacity: soil characteristics, topography, geology, waste disposal space, and ecosystem maintenance. Therefore, carrying capacity analysis is a valuable planning tool for growth and development.[2]

Sustainable Living and Sustainable Development

Dulal Chandra Goswami of Guwahati discussed sustainability and environment at the global level in his article "Sustainable Living and Sustainable Development", published in *The Assam Tribune* on June 5, 2003 on the occasion of World Environment Day. This outstanding article is reprinted below:

"Sustainable living denotes a lifestyle where the various social, cultural, economic and other human activities are compatible with the preservation of environment. It is centered on the concept of interdependence, of respect for both living and non-living components of nature, and of responsibilities for future generations. Another paradigm akin to and, to a great extent, dependent on it is sustainable development that has been dominating the realm of nature conservation and environmental protection vis-à-vis economic development since the 1980's. However, the concept of sustainability has since long past been a part of our cultural, social and religious ethos as evidenced by numerous reverberations of these ideas in our ancient literature, legends, scriptures and philosophical treatises. The *Upanishad* emphasis the use of nature without greed and cautioned that no creature is superior to others and hence human beings should not have absolute power over nature. Similarly, Kalidasa in *Kumar Sambhabarn* talks of milking the earth on a long-term basis by feeding and caring for the cow before we go to milk it.

Many scholars have observed that the ideas of sustainable development are rooted in perennial themes of responsibility to others, providing for the future and dependence of life on the natural environment. Daly (1992) cautioned that it is both morally and economically wrong to treat the world as if it were a business in liquidation. Someone has rightly compared the way the present generation has started wanton plundering of the earth to the 'scorched earth policy' followed by an occupation army in an occupied territory. Mahatma Gandhi's golden words of wisdom on the ethical and ecological aspects of the code of conduct of our life on earth become the most frequently uttered bywords of our time. In his beguilingly simple words he summarized it all when he wrote, "Nature has enough to satisfy everyone's need, but not everyone's greed." These words have more relevance today than ever before.

The term 'sustainable development' first came into prominence in the report entitled World Conservation Strategy published by the International Union for Conservation of Nature (IUCN) in 1980. As stated in the report, we are morally obliged to our descendants and to other creatures to act prudently because "we have not inherited the earth from our parents, rather we have borrowed it from our children". The usage of the term has gained greater currency since the publication of the Bruntdland Report, *Our Common Future,* in 1987 under the auspices of the World Commission on Environment and Development (WCED). Sustainable development, according to Bruntdland, is development that meets the needs of the present without usurping those of the future generation.

The concept got further boost and greater attention since the United Nations Conference on Environment and Development, popularly known as the Earth Summit, held in Rio de Janeiro in June 1992. A follow-up of this has taken place in the last World Summit on Sustainable Development held at Johannesburg, South Africa, in August/September 2002.

There have been several other efforts in the broad area of environment and conservation, besides the major global initiatives discussed above that have significantly contributed towards consolidation of the concept of sustainable development. The most prominent one among these is the UN Conference on Human Environment held in Stockholm in 1972, which is undoubtedly a major milestone in the development of global responses to environmental issues. The significance of this event is being remembered every year when we observe the Environment Day on June 5. Among the many ideas that transpired from the conference some of the major ones are: (i) environment and development could be managed to the advantage of both, (ii) lack of development could be as important an agent of environmental damage as development and (iii) pollution of poverty that is rampant in the developing world is a serious challenge to environmental preservation.

In 1991, IUCN published a second major policy statement. The focus on caring for the earth, had shifted from conservation to sustainable living. One of the cardinal principles of this concept is respect and care for the community of life.

The UN's Earth Charter of Principles of Environmental Protection and Sustainable Development, a sequel to the 1992 Rio Earth Summit, sought to promote environmental protection and sustainable livelihoods drawing heavily on indigenous cultures, traditional wisdom, belief and practices. Among the key provisions of the Earth Charter a few relevant ones are: (i) respect the earth, recognizing the intrinsic worth of all living beings independent of their value to humanity, (ii) protect and restore the diversity, integrity and beauty of the planet's ecosystem and (iii) share natural resources equitably among all – rich and poor, males and females, present and future generation.

It is increasingly being recognized that the lifestyles of the affluent classes in the western countries in particular and in other countries in general (where it is molded through mindless initiations and wayward consumerism in the model of the West) have considerable ecological and social costs bringing thereby tremendous stress on the earth's life-support system and the quality of life. The prime reasons for our destructive impact on environment are our unsupportable rates of consumption of resources and excessive disposal of wastes. Over consumption, a dominant trait of the modern affluent society, means using more than the environment can sustainable support. It appears as though right to consume has become the guiding spirit for the modern man. It is estimated that if the global population were to live at the level of the US, we would need at least three worlds! The global gross domestic product has increased more than ten fold over the last 50 years, but more than a billion people live today in abject poverty without the basic necessities of life. Recent reports suggest that the quality of life in the US (as measured by the Index of Social Health) in the last three decades has gone down by 52 percent while the per capita consumption has risen by 45 percent. The product-oriented lifestyles of the West are being aggressively marketed through the media causing considerable impact on the people of the emerging economies who are fast losing their moorings on the traditional conservationist ethos cultural value systems.

It is rightly being apprehended that if the present trend of over consumerism and environmental degradation continues, we will soon overshoot the carrying capacity of the earth causing irreversible damage to it and to all life forms it supports. Culture, more than nature, is the principal detriment of earth's future. With the passing time, this realization will become increasingly obvious to us.

In recent times, several innovative policy analysis tools are available for evaluating policy options for environmentally sound decision-making process. The three most outstanding ones among them are: (i) the Ecological Footprint, (ii) Environmental Space, and (iii) Genuine Progress Indicators (GPI). Developed by Mathis Wakernagel and William Rees of the University of British Columbia, the Ecological Footprint is an accounting tool that calculates the area of productive land needed to support, on a long-term basis, the lifestyles of an individual or a population. Environmental Space is another innovative tool developed by the Friends of the Earth in Netherlands. The concept includes the entire gamut of materials produced, consumed and thrown away (i.e. economic throughput) that could be sustained indefinitely. As an example, it is shown that by 2010, the people of Netherlands would need to reduce consumption of energy by 60 percent, fresh water by 38 percent, aluminum by 80 percent, wood use by 65 percent and land used for agriculture by 45 percent to attain the equitable sharing of resource at the global level. The Gamine Progress Indicator is developed by the San Francisco Organization, Redefining Progress, as an alternative to the Gross Economic Product. While GDP assumes all economic activities are good for the economy and for people, GPI incorporates the measures of well-being and sustainability taking into consideration environmental and social impacts of development. As an example, it is cited that while the GDP in the US has risen steadily in the last fifty years, the DPI has declined considerably indicating a slump in the nation's well-being.

No doubt, our ever-increasing power to change and shape the world around us enjoins upon us an equally finding responsibility to be a conscientious caretaker and a watchful steward of the various national endowments that have been bequeathed to us for sustaining ourselves and keeping the continuity of life and civilization on this only habitable planet for us.

Let us remember two Chinese proverbs that may appear relevant in the context of what is discussed above (i) if we do not change our course, we will arrive where we are going, (ii) one who ties the knot must know how to untie it.

STRATEGIC PLANNING

Strategic planning is akin to military strategy employed to win a war or battle. It is a short-term objective to accomplish the goal leading to a vision. Community Action Plan is another term used in the same context. The purpose is the same, to do what we need to do to accomplish our objective, goal, and vision. The term strategic planning has been used since 1990 or so. It is a community capital building process. While a comprehensive plan provides general guidance for the long term, a strategic plan is specific to short-term initiatives and actions within the context of the comprehensive plan.

Moving from Vision to Action

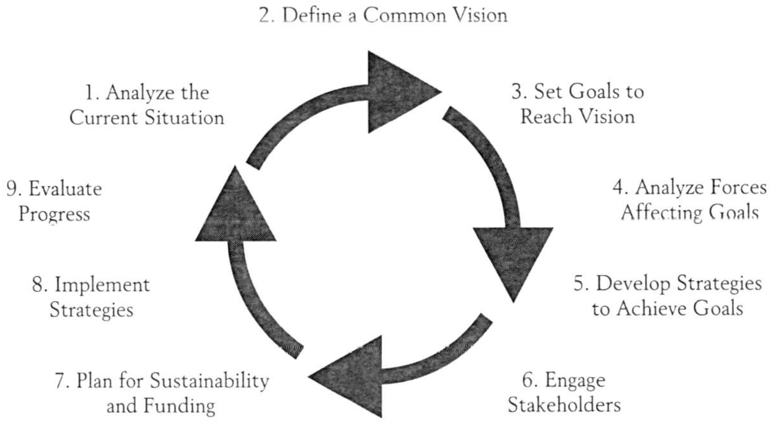

Source: Moving from Vision to Action: A Guide for Planning Community Change, ©June 2002 MDC, Inc.

There are some strategic planning models but each community should develop or modify its own model to be effective. Appalachian Regional Commission in the United States uses a model called *Moving from Vision to Action: A Guide for Planning Community Change*, developed by MDC, Inc., a private nonprofit organization. There are nine steps in the model, which is easy to understand. This model has wide ranging applicability in business, industry, and government.

Moving from Vision to Action: Summary

Step	*Purpose*	*Key Questions*
1. Analyze the current situation	Understand the current situation and determine assets and challenges to address.	Where are our strengths, weaknesses, opportunities, and threats? What assets should we build on? What challenges must we overcome?
2. Define a common vision	Develop consensus on a vision for the community's future.	At its ideal, what would our community be like?
3. Set goals to reach vision	Define goals that will move the community toward the ideal future.	To bring about our vision, what specific outcomes must we achieve?
4. Analyze forces affecting goals	Determine the forces working for and against the goals.	What forces will affect our efforts to achieve these goals, and how do we address them?
5. Develop strategies to achieve goals	Determine what actions will achieve the goals and what measures will indicate their achievement.	What is the most effective approach to reach those outcomes? What are the measures of success?
6. Engage Stakeholders	Ensure that those critical to success are involved.	Have we engaged the people and organizations that need to be involved?
7. Plan for sustainability and funding	Ensure long-term sustainability of the process and strategies.	How will we administer, maintain, and pay for our work – short term and long term?
8. Implement strategies	Develop work plans and define responsibilities and timeline. Implement work plans.	Who will do what, when? How do we ensure accountability to our group and the community?
9. Evaluate progress	Design an approach to measure and evaluate progress. Provide data for return to step 1, analyzing the new current situation.	Are our strategies moving us effectively and efficiently toward our goals? How much progress have we made so far? What else needs to be done?

Source: MDC, Inc., Appalachian Regional Commission

PUBLIC PARTICIPATION AND CONSENSUS BUILDING

Urban planning is a local government function. For any urban planning effort to be successful, partnership between the planning function of the government and the local community is a must. The collective wisdom of the community and the professional wisdom of the planning agency must converge to produce a desirable city.

Once public partnership is accomplished, the rest of the planning solutions will fall in line.

In the democratic sense, planning is for the people and by the people. Therefore, in a democratic society, citizens must express their desire through community associations. Conflicts will arise but must be resolved in the spirit of greater community interest and not in the interest of influential groups. A pitfall of the democratic process is that often the majority is wrong, because they are guided by sentiments, wrong information, and short sightedness.

The problem of reaching a just solution multiplies, because there are too many agencies, departments, jurisdictions, citizen groups, community activists, and special interest groups. They are interconnected but none of them has enough authority, influence, or resources to arrive at just solutions.

The necessity of a catalytic leadership is realized in this situation. A leader who will take charge like a corporate leader and dictate visionary solutions is needed. He forges active partnerships, gives hope, inspiration and spirit to the citizens. He is an expert on conflict resolution; his style is artistic and organic rather than mechanical. J. Luke in his book *Catalytic Leadership* listed four tasks to have a catalytic impact:

1. Focus attention by elevating the issue to the public and policy agency agendas.
2. Engage people in the effort by convening the diverse set of individuals, agencies and interests needed to address the issue.
3. Stimulate multiple strategies and options for action.
4. Sustain action and maintain momentum by managing the interconnections through appropriate institutionalization and rapid information sharing and feedback.

Public participation is necessary in both plan formulation and implementation stages. Public participation is accomplished by public hearings and encouraging individual citizens, civic clubs, neighborhood associations, businesses and professional organizations to participate in planning commission discussions. Civic leaders should be included in the planning commission and advisory committee. Such participation shall lead to intelligent understanding of public problems. They should be informed of planning objectives, procedures and methods of accomplishing them. Unless the public understands and is prepared to accept planning objectives, they will not conform to public control and public policies cannot be successfully enforced. There are three important factors in public participation: (a) People will be interested in planning if they understand the basic essential characteristics of objectives, methods and long-range planning. (b) They will take action if they feel a sense of personal participation and responsibility. (c) Some people are interested in some special aspects of city development. If they are made aware of the inter relationship between their special interest and the city development plan, they may be supportive of planning decisions.

Civic education in planning is therefore very important. Residents may become informed through news media and public meetings in neighborhoods. Maintenance of public relation with news media such as newspaper, radio, television, news reporters, feature writers, and program directors, therefore, is a necessary part of any planning effort.

The purpose of public participation is coalition building. A coalition is a set of diverse groups working together to form an alliance to accomplish a set goal and objectives, formulate policies, and accomplish them. While the goal may be the same or similar, the objectives and methods of accomplishing them may be different. In such situations, skillfull and effective leadership style, mediation, conflict resolution and decision-making capabilities are needed. The coalition must sustain its vitality, recruit new members, train new members, and prepare current members for future leadership roles. It must sustain hype and momentum surrounding target activities. The coalition members must have patience, because they will be dealing with long range plans. The land survey methodology of going from whole to parts is applicable in case of urban planning. That is going from broad planning to details.

Demonstration of success on a small level creates public interest and has a ripple effect. For example, start a renewal project in one neighborhood and provide wider roads, drainage, water, solid waste collection, park, community gathering facilities, etc. Seeing the success of this project the public would give land for road widening. Other small projects like parks and playgrounds, parking garage, school relocation, drainage, etc. will get public attention and create faith in the planning effort.

A group of people like retirees may be most useful and effective in citizen partnership. They have plenty of active life left, have a wealth of knowledge in the real word, and have plenty of time and desire to engage in social activities. They should be encouraged to join the better city building effort. However, they must be progressive minded and imaginative. Albert Einstein said "Imagination is more important than knowledge".

THE PLANNING PROCESS (THE URBAN PLANNING SYSTEM)

The planning process is very complex and needs thorough understanding. An outline is presented here, with detailed explanations in the coming chapters. One may start anywhere but must finish reading all of it.

The Planning Universe

1. The legal authority to plan and enforce plan. This is discussed in more detail in Chapter 8: Planning Laws.
2. The planning elements. This includes the subject matter that must be addressed in a general plan or comprehensive plan for a town, city, region, or a state.
3. The plan shall have a vision statement about the city. Each planning element shall have goals, objectives, policies, and projects. This is discussed in Chapter 4: The General Plan Preparation.
4. Planning tools and the use of modern technology. Different tools or techniques are employed to accomplish objectives. Modern technology as well as traditional methods aid the planning process.
5. Regulatory control in plan implementation. This includes zoning, subdivision regulation, building codes, capital improvement and budgeting.
6. Planning organization. How the planning organization is structured, the legal authority it has, and how it will operate.
7. Public participation. In every step public opinion, comments and input should be considered. Planning is a democratic process. It should be acceptable to the public. Without public understanding and cooperation planning cannot be successful.

INNOVATIVE PLANNING TOOLS

Application of Geographic Information System (GIS) in Urban Planning

In the late 1980s, with the advent of Geographic Information Technologies like Geographic Information System (GIS) and Remote Sensing technology, the process of urban planning in India received a new impetus. In the mid 1990s, Global Positioning System (GPS) technology brought a new dimension to the Spatial Data Collection Methodologies. GIS is a system of integrated computer-based tools for end-to-end processing (capture, storage, retrieval, analysis, display) of data using location on the earth's surface for interrelation in support of operations management, analysis and decision-making.

Geographic Information System at a minimum comprises a capability for input, storage, manipulation and output of geographic information. Remote sensing technology involves the use of satellites or aircraft to capture information about the earth's surface. Capturing spatial information based on remote sensing, either through satellite imagery or aerial photographs, or organizing that data with corresponding attribute data using GIS technology offers tremendous ease in undertaking many urban planning activities. Global Positioning Systems (GPS) is a system of earth-orbiting satellites which can provide precise (100 meter to sub-cm.) location on the earth's surface (in latitudinal and longitudinal coordinates or equivalent). A well-planned and well-developed GIS can significantly improve the decision-making and planning efforts of the professionals who rely on accurate, readily available data. It eliminates conventional manual surveying and therefore is faster. It is a very sophisticated technology aided by computer software. The ability of a GIS to combine information stored in separate map layers is extremely useful in urban planning and other disciplines.

In India, ISRO (India Space Research Organization) Bangalore, designs, launches, and manages the satellites, whereas NRSA (National Remote Sensing Agency) Hyderabad, under Department of Space, Government of India collects and distributes the satellite images data in digital and analog format. Today, GIS has been used in India by many government departments and in various places out of which ISRO itself has regional centres in places like Bangalore, Hyderabad, Ahmedabad, Dehradun, Nagpur, Kharagpur, Shillong etc. besides State Remote Sensing Application Centres. GIS is used in geology, agriculture, forestry, defense, flood management, transportation, urban and regional planning etc. where spatial information is needed.

It is the most essential tool in planning for identifying terrain, environmentally sensitive areas, site selection, existing road identification, finding the optimum road route between two points, analyzing transportation issues, finding buildings effected by a road widening project, monitoring development permits, land use mapping and changes, preparing zoning atlas, identifying urban sprawl, determining feasibility of a project, measuring population density, taking land inventory, etc. It also can help in deciding alignment of water, sewer, and electric lines on site and identifying individual property for tax collection. Almost anything can be identified in a GIS map. Spatial decision support system (SDSS) is specially designed for site analysis.

GIS is now a required subject in planning schools and many universities offer the courses as a professional career. A more detailed description of the complexity of this new technology is beyond the scope of this introduction.

Transfer of Development Rights (TDR)

Most land can be developed for human settlements, but some land cannot be developed because of environmental constraints. For the human race to survive there must be a balance between natural resources and environment. For example, wetlands, hills, and forests cannot be developed to the fullest extent of human desires. So there must be restrictions on development, given that we understand the consequences. The owners of wetlands, hills, and forests should be given options to utilize the property for some economic use of the properties. They may develop forestry of valuable species of trees, fisheries, nurseries, animals farming, or any other use, but not for human settlements. Therefore, the property owners may not have development rights.

Zoning regulation allows and restricts certain land uses depending upon the characteristics of land. The extent of development permitted on land by floor area to land area ratio is known as the development right. Since zoning regulation is legal, the development right is also legal and can be sold and bought like land. If a land owner decides not to use all the development rights, the unused part may be sold. The sale of development rights must be registered and recorded. The buyer shall transfer the development right to his/her land and is allowed to build more for the development right purchased. The ground coverage of the building is not allowed to increase but it can be built higher. TDR zones, the areas within which the development rights can be transferred, are predetermined. Normally a TDR zone consists of several city blocks.

TDR serves four purposes. (1) Allows flexibility of building heights while overall building density of TDR zone remains the same. Building densities are predetermined based on carrying capacity of the land. A city block has a designed capacity (if properly planned) of water supply, of sewers, and capacity of roads to carry certain volume of traffic. (2) Allows land owners to make partial use of development rights while allowing them to sell the remainder. (3) Sites of historic, religious, or other importance can be preserved from dense development by sale of development rights. (4) To preserve green spaces and agricultural land, development rights can be purchased at a lower cost than buying the land. Public access to such land can be negotiated.

Planned Unit Development (PUD)

PUD is a land use control technique which developed in mid 1960s. It is an alternative to the traditional single family development on each lot. An area of several lots together can be designed as a PUD. Units, like town houses, are built on zero lot lines in one or more buildings and have common open space around the buildings. Additional development rights can be granted to the PUD area as an incentive. It has several advantages. (1) The land is planned in an orderly fashion, can be developed in stages, and economical in construction cost. (2) The open space provides some recreational facility for the residents. (3) Fewer roads, water supply mains, and sewer mains are needed which reduce development cost. (4) Low lying areas and animal habitats can be left as open space.

PUD can be residential, office, commercial, or a mix of those if the PUD is large. State legislation must authorize the local planning agency to pass PUD ordinances.

Development of Regional Impact (DRI)

"Development of Regional Impact means any development which, because of its character, magnitude, or location would have a substantial effect upon health, safety, or welfare of citizens of more than one county".[3] Here county is an area of about a taluk. The development project has to undergo DRI review. The review includes: (1) environmental Resource Impact on vegetation and wild life, wetland, water, soils, flood plains, stormwater management; (2) burden on water supply, sewer disposal, solid waste/hazardous waste/medical waste disposal, and other public facilities; (3) impact on public transportation facilities and on roads, accessibility to places of employment; (4) ability of people to find adequate housing; (5) additional schools and other services for the new residents; and (6) economic impact on the region.

The developer or industry wants to locate the project in a particular location for some advantage. Therefore the developer has to mitigate concerns raised by the PRI review. The city also wants economic development. Generally, there is negotiation between the two parties about expense sharing and planning changes on these issues. If the concerns are not addressed, the development may need to move somewhere else. There must be state law and regulations on DRI.

Public Land Banking

"Public land banking is a system whereby governmental entity acquires land available for future development for the purpose of controlling the pace and direction of urban growth. By acquiring or leasing land in the path of urban expansion, and hence immunizing it from premature development, at propitious time for development and with use restrictions consonant with a publicly adopted plan for the area".[4]

Traditional land use controls have enormous problems to plan on private land. If the land is acquired, the city can plan freely, develop infrastructures, and sell developed lots for construction. This can be phased out as necessary over time. The zoning can be established as necessary without long range commitment. During the undeveloped period, the land can be leased for agricultural, nursery, or other purposes without permanent structures. The leased amount will pay for the interest on loans. As the land prices increase, the sale proceeds will pay for the loans. This will keep the land speculators out and the consumer will benefit from low price and well planned lots. This will also stop urban sprawl. This is an alternative to regulating private property, and is much easier but needs bold steps and heavy financing.

"Proponents of land banking assert two principal objectives for which land banking is well suited: 1. The promotion of more rational patterns of development in lieu of urban sprawl, and, 2. The reduction in cost of land through a more perfect land market and elimination of land speculation".[5]

This is not a new planning tool. It has been used in Sweden, the Netherlands, Finland, Israel, and Puerto Rico for more than fifty years. The British new towns were built by acquiring land through town corporations. In the United States public land banking was not used because: (1) It is less costly to control growth through police power. (2) Private land holdings are big, so it is easier to deal with fewer land owners. In India, small land owners are numerous. A state enabled legislation needs to authorize acquisition of private land for public land banking for urban development.

The laws allow acquisition of land for public purpose. There is no authorization to acquire land for public interest. There is a big difference between 'public purpose' and 'public interest'. When land is acquired for public purpose, it means that the land will be used to build a public necessity. In case of land banking it is a public interest, though the land is not required to build any public project or faculty. Therefore, laws must include the ability to purchase land in public interest. Otherwise it will have no legal backing to deal with the land owners who refuse to sell the land for land banking.

Timing Developments

All the land areas under planning control will not develop simultaneously in a short time – say five to ten years. Neither it is (a) a technical possibility to study the sites and create plans; (b) economically wise to install roads, water supply, sewer system, electricity, drainage, etc. before expecting any revenue; nor (c) desirable to zone and plan too many years ahead, before the demand for future land use is known. Keep the flexibility to accommodate new demands for land. Developments should be planned in a sequence as infrastructure can be provided and demand for land development increases.

It is unwise to fill up the entire future land use map with set land use designations. As stated above, the future is unpredictable. So keep options open. Zone it for agricultural use, or call it a floating zone – which means land use zoning will be decided at a latter time. When the demand for land for a particular land use becomes clear, the area will be zoned for that use, the area will have a detailed plan, and urban infrastructures will be provided. Phased developments are ideal.

There is no legal obligation to permit a land owner to build on his/her land if the land is not planned in a development scheme. It is legal and prudent to declare a construction moratorium on land unplanned, undeveloped, and without infrastructure. The cities which grant permits to land owners for construction on their land without planning, zoning, and development of infrastructure, are not planning but inviting sprawl developments and future problems including bad precedents.

Notes

1. *The Practice of Local Government Planning,* p. 380.
2. Scott, Randal W. (Ed.), *Management and Control of Growth,* Volume III, The Urban Land Institute, Washington D.C., 1975.
3. Florida Administrative Code, Chapter 9J-5, Rules of Procedure and Practice Pertaining to Developments of Regional Impact, 1998.
4. Scott, Randal W. (Ed.), *Management and Control of Growth,* Volume III, The Urban Land Institute, Washington D.C., 1975.
5. Ibid.

3

The General Plan Preparation

Planning for improvement of an existing city and its future expansions are being discussed in this chapter. A new town or city on an open land are not included.

The concept of master plan is very simplistic and devoid of many details and issues that are included in the contemporary urban plans. So, the urban plan is no longer called a master plan, which denotes an engineering scheme. The term "master plan" is still used for a plan of a development scheme such as a shopping center, office complex, a company township, a housing complex, etc.

First, plan how to prepare the General Plan. The General Plan is a tool for guidance of future development and improvement of the existing city. Professor T. J. Kent, Jr. of the University of California in Berkeley discussed the concept of General Plan in his book *The Urban General Plan* in 1964. Almost the same concept was carried forward as Comprehensive Plan, which includes all aspects of planning, and comprehensive in nature. In later part of 20th century, some cities in the United States started calling their city plan 'Growth Management Plan'. The plan is under constant evaluation and adjustment to improve. It is revised every five years.

Growth and development of an existing urban settlement is complex. In this chapter development of Modern Urban Planning and the complexities is discussed. The general plan preparation of a city or town involves many steps. Specific disciplinary knowledge and skills in addition to urban planning is required in environmental ecology, architecture, engineering, anthropology, land economics, geography, human ecology, sociology, social psychology, politics, etc. in the preparation of plans. The built up environment of the city that you see is an outcome of considerations or failure of considerations that has roots in all these disciplines. The flowing topics are suggested as a prototype of the General Plan.

PLANNING ANALYSIS OF CURRENT SITUATION

First, get to know the city just like a doctor would know a patient before he treats or operates. A planner gets to know a city through inspection, survey, data analysis and so on.

Technical Studies

(1) Delineate the study area and determine growth potential – Every city or town has a regional setting and a hinterland. Either the city under planning consideration is dependent upon surrounding cities or villages or the city is dependent on other big cities in the region. This study shall indicate if the city is going to be a dormitory town, a sub-regional center, or a center of a large region. Accordingly the growth potential can be envisaged and planned accordingly.

(2) Define the Planning Area – Once the built-up area of the city is defined, the outline is extended outward to open countryside for study and reservation of land for future expansion of the city for next 25 years. General growth prospect and likely directions of expansion affected by natural and man made features are considered. These features will include rivers, natural drains, lakes and hills. Civil divisions such as of villages, subdivision, etc. also may be considered. Keeping a greenbelt of agricultural area around the city for future planned development is very prudent.

(3) Define Planning Districts – The planning area is divided to planning districts of one square mile approximately. This area can accommodate 1,000 to 5,000 persons with an elementary school in walking distance. The planning districts may be established according to established neighborhoods, growing neighborhoods, commercial areas, industrial areas, and so on. Planning districts should be bounded by physical barriers such as railroad, thoroughfares, watercourses, and hills or by arbitrary division. It will be well and good if the planning districts coincide with municipal wards for community participation purpose. Undeveloped areas should be kept separate for future planning. There are several advantages of establishing planning districts. It is very useful for urban studies, data collection, analysis, detail planning and zoning, and reference in the plan.

(4) Prerequisite Studies – These studies should be done for each planning district and then compiled for the entire city.

   (a) The population study shall show: population growth, population distribution, population density, profile of the population by age, sex, education and skill level; direction of growth; social stratification; and so on.

(b) Economic study shall show: employment opportunities, economic stability, expansion of job opportunities, and unemployment level.

(c) Land use study should show by land use classification categories: residence (low density, medium density, high density), retail business, transportation and utilities, industry and related use, wholesale and related use, public buildings and open spaces, industrial buildings, public parks and play grounds, vacant and non-urban land (suitable and unsuitable for building classified).

(d) Structural conditions shall show: excellent to good, acceptable, substandard, and unfit for habitation.

(e) Roads and transportation study shall include: paved road width, right of way width, traffic volume and congestion, quality of road surface, turning radius at intersections of roads, pedestrian walk, and drainage.

(f) Study of existing educational facilities shall show any future need of physical facilities.

(g) Study of existing public infrastructures such as water supply, sanitation, and electricity shall show the adequacy of them.

(h) Study of existing parks, recreational and sports facilities shall show the need for the future.

(i) Study of environmental conditions is needed for improvement.

The analysis includes written texts, charts, diagrams and maps. Planners use statistical models, survey, census data, geographic information system, and many analytical tools to understand how a city is changing to arrive at realistic proposals for improvements. Alternative solutions should be evaluated for best results and how they will accomplish goals and objectives.

The analysis of current problems may be very extensive and intensive. The analysis should be limited to such information that will give definitive conclusions without meaningless details. Every analysis must therefore be usable. The analysis must be concerning the planning elements at a minimum.

PHYSICAL PLANNING AND COMMUNITY DEVELOPMENT ELEMENTS

There are certain topics or elements of concern in every town or city that must be addressed in the plan. Each element is analyzed; problems are detected; and goals, objectives, policies and projects are suggested. These elements are outlined below. Elements that have no relevance to a city may be omitted.

In India, emphasis is given to physical plan without including goals, objectives, and policies. In the United States emphasis is given to policy plan which includes

Figure 3.1
Basic Elements of the General Plan

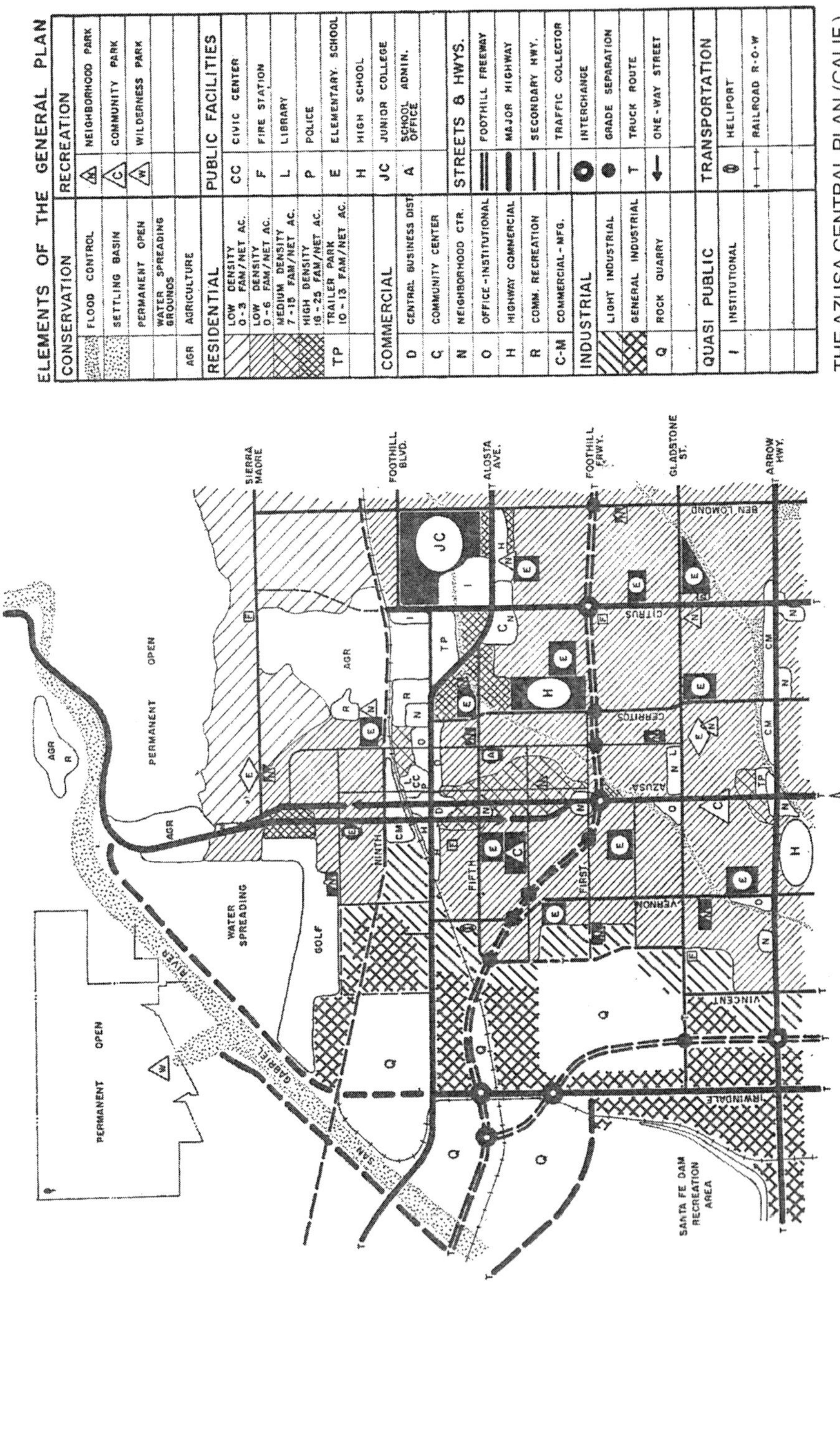

Source: Gallion and Eisner, *The Urban Pattern.*

Figure 3.2

Residential Subdivisions: Planning Influenced by garden city movement

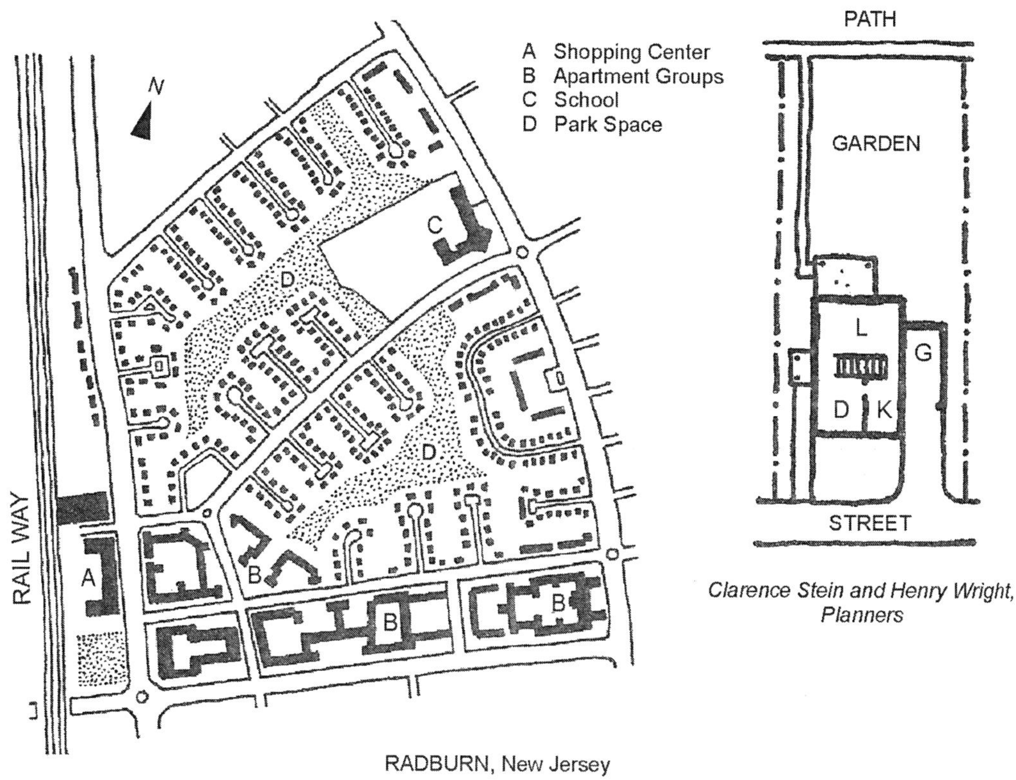

The Radburn plan became synonymous with "the town of the motor age." In this plan the cul-de-sec (dead-end) residential streets became service roads rather than traffic ways, the house being reversed so that the living rooms face on the rear gardens with pedestrian paths leading to the continuous park space.

Source: Gallion and Eisner, *The Urban Pattern.*

goals, objectives, and policies and deals with physical plan on the basis of the policy plan. Actually, physical plan should be supported by policy plan. Hence, both should be integrated. Physical plan implementation may be compared to a game we play and policy plan may be compared to the rules of the game. We should enforce a plan based on established goals, objective, and policies such that guidance is available and disputes are kept to a minimum in the enforcement. Therefore, defining goals, objective, and policies very clearly is very important.

The planning elements may be categorized to (1) city functions or activity pattern of the people, and (2) the infrastructure or physical facilities supporting the city functions.

Figure 3.3
Chatham Village

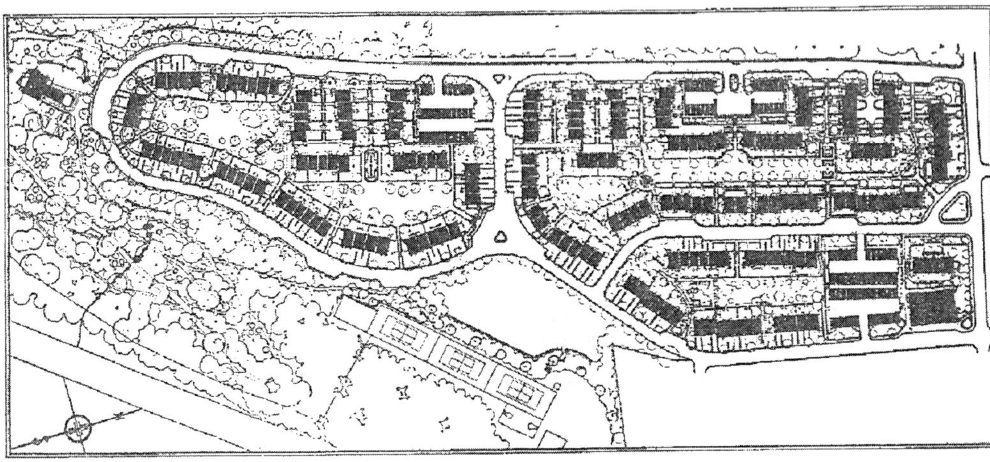

CHATHAM VILLAGE, Pitsburgh
Ingham and Boyd, Architects

A limited-dividend project originally planned for 300 units within reach of the $2,200-3,600 per year income group. The first stage of development was 128 dwellings. The density is about 12 families per acre in two-story group houses, demonstrating the theory of Henry Wright who espoused the cause of the group house on urban land which had not yet reached the high levels of many areas. This project was built as an investment by the Buhl Foundation.

Source: Gallion and Eisner, *The Urban Pattern.*

Vision, Goals, Objectives and Policies

A vision is an imagination, a dream, a fantasy, a foresight, a perception, which unleashes reality. Any grand thing or noble cause starts with a vision. It conveys a powerful revelation. It crystallizes a visual image and may include maps and sketches. A vision statement may consist of images such as: both man made and natural environment, place to live and raise a family, work, urban facilities, conveniences of modern life, and elite architectural and landscape designs for the city.

A goal is the end toward which effort is directed. Planning goals cannot be specified precisely. Goals are desires or intentions. It is general, indefinite, and not absolute. Yet it sets the direction of planning efforts. It follows the vision statements and set directions to planning objectives. Goals can be short, intermediate, or long-term period depending on urgency and complexity.

An objective is an effort or aim directed to a goal for an end action and result. Through planning analysis we can arrive at more conclusive objectives. The objectives are usable if the underlying assumptions concerning human behavior, need, technical

Figure 3.4
Environmentally Conscious Subdivision Plan – Piney-Z Plantation

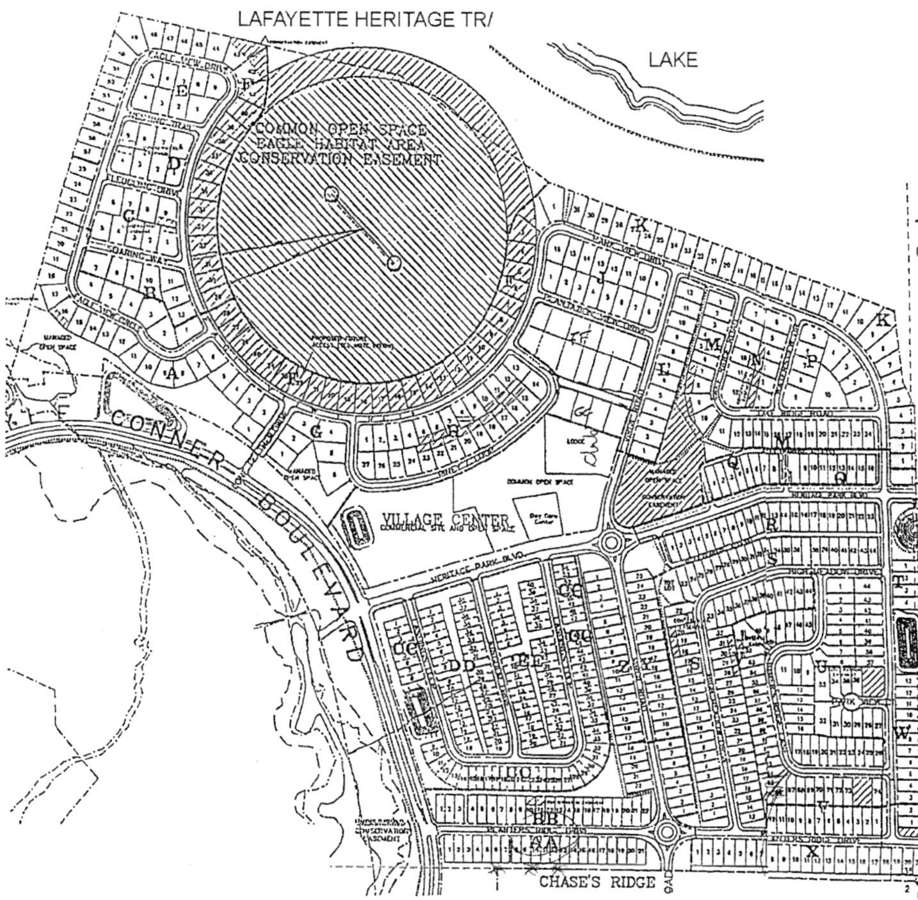

Source: Piney-Z Plantation, Tallahassee, Florida.

validity, value judgments, and decisions are valid. Metropolitan region, regional planning council, state planning, national planning, and even international ideas also influence local government decisions. Since planning is related to population growth, economic development, consumer-customer requirements, taste and attitudes, employment skills, technology, government politics and policy, objectives are influenced by these factors. Planning objectives differ in probable time required for their attainment. Short-term objectives are 1 to 5 years, intermediate-term objectives are 5 to 10 years, and long-term objectives are 10 to 25 years.

Each objective is followed by policies. A policy is a defined course or method of action selected from among alternatives and in light of given conditions to guide and

Figure 3.5
Planning Ingredients

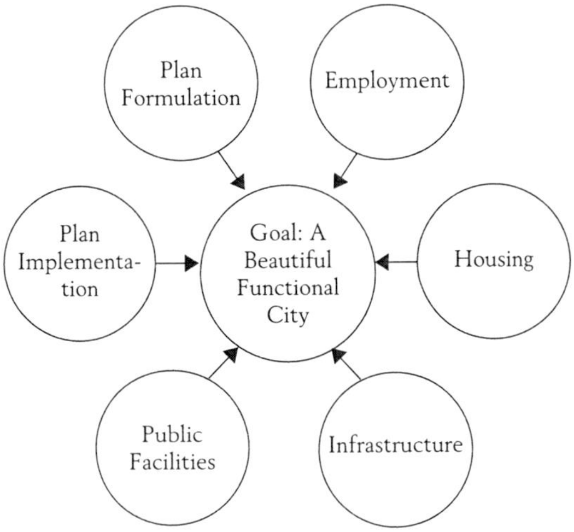

Which contribute to a beautiful and functional city.

Plan Formulation	*Plan Implementation*	*Employment*
-National Constitution	-Zoning Plan	-Economic Base
-State Planning Law	-Zoning Regulation	-Industry
-City Council	-Building Codes	-Office
-Planning Agency	-Subdivision Regulations	-Business
-Growth Management	-Slum Clearance	-Commercial
-Environmental Concerns	-Urban Renewal	-Service Industry
-General Plan	-Project Budgeting & Financing	-Government offices
-Strategic Plan	-Inter- & Intra-Government coordination	-Institutions
-Sustainable Community	-New Towns	
-Future Land Use Plan	-Satellite Towns	
-Timing Developments		
-Citizen Participation		

Housing	*Infrastructure*	*Public Facilities*
-Housing & Subdivisions	-Electricity	-Civic Center
-Homes	-Communications	-Entertainment
-Townhomes	-Roads	-Parks & Recreation
-Flats	-Drainage	-Sports facilities
-Apartments	-Water	-Educational Institutions
-Low Income Housing	-Sewer	-Historic Preservation
-Shopping Centers	-Solid waste Disposal	-Post Office
-Schools within residential areas	-Mass Transit	-Health Facilities
-Playgrounds & green areas	-Capital Improvements	-Crematoriums & burial

determine present and future decisions. Essentially it becomes the rule what to do and what not to do, until it is amended for a justified reason.

A strategy is a careful plan or method, a claver stratagem, the art of devising or employing plan or stratagems toward a goal. It is essentially similar to military strategy.

A project is a specific plan or design to accomplish an objective. This is the end product in urban planning after goals, objectives, policies and strategies. Projects precipitate from goals, objectives, and policies and implemented as funding sources are found.

Planning Elements

These planning elements must be addressed in the Urban General Plan. Tentative goals, objectives, and policies are given as examples. These should be refined for town or city concerned.

(a) Environmental Protection Element

Environmental degradation may occur from air pollution, disposition of chemicals, disposition of sewer in open pits and drains, mud sliding, trash deposited in open pits, etc. These environmental hazards cause respiratory diseases, cancer, bacterial infection, premature death, deforestation, soil erosion, water pollution, land degradation, etc. New Delhi is one of the top ten most polluted cities in the world. In New Delhi the incidence of respiratory diseases due to air pollution is about 12 times the national average. The obstacles, which will come on the way, are: private ownership of land, lack of political muscles or willingness to take right steps, lack of regulatory control, lack of wise technical advice or financial difficulties or any combination of the above. The Government of India adopted Environment Protection Act in 1986.

Human settlements cannot be built without modifying the natural environment. It will consume natural resources and generate pollution. The impact of development on environment could be minimized by design creativity and regulations based on environmental science. The planners should study environmental degradation and recommend actions to eliminate the existing problems and to make policies for future protection.

Goal: Minimize impact of human settlements on natural resources and environment, and human.

Objective 1: Conserve natural resources such as wetland; flood plain; natural drainage systems; river front; beaches; ground water; hills; forests; areas of scenic beauty;

and animal, bird and fish habitats shall be prevented from exploitation, destruction or neglect and therefore undevelopable.

Policy 1: Natural resources shall be identified; set aside from development; and device a management plan.

Policy 2: Contaminated water and pollutants from industries and other sources shall not be discharged to rivers, lakes, and wetlands.

Policy 3: Landfill shall not be permitted on rivers, lakes, ponds, and wetland as they serve as rain water retention tanks and reduce flooding.

Policy 4: Indiscriminate cutting of hills shall not be permitted. If permitted, the surface shall be restored to gentle slopes and covered with grass and plants to prevent erosion.

Objective 2: Air pollution shall be reduced or eliminated.

Policy 1: Automobile exhaust pollution shall be controlled by disallowing automobiles producing high levels of carbon dioxides.

Policy 2: Point sources of pollution, such as power plants and factories, shall be managed effectively.

Objective 3: Chemicals having long term effect on environment or people shall not be allowed to be used or disposed with out satisfactory remedy.

Policy 1: The chemical user must provide scientific evaluation of the chemical to prove that it will not effect the natural environment, human, global climate change, and ozone depletion.

(b) Historic Preservation Element

The obstacles to historic preservation are: lack of historical value judgment of the trustees, lack of revenue to support the preservation, and more construction of income producing structures on the site by the trustees.

Goal 1: Sites or buildings of historical, religious, cultural, architectural and archeological importance shall be identified and preserved.

Objective 1: A formal registry shall be prepared declaring sites of historic preservation by the year X. No further development shall be allowed on the site and a management plan shall be made for each site.

Policy 1: Transfer of development right (discussed in the previous chapter) shall be encouraged.

Policy 2: The city shall help development of the sites as centers of tourist attraction.

(c) Housing Element

India has severe housing shortage. The housing industry will grow if proper financial mechanisms are available for home mortgage loans. Residential lots should be made available by planning residential subdivisions. Provision of housing for all income groups should be made available. Land and home sale and registration should be made easy and fraud proof. Unfair laws such as landlord tenant acts and rent control acts should be amended such that the owner do not lose property and rent, and the rent defaulters can be evicted on reasonable grounds. If these barriers are removed, rental housing including apartments will be available. Housing sector is a big employer in building construction and manufacturing building materials and components. Development of the housing sector is good for the economy, employment, and organized urban development. There is a social stigma, never to sale or remodel ancestral property. This has a profound impact on mobility in the housing market. Some people want large lots, personal space, garden, and prestige. Most others want just a modest house to live and raise family. Yet many other cannot afford to own a home but to rent one, which is also not easily available. All these people must have accommodations to live.

Goal 1: Provide for safe and sanitary dwellings at affordable cost for all income groups.

Objective 1: Provide varieties of choices for single family homes, duplexes, town houses, multifamily buildings, and flats for homeownership.

Policy 1: Make lots available by zoning or lot review process for all types of housing – home sizes and price ranges.

Policy 2: Housing shall not be segregated by income level, race, or religion.

Policy 3: Make home mortgage loan available through lending institutions.

Objective 2: All dwellings shall have adequate infrastructure such as: adequate roads, water supply, sanitary sewer, stormwater drainage, electricity, telephone, school, neighborhood park and playground, neighborhood shopping center, and community center.

Policy 1: The costs of first time development of infrastructure shall be bourn by home owners or land developers.

Goal 2: Rental dwellings of various sizes and rents shall be made available.

Objective 1: Encourage construction of rental units of various sizes: 4 bed rooms, 3 bed rooms, 2 bed rooms, 1 bed room, and efficiency units.

Policy 1: Lots shall be zoned or made available through lot review process for rental units.

Policy 2: Landlord tenant act shall be revised making it easier to evict tenants for default of rents, and to increase or decrease rent as market conditions change.

Goal 3: Hotels, guesthouses, and hostels run by private owners, companies, government, philanthropic organizations and religious organizations shall be encouraged to accommodate transient population who come to the city for official work, business, conference, or as tourists, must have affordable, safe and sanitary rooms for rent at convenient locations. A metropolitan city must have thousands of hotel rooms to host any big events such as sports events, conferences, conventions, and cultural programs.

Objective 1: Encourage construction of these facilities as business ventures which brings employment and sales tax revenue to the city.

Policy 1: Help the owners to acquire land at locations close to public transportation routes.

Policy 2: Provide infrastructures promptly.

Policy 3: The facilities accommodating transient population shall not be located inside residential neighborhoods.

Goal 4: Remove slums and provide safe and sanitary housing to the dwellers.

Objective 1: Study the existing slums (number of families, income level, land ownership, land areas), and assess the extent of the problem.

Objective 2: Plan housing projects to relocate the slum dwellers. Make cost estimates, explore possible funding sources. Execute projects.

Objective 3: Relocate slum dwellers, clear slums, plan for the cleared land.

Policy 1: Help slum dwellers who can afford to pay monthly mortgage, to obtain loans for home ownership.

Policy 2: Give option for lease purchase. One can pay rent and purchase when money is available.

Policy 3: Provide rental housing at subsidized rate with the help of governmental or international programs.

Policy 4: Prevent formation of new slums.

(d) Office Element

Offices may be categorized as public offices, corporate offices, and commercial and business offices which have different functions, number of employees and visitors. (1) Public offices, banks, and doctors offices deal with general public. They may be government or non-government offices. These offices generate high volume of visitors and require high accessibility by public transportation systems, lots of parking spaces, and some ancillary services such as restaurants, stationary supplies, typing services, etc. (2) Corporate offices, consulting firms, and some government offices engaged in operations or client services and infrequently visited by public and customers and require medium accessibility from public transportation system and parking demand is medium. (3) Commercial and business offices generally do commercial transactions by telephone or electronic communications. These offices generate little office visits and parking is required mostly for employees.

Goal 1: Provide ample office spaces at convenient locations.

Objective 1: Public offices shall be planned along major roads having public transportation systems.

Objective 2: Develop office parks for corporate offices and commercial/business offices.

Policy 1: Offices shall not infringe into residential areas.

Policy 2: Big office complexes shall be encouraged with common parking spaces and well landscaped areas.

Policy 3: Movie theaters which open after office hours shall be permitted in office zone such that the parking spaces can be utilized in the evening hours.

(e) Wholesale and Retail Business Element

Four levels of shopping facilities are needed. (1) The Central Business District may sale every consumer goods but specialize in expensive and rarely available consumer goods. It is a regional shopping center. It generates high volume of automobile traffic and customers. (2) Sub-Business Districts, where most of the consumer goods are sold, are necessary for convenience and traffic distribution. They may be four or five miles apart. (3) Neighborhood shopping centers cater the daily needs of residential areas. (4) Convenient stores within residential areas in walking distance are needed to cater the immediate needs of small items for the residents. The principal factor determining location is customer convenience. They will not make long trips to rent videos if available at convenient store. But for jewelry or appliances they do not mind going to the central business district.

Floor spaces, rooms, or stalls are in short supply. Therefore, exorbitant *pagri* (money for giving possession) money is prevalent. Since there is a great demand for store space, the landlords are not motivated to improve or rebuild the rental property. Many traders resort to street side carts making the roads congested and dangerous. Many homeowners also build stalls on the road front for rent, customers standing on the footpath, making the roads congested and unhygienic. Shortage of store space is one big reason for road congestion.

Goal 1: Separate shopping areas and roads for public safety and smooth flow of automobiles.

Goal 2: Provide for plenty of shopping areas and floor spaces to overcome shortage and overcrowding.

Goal 3: Distribute shopping centers throughout the planning area for convenience and distribution of shopping traffic.

Objective 1: Provide for development of central business district, sub-business districts, neighborhood shopping centers, and convenient stores within the neighborhoods with separation of shoppers and automobile traffic.

Policy 1: Build new shopping centers with separation of shopping areas and automobile ways, plenty of shops, and parking spaces. Use mall concept for design.

Policy 2: In existing shopping areas, no new shop shall directly open to footpath.

Policy 3: Existing shops which directly open to the footpath, shall comply with policy 2 within five years from the date of publication of the General Plan.

Policy 4: Parking – Property owners shall be responsible for providing parking spaces for the customers as provided in the zoning ordinance. The existing shop owners, if they cannot provide spaces, will contribute money for construction of multistory parking garages.

Policy 5: Construction of stalls on road front is prohibited. Existing stalls shall be removed.

(f) Industrial and Economic Development Element

Economic prosperity is sought by all communities. Primarily employment is created by various industries, government, education, research, trade and commerce, construction, healthcare, etc. These employees create secondary and tertiary employments in service sector and consumer oriented retail mercantile. Industrial and economic developments contribute to the local and regional employment, production of goods and services, and tax base to the local government. The big employers always look for advantageous locations in a state and availability of infrastructures such as major highways, water, power, transportation, communication, and information technology infrastructure. Places compete to bring employers by providing quality of life and physical amenities. Industrial and economic developments also bring some problems and challenges for the local municipal government: pollution, more traffic, and more loads on existing infrastructure and amenities.

The physical environment influences economic and social structure of the community. Therefore, the scope of urban planning is broader and should include integration of physical and socioeconomic planning. This is an age of global economy. Many things locally manufactured can be marketed elsewhere in the world, provided it is creative in design, good quality, and reasonable in price.

The planner's role is to facilitate land and infrastructure. Local government, state government, and community leaders need to take initiatives to attract employers. Some municipalities in U.S.A. lease land at nominal rate, forgive property tax for few years, or even give seed money to attract industries.

Goal 1: Attract large employers which fit into the local economic picture.

Objective 1: Create opportunity for employment of local people and create local tax base.

Policy 1: Provide land, infrastructures, amenities, and local human resources.

Policy 2: Give opportunity to promising local enterprises.

Policy 3: Harness local human resources by training them through local institutions.

Goal 2: Zone appropriate land areas for industrial locations.

Objective 1: Land and infrastructure shall be in place to facilitate timely construction of industries.

Policy 1: Heavy and medium industries shall be located in the outer ring of the city. General wind direction shall be considered such that smokes do not blow into the city.

Policy 2: Light Industries – Industrial Estates may be locate inside the city but away from residential neighborhoods.

Policy 3: Service Industries automobile repair and servicing shops, carpentry and cabinet making, welding shop, etc. produce noise and should be separated from residential areas.

Policy 4: All industries must be accessible by highways, and infrastructure must be in place.

Policy 5: Create a land bank for this purpose.

(g) Transportation Element

Street plan has always been regarded as the foundation of all city planning. Streets carry almost all traffic. Until about 1950s city streets were planned to serve three principal purposes: (1) to move traffic, (2) to provide access, light and air to abutting buildings, and (3) to provide for street parking. As the number of automobiles and population increased, traffic congestion increased. Most cities suffer from chronic traffic congestion, lack of parking, and high rate of accidents. This is the situation allover the world. The first effort was to widen the roads by tearing down expensive buildings. This effort also failed to ease the traffic, as more traffic came. The next effort was to provide freeways for through automobile traffic, such that local and through traffic are separated with movement efficiency. Now more freeways are required as the traffic kept increasing. The cities are out of land and money to building more freeways and parking. So the big cities are running out of caring capacities for traffic and also for water, sewer, and electricity. Upgrading cost of these is very high so other solutions are needed.

Possible solutions include: (1) Encourage greater use of public transportation and discourage private automobiles. (2) Encourage growth of counter magnet cities in the region to discourage further growth of large cities. (3) Redevelop existing large cities without encouraging further population growth.

Tasks: (1) Estimate future demand for transportation facilities and services; (2) propose and evaluate alternative ways to meet demands and services; (3) Calculate costs of alternatives; and (4) Evaluate options and recommend the appropriate solution.

Recommendations are made based on judgment and experience with the help of elaborate computer models and simulations. Transportation planning is coordinated with state and national highway agency, civil aviation, railway agency, inland water transport authority, port authority, mass transit including bus service, subways, economic development plan, environmental plan, and many departments of the municipality.

The planning area is divided into small areas called *traffic analysis zones*. The region's transportation network is represented with links and nodes. Studies also include traffic capacity, speed, direction, trip generation, trip distribution, model split (bus, train, private automobile, etc), traffic assignment, etc. Nowadays, geographic information system (GIS) technology is used very precisely.

Transportation connects all functions and land uses within the city and the region around the city. Daily commuters from other cities within a radius of 50 miles or so are quite common. Inter-city long distance travel is also very common. Transportation planning is the most technical and quantitative element in planning. Transportation planning has developed to a very specialized field within the planning profession. Transportation deals with increased travel demand, congestion, pollution, accidents, even distribution of facilities and services, consumption of energy, providing alternative to private automobiles, safety to pedestrians, public transportation, parking, etc.

Goal: Develop transportation systems that will carry vehicles, people, and goods smoothly and efficiently.

Objective 1: Develop freeways connecting regional roads and passing through the city for through traffic.

Policy 1: At a minimum plan for two lanes each way and keep enough land for future increase of lanes.

Policy 2: Entrees and exits shall be limited to arterial roads and major activity centers.

Policy 3: Right of ways for freeways shall be fenced to prevent accidents from animals or people crossing the freeways, and landscaped to prevent noise and pollution, and beautification.

Objective 2: Arterial roads shall be planned to move inner city traffic fast without interruption of too many traffic lights, any development creating pedestrians.

Policy 1: Provide entry and exit only at road crossings.

Policy 2: No development shall be permitted along arterial roads that have direct entrance or exit from the arterial roads.

Policy 3: Each arterial road shall have at least two lanes in each direction, and turning lanes.

Objective 3: Feeder roads or collector roads to the arterial roads shall have minimum of two lanes in each direction; and can have developments on both sides.

Policy 1: Each property shall have only one vehicular entrance from the feeder road. If the property is at an intersection of two roads it may have entrance from both roads, but farthest from the intersection.

Policy 2: Since the feeder roads will attract lot of pedestrians, wide side walks, say 20' or more, shall be required. Side walks shall be landscaped with trees and shrubs.

Policy 3: No street side parking except on metered lots shall be permitted. Parking spaces as required by zoning ordinance shall be provided by each land owner.

Objective 4: Local roads for residential, office, industrial, or other land uses shall have at least two lanes, side walks, and space for drainage and utility installations.

Policy 1: The initial construction costs for roads, drainage, water pipes, sewer lines, and electric line shall be borne by the property owners or property developer.

Objective 5: Commuter trains, subways, and buses for public transportation shall be provided to reduce use of personal automobiles.

Policy 1: Encourage railways and private enterprises to provide this service.

Policy 2: Provide terminals and bus stop lanes.

Objective 6: Eliminate traffic congestions and reduce accidents.

Policy 1: Clear road right of way of any illegal occupation.

Policy 2: Reduce number of entry, exit, and turns to the road.

Benefit of Policy Plan – This includes goals, objectives, and policies and removes the vagueness of master plan. The planners and municipal government exactly know what they are shooting for and the citizens know what they are expecting. Therefore, there is more understanding and less resistance form all sides.

PLANNING MUNICIPAL AND OTHER GOVERNMENTAL SERVICES ELEMENTS

The elements which are mostly under public or government control are grouped here. These services are provided under government ownership or privatized under government regulations. As long as the services are adequate and the rates are reasonable it should not be a concern whether they are operated by government, private companies, or non-governmental organizations.

(h) Public Utility and Sanitation Services Element

Water Supply

Water supply system is one of the most vital necessities of every community. Water is required for sustaining life, safeguarding health, promoting sanitation, providing fire protection, maintaining beauty of lawns and gardens by sprinkling water, and supplying the needs of industry, commerce, and agriculture. Water usage varies from city to city and is determined by domestic, commercial and industrial demands. Domestic demand for kitchen, bathrooms, drinking, cloth washing, and lawn sprinkling does not exceed 60 gallons per day per person. Public use demand includes water for fire fighting, street cleaning, fountains, swimming pools, sprinklers in parks, and maintaining water level in lakes. Industrial demands vary depending on type of industry such as textiles, power plants, paper mills, railroad terminal, etc. Water loss through waste and leakage could be 15 to 25 percent. Total consumption rate will vary from 100 to 200 gallons per person per day.

Water quality is to be maintained against contamination, odor, and color. Facilities are required for purifying, storage, and distribution. Treatment may include filtration, aeration, chlorination, and adding minerals to improve taste.

Water supply system may include water mains and branch lines, pumping stations, reservoirs, and standpipes. Water supply planning requires coordination with street planning since water pipes are normally laid under streets. Water pressure in the mains is established according to present and anticipated demand. Residential areas require 20 to 30 pounds per square inch pressure; high-rise buildings require 50 to 80 pounds per square inch pressure. For fire fighting pressure up to 300 pounds may be required.

The water supply system is very expensive, once built it would last for a hundred years, and cannot be rebuilt without very major expenses. Therefore, it is very critical to consider; ultimate capacity in terms of population and area to be served; population density it is designed for; how high the buildings can be; is it going to serve areas outside municipal area or to other surrounding towns, etc. It is a political and technical decision that will affect the city for several generations to come.

Some cities provide intermittent water supply. It is unacceptable. All water systems should have 24 hour supply. Otherwise the customers incur expenses to build individual water tanks, buy water pumps, use electricity to pump, and have inconvenience of attending to it. Because of irregularity in water supply, most residents install wells, which is an additional expense. The water from the wells is polluted since septic tank effluents disposed to the drain enter the underground water table. The water pipe system is already in place, only water treatment and supply need to be increased.

Sewerage System and Sewage Disposal

The system used for disposing liquid wastes is called the sewerage system. In combined system, which exists in Kolkata and other older cities, sanitary sewer and stormwater is carried in the same set of mains and disposed to a river or sea without treatment. In combines system mains are very large and expensive, disposal is least expensive, but disposed sewerage contaminates the rivers and seawater. The contaminated water is harmful for swimming or any human use, irrigation, and fish for human consumption. Therefore, combined sewerage is not used nowadays. Stormwater sewers and sanitary sewers are now separated. Stormwater is dealt with natural drainage system.

Sanitary sewers are designed to carry domestic household wastes from toilets, bathrooms, kitchens, laundries, and industrial liquid wastes needing treatment. The sanitary sewer is collected in a treatment plant. The plant is located away from residential and commercial developments due to odor and requires huge land area for the plant and spray field. Sandy soil in the vicinity of airfield seems to be a good location. The sewage treatment is a complex process involving chemistry, bacteriology, biology, and engineering.

Septic tanks may be used when the lots are big and have enough room to provide drain fields. Disposing effluents from septic tanks to drains is unhygienic. Therefore, high-density developments must have sanitary sewers.

Solid Waste Disposal

To protect public health, efficient garbage collection and disposal system is required. Garbage and dead animals unless promptly collected and properly disposed; decompose and create disagreeable odor; and become a breeding place for insects, mosquito, rodents, and vermin. Combustible garbage create fire hazard. Rubbish and trash such as wasted building materials, metal, rubber, wood, and rags create hiding and breeding rooms for insects, rodents and vermin. Due to unhygienic conditions, many epidemics erupt. Industrial waste is another category of garbage. It is also a public concern for public convenience, orderliness, community appearance, aesthetics, and general liability.

Garbage collection is a municipal responsibility. It may be collected by municipal employees or under private contract. Garbage is collected at least once or twice every week if garbage collection containers are provided. In commercial areas garbage collection and street cleaning may be required every day. In the United States two containers with covers are provided to each household by the municipalities. One container is for recycled materials such as glass, plastics, and paper. The other container is for biodegradable garbage. Big trucks empty the containers and take to the disposal site. Recycled materials are picked up every two weeks and sent to plants. The separation of garbage to biodegradable and recycled materials makes sense. If both are taken to landfills more landfill space is required. The recycled materials have economic value and otherwise would have been wasted. In sparely populated areas garbage collection centers are provided where households can deposit garbage. Industrial garbage collection is generally the responsibility of the industries and regulated by ordinance.

Garbage disposal is a municipal responsibility. Garbage open dump and incineration are unacceptable due to foul smell and smokes. Sanitary landfill is the most acceptable method of garbage disposal. Trenches are dug, filled with daily garbage, compacted and covered with soil every day. Trenches may be used more than once as the garbage decompose and shrink. A very large area is required for sanitary landfill. Since urban land is expensive, sanitary landfills are located in the outskirts of the urban areas. If the sanitary landfills are too far, the cost of hauling the garbage is increased. The sanitary landfills may eventually be used for public parks and recreational purpose. Selecting the location of sanitary landfill the following factors should be considered: (1) It does not pollute streams or watersheds; (2) It does not create a nuisance to the general public; (3) It is consistent with the surrounding land use; and (4) The cost of land and unintended consequences are at a minimum.

(i) Stormwater and Drainage Element

Flooding in monsoon, damage homes and other properties. It also disrupts traffic. It is a public health problem since water contaminated by effluents from septic tanks and latrines bring germs and bacteria.

The plan should identify natural drains and water retention ponds, lakes and rivers for preservation; Develop regulatory controls such as zoning, lot coverage, building code, and requirement of construction of retention ponds.

Goal: The volume and rate of post land development runoff from a site should not exceed the site's pre-development volume and rate of runoff.

Objective 1: Stop construction in wetlands and preserve natural drains, canals, rivers, lakes and ponds.

Objective 2: Reduce coverage of land by buildings and pavements.

Objective 3: Construct stormwater retention ponds and underground drainage in developed areas.

Objective 4: Drainage must be evaluated and found satisfactory before issuing building permit.

(j) Gas

Cooking with wood fire is outdated. Wood is hard to find, wood fire create smokes and air pollution and is a fire hazard in densely populated areas. In the western world either electricity or gas is used for cooking. Many cities distribute natural gas by pipes on every street.

The plan should evaluate this possibility and make recommendation.

Goal: To provide natural gas through pipes for 24-hour supply.

Objective: Should be developed based on need.

(k) Electricity

Adequate electricity supply is prerequisite for modern development. The progress of a country can be measured by the consumption of electricity per person. We need electricity for everything: to light buildings and streets; to run computers, televisions, appliances, water supply; in hospital operating rooms; research laboratories;

industrial operations; air conditioning; etc. Any interruption in electricity supply causes difficulties in productivity, delay and inconvenience. Customers are forced to buy standby generators at an additional cost.

Consumption of electricity varies from household to household, season of the year, number of occupants, appliance used and geographic location of the city. In North Florida, at my home we used 1577 KWH average per month. Electricity use is high in January (2168 KWH) because of heating the home, and in August (2335 KWH) for cooling the home. The months of April and November have moderate temperature and therefore electric consumption is less for cooling or heating homes. Similarly industrial consumption will vary with development of industries. In India electric consumption is very small.

Total energy consumption by countries in 2001 in billion KWH was: United States 3602, China 1312, Japan 964, Russia 773, Germany 506, Canada 504, India 497, and other countries followed. India is not one of the top 100 countries in energy consumption per capita per year. Iceland toped the list with 26143 KWH per person annually, Turkey ranked 100th with 1653 KWH per person annually, and India had about 490 KWH per person annually, which is very low. India needs a strong national energy production policy to get out of kerosene lamp age.

Goal: To provide reliable 24-hour electric supply to residents, business, commerce, institutions, and industries at a reasonable cost.

Objective: Provide reliable 24-hour electric supply by the year XY.

Policy 1: Give building permits only if electricity is available in the area.

Policy 2: Provide electricity only if the building is constructed as per building permit.

Policy 3: Conserve energy by promoting energy efficient appliances and reducing wastage.

Tasks: (1) Estimate current and future electricity demand for all sectors in and outside incorporated area. (2) The municipality must take measures to fulfill the demand as soon as possible.

The Costs of Public Utility and Sanitation Services

The electric supply, water supply, sewers, and garbage collection and disposal is very expensive. The municipalities may sale bonds or may get loans from many financial institutions. The costs are easily recovered from customers. The customers are charged for electricity, water and sewer connections and monthly service fees are charged for each of the three services and garbage collection. Electricity and water charges are determined by meter readings. Sewage charge is also based on water meter reading. It is assumed that all the used water goes back to sewers.

(l) Recreation, Open Space and Playgrounds Element

Parks and open spaces are oasis in the concrete jungles of the cities. Please see Changing Emphasis in Planning in Chapter 3, why parks and open spaces are so important.

Goal: To provide parks, recreation, open space, and play grounds for all citizens for the current and future population.

Objective 1: At least one neighborhood park and playground shall be developed in every neighborhood. Park size shall be minimum .75 acre per 1,000 people.

Objective 2: Community parks (for several neighborhoods) including playgrounds shall have a minimum of 1 acre per 1,000 populations.

Objective 3: The area of city parks and play grounds (for the entire city) shall be at least 1 acre per 1,000 populations of the city. These parks should be designed for recreation, sports, and public events such as public meetings, public rally, and fair.

Policy: The city shall acquire and develop parks of all three levels: neighborhood parks, community parks, and city parks.

Tasks: The plan shall identify existing parks and recreational facilities; propose extension and improvement of them; and plan for new parks and play grounds.

(m) Civic Facilities Element

We live in a congested environment in our urban places. Often our living environment is filled with foul air and we live a stress filled life. It is rejuvenating to get out to a park or playground for both physical and mental health. It is nice to run or walk for exercise, have a family picnic, or to sit in solitude in a public recreational park, without noise, smokes and fear of being run over by cars. Playgrounds give an outlet to children and adults to use energy or to recuperate energy taking the mind away from routine works.

Public recreational parks need not be with manicured lawns and rows of flowers. Those can be aesthetically landscaped with shrubs, flowering trees, hills, stones, ponds, benches, fountain, etc. giving the relaxing qualities and easy to maintain. It brings together all classes of people. It is the breathing space for everybody. Occasionally, it also provides the space for community meetings and cultural events.

Parks can be of different forms and functions such as neighborhood parks, community parks, city parks, riverside parks, rock garden, hill garden, Japanese garden, and botanical gardens. India has many beautiful recreational formal gardens built by the Maharajahs and many modern gardens. Many city parks also include zoo, aquarium, planetarium, museum, music stand, playgrounds, sports stadium, and botanical garden. Community parks generally include swimming pool and sports fields. Ponds with ducks, fish, birds and landscaping give refreshing and educational experience. Environmentally it is a very good idea to bring rural setting to urban areas.

Goal: To provide rich and high quality cultural opportunities for the citizens and visitors including convention center, sports center, theaters, visual and performing art and cultural centers, museums, exhibition halls etc. and contribute to the economic development of the city.

Objectives: (1) Maintain a comprehensive inventory of the community's civic facilities and amenities. (2) Explore the current and future civic needs and requirements and explore financial feasibility.

Policies: (1) Encourage private owners and local organizations to build such facilities and help by acquiring land, zoning, collaboration, sponsorship, and even financial grant or loan with some regulations. (2) Help the civic facilities marketing, programming, management and promotion. Seek help from Chamber of Commerce and other organizations.

Tasks: The plan shall determine and propose civic facility needs.

(n) Education Element

Government supported and private educational institutions should be addressed in this element. Adequacy of existing educational facilities as well as expansion and new facilities should be considered

(1) Primary Schools should be located within residential areas in walking distance without crossing busy streets. School premises should be large enough to accommodate classrooms and playground.

(2) Middle Schools and High Schools should be located within walking distance (say one mile) and without crossing major streets, and school premises need to be large enough to accommodate classrooms and playground.

(3) Special Education Schools: Schools for blind, deaf and dumb and mentally disturbed may be necessary.

(4) Colleges should be conveniently located and college premises must be large enough to accommodate classrooms and playgrounds.

(5) Universities, Research Institutions, and Special Education: These institutions are of regional and state importance. Hence residential accommodations are required for students.

Goal: To provide adequate educational opportunities to children and adults at affordable costs and at easily commutable distances. Develop objectives and policies.

(o) Public Health Protection Element

It is the responsibility of the state and municipal governments to provide hospitals and clinics for the public. Private hospitals and clinics are also allowed under government regulations. The planner's duty is to identify the existing facilities and forecast the current and future needs. The future land use plan also should identify appropriate locations. Large complexes are desirable as medical centers associated with medical college, health research facilities, laboratories, hospitals, specialized doctors' offices, hotels for the patient's families, medical supplies and pharmacies.

The government is no longer a public health provider for all but a limited provider, regulator, and facilitator. The providers are privatized. There are groups of doctors and private nursing homes in cities. The present trend is specialized doctors practice as a group. This has several advantages: share the same examination rooms, use the same diagnostic machines and tools, use same office staff for office maintenance and accounting, avoid duplication of space and staff, doctors as a group can have free consultations among themselves, and can cover patients in absence of any doctor. The planners should note that for group practice bigger office buildings and more parking spaces are needed. These buildings also generate medium traffic.

(p) Public Safety Element

Police protection, fire protection, ambulance service and emergency services for natural and manmade disasters are government responsibilities. The plan should assess if these services and locations are adequate. Otherwise locations and land needed should be proposed. Actual planning and administration of these services remains with the individual departments. However planning agency must coordinate with these departments.

(q) Post and Telegraph Offices Element

These are central government services. Planning Department should coordinate for even distribution and locations of Post and Telegraph Offices. Location is critical for public convenience and traffic generation.

(r) Property Identification and Address Element

The property address is very critical for emergency response by the police, ambulance, and fire trucks; to deliver mails; tax record; billing for municipal services; telephone and others; repair services; serving legal notice; and finding an occupant.

Property addresses should also be matched with land revenue maps and subdivision plan.

All streets should be named and marked in the city map. Properties (buildings and vacant lots) should be numbered – odd numbers assigned on one side of the street and even numbers assigned on the other side of the street. Numbers should be in sequence such as 1, 3, 5, 7, etc. on one side and 2, 4, 6, 8, etc. on the other side of the street. Odd and even numbers of equal value (plus or minus one) should be on the opposite side approximately. For larger lots one or more number may be skipped. If the land is subdivided the skipped numbers should be used. This is the most systematic and simple property numbering system.

The plan should call for property numbering system. Streets should be named in neighborhood meetings or in hearings in the municipal office. Legal notices should be published in local newspapers about hearings and final naming of streets. Each street should have names engraved at each intersection of streets. Letters should not be less than 3" high and the sign should be placed conspicuously. Property numbers should be displayed on the gate or on the building. The plan should specify these requirements.

COORDINATION OF GOVERNMENTS AND COMMUNITY PARTICIPATION

(s) Public Participation Element

This element shall state how public participation can be accomplished. Meetings may be held to get input from citizens, social clubs and institutions. Publicity through media is another option. Importance of public participation has been discussed in Chapter 2.

(t) Intra-Governmental Coordination

It is very important that various departments in the municipality coordinate plan, projects, budget and work with each other to avoid conflict. For example: the road department paves a road and the water department digs the road after a week to lay new pipes; the drainage department digs drain without consulting telephone department and cut underground cables; the electric department installs a light post without consulting traffic engineer and cause accidents. The budget for a drain is included in the drainage department and road department etc.

The plan should address how different departments shall coordinate. There may be a clearing house or other arrangements to avoid conflicting work schedule.

(u) Inter-Governmental Coordination

The municipality deals with many state departments for roads, electricity, drainage, flood, environment, health services, city parks, sports, etc. Municipality may provide water to unincorporated areas and neighboring towns. So, plans, projects and works must be coordinate with other governmental units.

The plan should address how different governmental units shall coordinate. There may be a clearing house or other arrangements to track down work schedule of all departments and give clearance or to reschedule.

FUTURE LAND USE AND TRANSPORTATION PLAN

The Future Land Use Plan and Transportation Plan is often misunderstood and confused with Zoning Plan and Regulation. This confusion leads to conflicts between landowners and the planning office. The readers must be aware of the differences.

The future land use plan is a guide and generalized proposal for physical expansion and renewal of an urban area. It represents the best possible physical environment for urban living. The land use plan embodies a proposal based on accepted principles of health, safety, convenience, economy, amenities of urban living, healthy environment and a balance between cost and revenue. It is more than a map. It represents land and structures built upon the land based on principles, assumptions and reasoning. It is a progressive planning approach. The land use plan is an estimate of land use requirements relative to location and amount of land to be reserved for each public and private use. The land use plan is a guide for day-to-day operational direction of the planning office. It is a guide for zoning, subdivision control, and urban renewal, land acquisition for public facilities, schools, plays grounds, and so on.

The land use plan is not rigid. There is some latitude for variations. It is preliminary. As the details are worked out, some changes will emerge. For example the alignment of utility lines and roads may change when detail studies and final decisions are made.

Zoning is one of several legal devises for implementing the land use plan. It is detailed by lot boundary base on the land use plan. The future land use plan must be translated into zoning regulation for implementation.

A very common mistake made in the future land use plan is that every square feet of land is designated for a particular land use. It is not necessary, rather unwise to plan on every vacant land. Some or most of undevelopable land should be reserved for future zoning called floating zoning. As the undeveloped land become ripe for development, the land use can be determined for appropriate use. This gives the flexibility for use as demand arises. Unforeseen land requirements for civic center, medical center, modern office complex, and so on can be accommodated in floating zoning areas.

REVISION OF GENERAL PLAN

The General Plan (planning elements and the future land use plan) is constantly monitored and evaluated for its success and failure during the plan implementation process. It is revised to update every five years. This means that one year before the revision is due, revision work shall start.

4

The Planning Agency: Organization and Structure

Urban planning can be a function of the state government or of the local government. There are advantages and disadvantages in both organizational patterns of planning agency. The statutory provisions of state planning laws dictate the organizational pattern of the planning agency and its structure. There are many options for organizing and structuring a planning agency.

STATE GOVERNMENT AS PLANNING AGENCY

The state planning law may require a State Planning Department to prepare plans for different cities within the state. A planning director heads the state planning organization. A Planning Advisory Council consisting of high officials from PWD, Health Department, Municipal Council, Chamber of Commerce, citizens etc., may guide the director. Field offices of the state planning department collect information, data, maps, and conduct surveys; study all aspects of planning; and based on these findings, prepare draft city plans for public comments. After considering public comments, the final city plan (master plan) is prepared. Both the draft and final plan are published in locally circulated newspapers. The government hands over the final plan to a development authority created in each town or city for execution. A chairman appointed by the government heads a development authority. The authority hires qualified staff such as a planner, engineer, surveyor, etc.

The advantage of state government as planning agency is that local governments are relieved from the financial burden of preparing the plan. The state government can mobilize the planning staff from one town to another. It is advantageous for small towns and cities.

The disadvantages are many: (1) The planners and planning advisory council members are transferable and have no permanent interest on planning and implementation. (2) There is not much public participation in the state agency planning process. (3) Detail planning such as zoning maps, community development projects, and capital improvement projects are left to the development authorities, which is again left to non-elected appointees. As a result, there is no continuity of ideas and thoughts from plan making to implementation. (4) The role of the city/town council/commission in making the plan and implementation is ignored. It is also against the principle of home rule. Therefore, the state government as a planning agency is not acceptable in most western democratic countries.

The State Planning Department has vital roles other than planning for cities/towns. It reviews local government plans for compliance with the State Planning Laws and gives approval on compliance. It conducts research and provides technical assistance to local planning agencies. The State Planning Department may recommend new planning laws or amendments to the existing planning laws. It may have the same responsibilities with regional planning and state land planning if such laws are passed.

LOCAL GOVERNMENT AS PLANNING AGENCY

The local government is a validly democratic entity. The City Council/Commission is the final policy making and budget authority in municipal government. Therefore, the City Planning Department/Commission should be under the City Council/ Commission as an advisory policy making department. The council is not a technical body and does not have enough time to give attention to planning details. The director of planning keeps the council apprised of the planning activities. The city planner is a technical expert and should not be subject to political influence.

If there are two or more cities adjacent to each other, a City Planning Commission or a Metropolitan Planning Organization may be formed covering all the cities/towns. Since the cities/towns are interdependent for urban services, activities and functions, planning activities need coordination and cooperation. This arrangement works best. This commission is represented by all constituent jurisdictions. The city planning staff works for the City Planning Commission. Each municipality is responsible for enforcement of the plan in its own jurisdiction.

The organizational structure may vary according to city size and political makeup of the city. Metropolitan cities will need a sophisticated planning agency structure. Functions of the planning agency must be grouped and detailed. Responsibilities are delegated according to different units of the planning agency. Staffing the agency with professional, trained, competent, and dedicated persons is another matter of

Table 4.1
PLANNING AGENCY
ORGANIZATION AND STRUCTURE

City Council

City Planning Commission (*Advisory*)

- Planning Dept. or Community Development Dept.
- PWD, Roads, Water, Sewer, Drainage, Solid Waste
- Parks and Recreation Dept.
- Utility Dept. ill collection for municipal services
- Other Departments
- Other Departments
- Other Departments
- Other Departments

Advance Planning Division	Plan Implementation Division	Zoning and Subdivision Division	Building Code Division	Housing Code Division	Urban Renewal Division
— Research — Reports — Planning — Plan Revision — Public Hearing — Land Use — GIS — Graphics — Zoning — Regulation — Transportation — Plan — Special Projects	— Public Relation — Land use Control — Approval of Special Projects — Environmental — Review and Permit — Zoning Map — Drainage — Special Projects — PUD, TRD, Parks & Play Grounds	— Zoning — Subdivision — Zoning Appeals — Hearing — Approval of Subdivision Plans	— Lot review: — Ownership — Dimension — Zoning — Drainage — Infrastructure — Plan review — Construction — Inspection — Occupancy Certificate	— Existing housing stock maintenance — Inspection of existing housing — Compliance with code — Slum clearance — Facilitate Housing Development — Housing Projects	— Identify areas for urban renewal — Initiate redevelopments — Negotiate with property owners. — Financial feasibility study — Prepare plan proposals — Implement

importance and success in planning. A very close coordination among the departments and divisions is necessary. In certain projects more than one department or more than one division is involved. A flow chart should be prepared for each project's activities showing the functional relationship with each of them.

FUNCTIONS OF A PLANNING AGENCY

The major burdens on planning staff are: (a) advance planning and research that must precede and support long-range planning; and (b) administration responsibilities. A local planning program may be classified into seven functions or categories as follows:[1]

1. To establish community development objectives.
2. To conduct research on the growth and development of the city.
3. To make development plans and programs.
4. To increase public understanding and acceptance of planning.
5. To provide technical service to other governmental agencies and private groups.
6. To coordinate development activities effecting city growth.
7. To administer land use controls (zoning and subdivision regulations).

The planning program needs a framework of officially approved development policies, which serve as both a checklist and directive for the planning agency's activities. Broad development objectives should be established, approved officially, and periodically reviewed and updated, (1) to give the government and public a clear sense of the future city, and (2) to give the agency a clear sense of direction for its activities.

The agency must be organized and staffed to collect and analyze pertinent data on a continuing basis on city growth, development and to provide a foundation for the planning program. It is a repository of data, statistics, and information, which may aid other city departments and citizens in making development decisions.

The central function of a planning agency is to make development plans and programs. After careful study and analysis city development objectives shall be written. These objectives shall provide a clear guide for governmental decisions in construction of public facilities and land development controls. The agency shall develop specific plans and programs to achieve these objectives. Goals, objectives, and policies are discussed in the previous chapter.

Understanding, acceptance, and support of planning activities by the citizens of the community and public officials are vital for success. It is a staff function of the agency. Publicity is very important.

Furnishing of technical information and advice to other municipal departments and public is a service activity. Staff members should be specifically assigned for publicity and distribution of technical information such that staff assigned to development of plan and programs are not disturbed.

Coordination, collaboration, and liaison with governments of different levels, other cities, other city departments, funding agencies, private organizations, and public is a continuing function. Some documents are also received by the agency for review and comment. The capital improvement programs especially need a great deal of coordination and collaboration.

Another important function of a planning agency is the administration of land use control, fairly and equitably enforced, based on plans and development policies for public interests. Separate staff members are assigned for this function.

THE CITY PLANNING COMMISSION OR BOARD AND METROPOLITAN PLANNING COMMISSION OR BOARD

The City Planning Commission (or Board) and Metropolitan Planning Commission (or Board) are unfamiliar bodies in India. Such bodies should be introduced in India for their effectiveness. In the United States, the first City Planning Commission started in the city of Hartford, Connecticut in 1907.[2] Because of its effectiveness in urban planning, this mechanism has spread, and now almost every city, metropolitan area, and regional planning area has a planning commission.

The role of the commission is very critical. The elected officials have the final responsibility for planning, policy, decision-making, and action. They may delegate administrative responsibility but not legislative authority. Therefore, the city council has the ultimate authority. If the council members are pro-planning, farsighted, and determined the planning activities will go well. But if not, they may take politically advantageous positions over logical solutions for the community. Because of highly contested political elections, the city council also may be unstable. Because of these situations, a planning commission or board acts as a safety valve and provides some stability, continuity, and public participation in the planning process. Citizens and concerned groups appear in the planning commission meetings to voice their concerns. By attending meetings they gain a better understanding of the problems and solutions in their community.

The governing body of the jurisdiction, authorized under the state planning law, must pass an ordinance creating a planning commission. This commission is comprised of a majority of citizens and neighborhood groups, along with public and elected officials. In case of a metropolitan planning commission, public officials and citizens of all jurisdictions will be represented in the commission. Cooperation and coordination among constituent cities in all aspects of planning and plan implementation are very important.

The planning commission serves as a reviewing and recommending body on current development proposals, zoning amendments, plan approval, etc. It also performs four other roles as follows:[3]

1. A representational role on behalf of the public, subjecting planning decisions to citizen examination, by establishing technical advisory committees of informed citizens and officials on specific subjects.
2. A promotional role to stimulate interest in planning.
3. An advisory role to municipal officials on development policies of local government.
4. A coordinative role in working with other public and private agencies to integrate the total governmental planning effort.

The planning commission may be independent or advisory. An independent or autonomous planning commission is independent from the local administration. It fosters an objective and neutral attitude, free from political influence, and pro-community activism. The planning staff works for the autonomous planning commission. The commission causes to implement the planning functions. It spends most of its time on development control administration and routine duties are left to the planning staff. The planning commission formally communicates with the chief executive (Mayor) of the municipality. Ultimately, the city governing body has to approve the actions of the planning commission. The advantage of an autonomous planning commission is that planning activities have less political and more citizen influence.

An advisory planning commission performs advisory function to the planning department, which is under the chief executive of the municipality. The planning department is not subject to supervision and control of the commission. The advisory role is performed by special ad hoc committees appointed to review and comment on certain problems under study. When the planning department is under the chief executive of the municipality, it is called the department form of organization. The advantage of the department form of organization is that the chief executive can coordinate physical planning policies with other administrative operations of local government.

Composition of the planning commission: Selection, election, or appointment of commissioners should be such that sincere and dedicated people who can effectuate planned changes to the community are representing the commission. Individuals' knowledge, experience and dedication are important considerations. The dedicated people may not know what is planning, but they learn fast. Many people want to be a commissioner to promote personal agenda such as: as a stepping stone to become a council member, to enhance value of their own land, to make money by favoring somebody, to improve economic livelihood, and become an influential person at the expense of the community and the general public. Unfortunately, such people always find political connections to become a commissioner.

ORGANIZATION OF ACTIVITIES

Planning, zoning, building code enforcement, and urban renewal or redevelopment activities may be organized under the planning department. It makes more sense to bring these activities under a community development department since they are inter-linked and need coordination. This will bring the planning and development functions together.

The structure of the department should be by division, bureau, and section, to reflect the division of responsibilities and chain of command. The objectives of the department should be clearly stated to the employees. Specific tasks should be assigned to each employee and they should be made aware of expected job performance. The director of the department must be competent in the technical and administrative work. As the workload increases, he may have to assign certain responsibilities to his assistants.

Need a Spark for Action

A spark starts a motor engine. Once started, the engine will do the work. This is an analogy. The spark for action can come from organized groups such as a neighborhood association, citizens committee, chamber of commerce, tax payers association, voters for action, association of professionals, or an individual citizen. Some unfortunate situations like accident, explosion, fire, or flood also may spark an action. But do we need to wait for it. People are accustomed to live in miserable conditions, because most of them have not traveled outside and have not seen any better. Or the citizens are unable to change the existing political atmosphere for better. Until the citizens are an effective force, it is unlikely that the politician on their own will improve their community.

Notes

1. William I. Goodman and Eric C. Freund, Editors, *Principles and Practice of Urban Planning,* International City Managers Association, Washington D.C., 1968.
2. Herbert H. Smith, *The Citizen's Guide to Planning,* American Planning Association, Chicago, 1972.
3. William I. Goodman and Eric C. Freund, Editors, *Principles and Practice of Urban Planning,* International City Managers Association, Washington D.C., 1968.

5

Plan Implementation

The preparation and adoption of the General Plan (the Master Plan) including the Future Land Use Plan is the beginning and not the end of planning. The success of building a beautiful and functional city depends on the formulation and implementation of the following major components: Zoning Ordinance; Sub-division Regulation; Building Codes; and Infrastructure Development. An excellent city plan may totally fail if the execution is poor. On the other hand, a poorly developed city plan may produce better results, at least a functional city, if the execution is good. It is like sports – the players know the techniques, but the players who can execute most techniques become winners. The ultimate goal of planning is implementation or execution of the plan.

ZONING

Often people confuse between the Future Land Use Plan and the Zoning Map. Zoning is not synonymous with the Future Land Use Plan. The Future Land Use Plan is an overall concept or idea of city development. Boundaries of land uses in the Future Land Use Plan are not precisely identified. The Zoning Maps precisely define the lots or parcels of land for each land use category in detail. Therefore, without preparation and adoption of zoning maps zoning cannot be enforced.

Each land use category, as shown in Table 5.1, has different characteristics and impact on the environment. Therefore, separation of land uses is necessary. Zoning is justified for the reasons: automobiles, rickshaws, animal drawn carts, and pedestrians create congested streets; high-density developments impact on narrow streets;

smokes from industries and automobiles, dust, odor, noise, and accumulated garbage pollute air; invasion of residential areas and open spaces by shops, factories, offices, and warehouses. This causes undesirable residential environment, social problems, and public safety problems. Hence, land use categories should be separated except when compatible uses may be desirable and should be allowed side by side.

These problems were experienced during the unrestricted land developments in the industrial revolution. Land use separation started in the eighteenth century. Paris started building height regulations. Many cities in Europe started controlling size, shape, height and open spaces around the buildings to ensure light and air. New York City's 1916 zoning regulation was the first formal zoning law. Edward Bassett, an attorney in New York City, defined zoning as "the regulation by districts under the police power of height, bulk, and use of land, and the density of population." Zoning was used extensively in European and American cities before Word War II.

Land uses categories and their characteristics are shown in Figure 5.1. By no means this is an exclusive list. Zoning is an instrument of plan implementation. It has three purposes: (a) to control land use, (b) to prevent overcrowding and (c) to set a limit for water supply, sewer, electricity, schools, roads, and other urban services. It accomplishes (a) orderly community growth, (b) general public welfare, (c) elimination of nuisance, (d) location of buildings in appropriate places, and (e) conservation of property value.

Zoning is an application of police power to regulate private land to carryout objectives of planning. Zoning divides the planning area into zones or districts to control the use and development of private land. Public land belonging to the State or Central Government also can be zoned but cannot be enforced without consent of the State or the Central Government and has superior legal jurisdiction over the Local Government.

The zoning enabling legislation must be passed by the state. Land uses shown in plan must be translated into zoning maps and have written special regulations for each zone classification. Rational of zoning are: promotion of health, safety, moral, and general welfare. Landowners may have to bear certain loss or hardship for greater advantage of the community. Existing nonconforming uses are allowed to continue, but not allowed to upgrade or expand.

Zoning is not a total segregation of land uses. Some land uses belonging to another classification may be compatible and desirable. Example 1: In a residential neighborhood a small convenient shopping center is desirable. It may include convenient shops, barber, tailor, laundromat, doctor's office, municipal tax collector's office, post office, place of worship, etc. for neighborhood use. This complex shall reduce travel to a commercial place and provide a venue for community interaction. Example 2: A nursery school in an office complex can be very useful for parents working in the complex. Proper zoning regulation can reduce travel distances and hence less traffic congestion, and less fuel consumption.

Residential zones are expected to be quiet. No large volume of through traffic, noise, or pollution is desired. Recreational parks, playgrounds and recreational facilities are desired in a residential neighborhood. Rental flats will have transient occupants and higher population density. So they may be permitted on the fringe of commercial and single family residences.

Business and commercial districts require high accessibility to traffic, parking, and higher level of municipal services, and higher protection from fire and police.

Industrial zoning can be classified as light and heavy industry. Industries produce noise and vibration, smoke, odor, dust and dirt, noxious gases, glare and heat, fire hazard, industrial wastes, transportation and traffic, aesthetic problems, and psychological effects. Either they may be zoned separately or define performance standards. Some industries cannot even be allowed in an urban area because of toxic emission or highly inflammable nature. For example, the world's worst industrial disaster happened in Bhopal on December 2, 1984. Union Carbide plant leaked 40 tons of lethal methyl isocyanate gas in Bhopal. It killed over 14,000 and over 150,000 people are suffering from reproductive complications, loss of ability to perform physical labor, rare cancer, and severe respiratory problems. The slum dwellers living next to the plant were the victims.

Zoning is also used to control population density and prevent overcrowding. Overcrowding has a direct relation to the protection of public health, public safety, moral, and general welfare. Zoning can control land uses and specify height restrictions, minimum lot size, percentage of built up area, floor area to lot area ratio, setback requirements, or any combination of these to limit construction, number of parking spaces and landscaping. Because of problem inherent with enforcement, population density is not prescribed. Special development standard such as sign regulations (number, location, type, height and lighting) is also included in the zoning regulations. Signs to identify businesses should maintain visual quality in the city. Zoning can be used to protect farmland, forest, animal habitat, scenic beauty, flood control, and cultural or historical sites.

Zoning Ordinance

A zoning ordinance has two parts: (1) a zoning map, and (2) a text containing definitions, general provisions, zoning district regulations, development standards, and administration and enforcement. Regulations must be reasonable and nondiscriminatory and give equal protection of law. It is adopted by the city. It also must be consistent with the general plan.

Figure 5.1
Land Use Characteristics

Land Use Category	*Characteristics*								
	Air pollution	*Noise Level*	*Pedestrian generated*	*Traffic generated*	*Fire hazard*	*Explosion hazard*	*Odor*	*Chemical/ Bio hazard*	*Strangers Encountered*
Residential	0	Low	Low	Low	Low	Low	Low	Low	Low
Educational institutions	0	Low	Medium	Medium	Low	Low	Low	Low	Medium
Neighborhood shopping center	Low	Medium	Medium	Medium	Low	Low	Low	Low	Medium
City shopping centers	Medium	High	High	High	Low	Medium	Low	Low	High
Cinema/ Theater	0	High	High	High	Low	Low	Low	Low	High
Offices	0	Low	High	High	Low	Low	Low	Low	High
Hospitals	Low	Low	Medium	Medium	Low	Low	Low	High	Medium
Warehouse low combustible	Low	Low	Low	Medium	Medium	Medium	Low	Low	Medium
Warehouse highly combustible	Medium	Medium	Low	Medium	High	High	Low	Medium	Medium
Light industry workshop	Low	Medium	Low	Medium	Medium	Medium	Low	Low	Medium
Medium industry	Medium	High	Low	Medium	High	High	Medium	Medium	Medium
Heavy industry	High	High	Low	High	High	High	Medium	High	Medium
Tannery, Sewage plant	High	Low	Low	Low	Low	Low	High	Medium	Low

Contemporary zoning district regulations are exclusive. This means that each land use category (zoning district) is exclusively for that land use. For example, an industrial district is for industry only and no residences can be built. Exclusive zoning preserves the area for future expansion and remains out of conflict with other land uses.

Certain areas of the planning district should be zoned agricultural, open space, and undetermined use (floating zone). These categories are not committed to any physical development. It is safe to do so because the future growth and land use requirements are unpredictable. As the city expands and urban services (water, electricity, sewer, garbage collection, etc.) are provided land use categories for development should be determined.

Houston, Texas is probably the only U.S. city that does not have zoning regulation. It controls land use through development permit. When a developer wants to develop a large parcel of land, the proposal is reviewed for land use compatibility. This however, may not be feasible in India since land holdings are very small.

Development Standards

Zoning regulation should contain development standards for roads, water supply, sewage, drainage, stormwater retention ponds, parking, etc.

Innovative Zoning Techniques

Development of roads and abutting lots is the prevalent pattern. This pattern is monotonous and not always possible. Planned unit developments (PUDs) are an innovative technique allowed in the zoning regulation. Instead of dividing a tract of land into lots, the developer gets lot of freedom in planning. In PUD buildings are clustered, building units can be connected without setbacks on sides, it can have mixed compatible land uses, open spaces are kept together, and clusters can have high density keeping the same overall density for the tract. Advantages of PUDs are: protect wetlands by using only a portion of the land; cost of construction of roads and utilities is reduced; self-contained residential or office community can be planned. Planning Commission has to review and approve the plan.

Zoning Administration

The local government should establish an office called Zoning Department or Planning and Zoning Department with a zoning administrator. This department reviews development applications for compliance with the zoning ordinance.

The local government should also appoint a Board of Zoning Appeals. This Board is authorized to grant minor variances to an individual property when enforcement of zoning ordinance would cause unnecessary hardship or practical difficulty. Variances are of two types: (1) Area or bulk variance include building setback and building height. (2) Land use variance is considered zoning amendment. It requires notification to the property owners of nearby properties and public hearing.

SUBDIVISION REGULATIONS

Zoning and subdivision regulations may be combined in a single development ordinance or they may be separate. If combined, it may be administered by a Land Development Agency. Subdivision regulations have to comply with the zoning regulations.

The division of land into two or more lots in an existing planned and developing area is a minor subdivision or lot split. It requires a brief approval process to see that divided lots are useful in considering building setbacks. There may be other implications of lot split such as creating new lots on wetland for development. Permit to divide land should be given if each lot can reasonably be developed.

Subdivision regulations are intended to control (a) design of subdivisions, the main key to planning development, and (b) construction standard of public improvements such as roads, water supply, sewage disposal system, drainage, electricity, public parks, playgrounds, open space, and community facilities. The term 'subdivision' is often misconstrued only as division of land. Subdivision also means a neighborhood, a section of the city, or a large area, which is designed and developed for homes, office complex, business, or any other land uses.

In western countries land holdings are large and land developers acquire large parcels of land, plan, develop land for construction according to subdivision regulations and sale the lots. This is a real estate business, which also serve land planning, and development in the construction of orderly cities. In India it is very difficult to develop a unified and integrated subdivision. Under the land ceiling act no body could keep large parcels of land. Land developers are nonexistent. Some alternative solutions to land planning and development are available. In some parts of India, landowners form housing cooperatives. The cooperatives plan and develop subdivisions, and distribute land among them. This gives systematically planed neighborhoods. Housing (ownership as well as rental apartments or flats) is the most important element in planning.

In Chapter 7, under the heading "Difficulties of Public Planning on Private Land", the problem solutions by different countries are being discussed.

Figure 5.2

Typical Lot Survey Information: Used in the United States

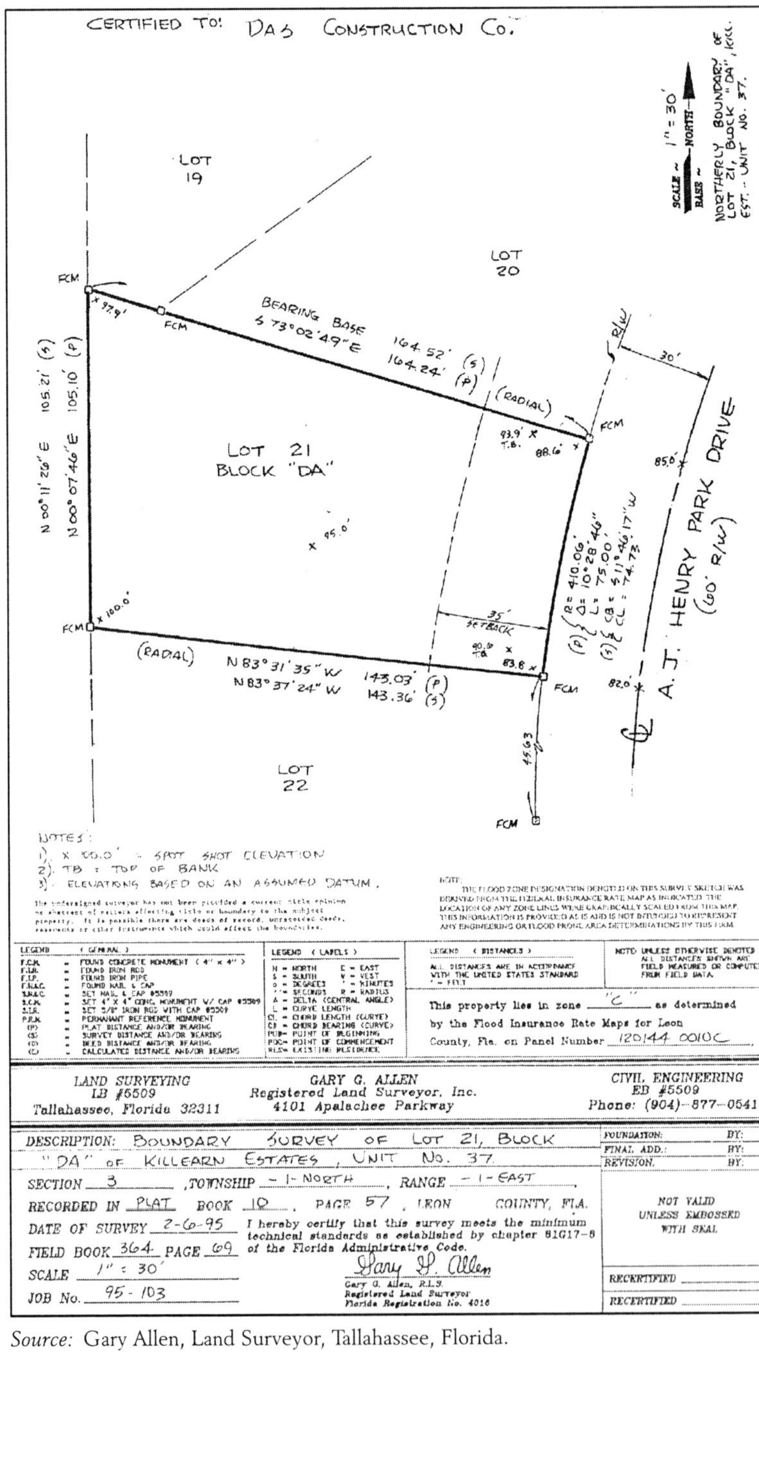

Source: Gary Allen, Land Surveyor, Tallahassee, Florida.

Figure 5.3

Typical Lot Platting in a Subdivision: Used in the United States

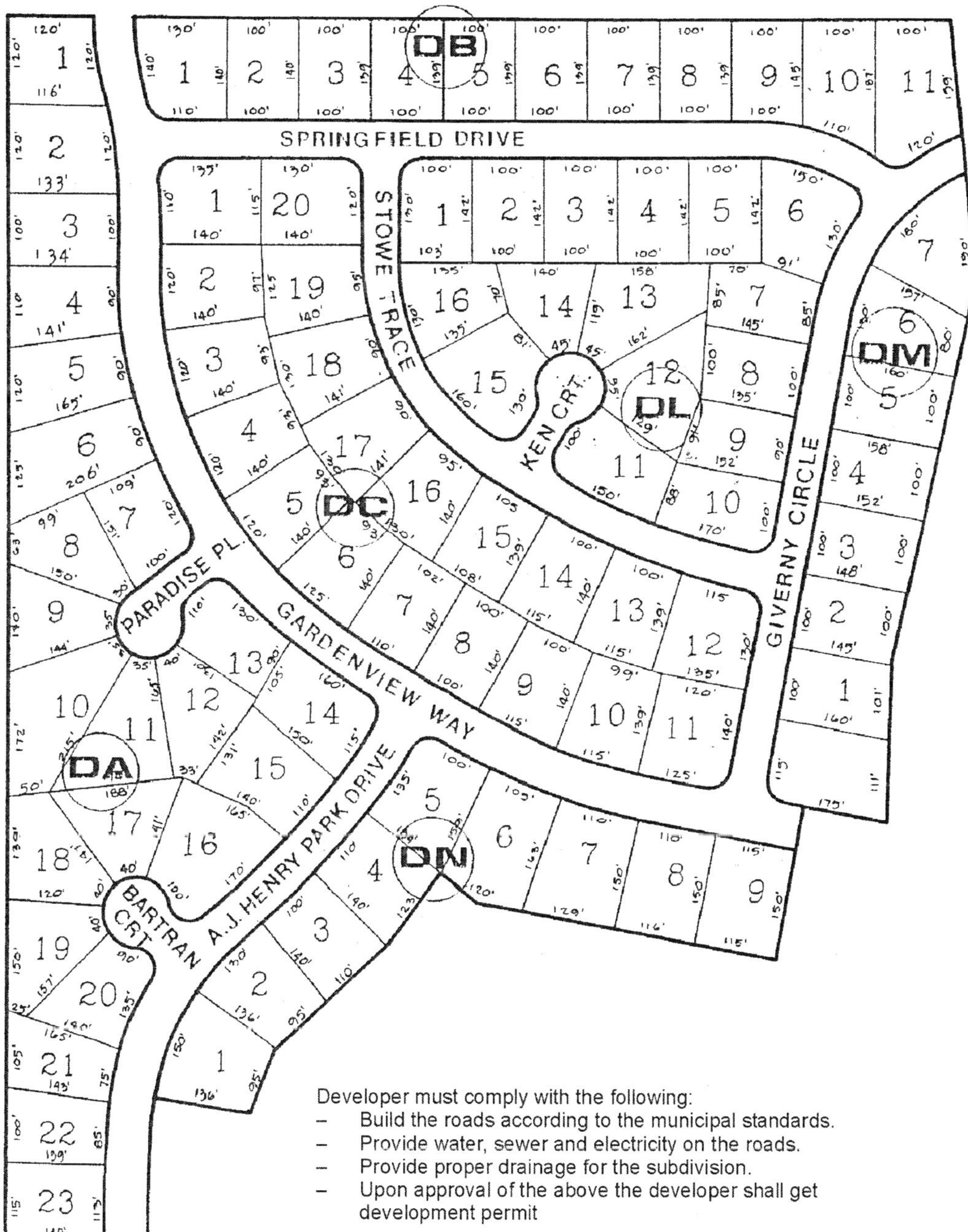

Source: Killearn Estates, Tallahassee, Florida.

Lot recording in plats – Each lot should be surveyed and map should show all of the following: lot boundaries measured in meters and centimeters, boundary latitude and longitude base on a bearing base or geographic positioning system (GPS), distance from the center line of the road to the front boundary, elevations at the corners, area of the lot in square meters, and lot number. The surveyor shall provide legal recording information and certify the survey by putting his name and seal. This method will replace the old method of survey. Encroachments can be easily detected and land disputes can be easily resolved.

BUILDING CODES

Purpose

The International Building Code in the United States and Canada stated the purpose as: "The purpose of this code is to establish the minimum requirements to safeguard the public health, safety and general welfare through structural strength, means of egress facilities, stability, sanitation, adequate light and ventilation, energy conservation, and safety to life and property from fire and other hazards attributed to the built environment and to provide safety to fire fighters and emergency responders during emergency operations."

Scope: "The provisions of this code shall apply to the construction, alteration, movement, enlargement, replacement, repair, equipment, use and occupancy, location, maintenance, removal and demolition of every building or structure or any appurtenances connected or attached to such buildings or structures."

The installation and maintenance of all electrical, gas, mechanical and plumbing systems, which may be referred to as service systems are also regulated.

Historical Development

People were concerned for safety of their building since ancient time. King Hammurabi of Babylon (in Iraq) codified laws around 1700 B.C. In Article 229 it reads "If a builder has built a house for a man, and his work is not strong, and if the house he has built falls in and kills the householder, that builder shall be slain". The collapse of a wooden amphitheater near Rome, which killed or injured 50,000 people in 27 A.D., moved the Senate to make new regulations for the safety of public places of entertainment. Fire hazards prompted building regulations in England and the United States. The Mayor of London promulgated a building code in 1189. After a fire in Boston in 1630, thatch roof and chimney with wood was no longer permitted.

After 1666 great fire of London, masonry firewalls were required between houses. Severe losses by fire in the USA, prompted the National Board of Fire Underwriters to publish the Recommended National Building Code in 1905.[1]

In the United States, National Building Code (1905), Uniform Building Code (1927), and Standard Building Code (1945) were developed. However, it remained up to local governments to adopt or not to adopt a building code. About 1975, most states required local governments to adopt a building code. Since too many model codes and different requirements confused the architects, engineers, contractors, and code officials, a unified International Building Code started developing in 1994 and completed in 2000 in collaboration with all model codes. All states are now adopting this code.

The Bureau of Indian Standards published *The National Building Code of India* (NBCI) in 1987. Adoption of this code is voluntary and therefore very few agencies has adopted some parts or the entire code. I see several problems why the NBCI is not successful. (1) There is an evolution process. Start with a simple minimum building code. When the people understand it, add more. Since the NBCI is very comprehensive, it is overwhelming to the general public, building departments, contractors, engineers and architects. In the United States, Building Codes were simple until 1990. (2) There are no trained building officials. They need to be trained through workshops and on the job experience. Some educational institutions should offer certificate courses on building codes. (3) Building code should be made mandatory by each state to towns and cities above certain population size. (4) The NBCI books are very expensive (about Rs. 1,400 per volume). (5) The NBCI is not amended since publication and it is stagnant. Building codes need amendments every year or every two years, for adjustment to practical problems, new building materials, and new construction technology.

Building code is relatively a very new field. It has developed tremendously in last 15 years. Building code is now widely recognized as remedial to: (a) disasters like fire, flood, hurricane, tornado, earthquake, and building collapse; (b) environmental degradation; and (c) public health and safety.

Subject Matter

Building codes are a combination of design performances and standard specifications. The designer of a building can prescribe materials and methods of construction to achieve the required result. Standard specifications include quality of materials, construction methods, and accepted engineering design criteria. Building codes include: building code, plumbing code, mechanical code, fuel gas code, and electrical code. The last four codes are also called service codes, since they provide services to the building. Building codes are legal documents. Following is a very brief discussion of each code.

Building Code

This code is about construction of buildings, and includes the following:

(1) Administration – Building department, building permits, plan review, building inspection, violations and penalties, and occupancy certificate.

(2) Occupancy classification – Assembly, business, educational, factory-industrial, hazardous, institutional, mercantile, residential, storage, etc. Each occupancy category has different code requirement.

(3) General building limitations – It defines allowable height and area.

(4) Construction types – Type I is made of non-combustible materials, type II is heavy timber construction, type III has exterior walls and structures non-combustible but interior is of combustible material, type IV exterior and interior walls and floors are made of wood or other combustible materials. Construction types are based on fire resistance values. The construction types may vary depending on local circumstances.

(5) Fire resistant materials and construction – It defines materials of different fire resistance and fire resistance separation.

(6) Fire protection systems – It deals with standpipes of water to fight fire, sprinklers, and fire alarm.

(7) Life safety – Means of egress – Safe exit – In case of emergency such as fire, earthquake, or riot the occupants must be able to evacuate the building or facility safely. Therefore, the code prescribes size, location, and number of exits for different occupancies. It also specifies construction of stairway, ramps, guardrails, and illumination and exits signs.

(8) Building environment – It covers natural and artificial light and ventilation, room sizes, ceiling heights, and sanitary facilities.

(9) Accessibility to the disabled – Persons on wheelchair has difficulty to visit any place with steps or without lifts. The code requires that public places as restaurants, shops, medical facilities, libraries, museums, parks, etc. should be accessible by wheelchairs.

(10) Structural design – Buildings shall be designed to withstand dead loads, live load and loads exerted by wind, snow, water, earthquake, etc. Structural design shall include foundation, retaining walls, and superstructure.

(11) Energy efficiency – Walls and roofs shall have certain insulation value to resist outside heat and cold such that the buildings are comfortable. In case of air

conditioning insulation is even more critical because of electricity consumption. Air infiltration from outside to inside to be reduced.

The plan examiner examines all these aspects and compliance to zoning and subdivision regulations before approval of the submitted plan. A building inspector examines the building at different stages of construction for compliance with the approved plan.

Plumbing Code

The plumbing code deals with safe supply of potable water and disposal of wastewater within the building premises. Public water lines and public sewers that run along the streets are not addressed in the plumbing code. Some of the features of the plumbing code are as follows. Detail technical requirements are not discussed here.

(1) Potable water lines shall be protected from infiltration of water from sewer lines and sanitary drain field. Therefore, separation is required.

(2) Pipes shall be supported firmly such that there will not be sagging or damage.

(3) Pipe joints shall be perfect such that potable water is not contaminated by infiltration of wastewater.

(4) Building water distribution and building sewer systems shall be designed as per plumbing code. Water pressure and rate of flow shall be maintained as required by plumbing code.

(5) Minimum number of plumbing fixtures (toilets, urinals, baths, sinks, etc.) shall be provided as per plumbing code for different types of occupancy and number of occupants.

(6) Certain number of fixtures shall be accessible by persons with physical disability.

(7) Vents shall be provided for foul gas to escape from plumbing fixtures.

(8) Stormwater and industrial wastewater shall not be disposed into public sewer system.

Mechanical Code

The mechanical code became necessary with modern living when building heating, air conditioning, mechanical ventilation, and different equipments and appliances became parts of the building. Heating, ventilation, and air conditioning (HVAC) is not a luxury, but a necessity for productivity. People are most comfortable and productive when the temperature is between 21-23°C (69-73°F) and relative humidity is about 50 percent. This may vary a little for different persons and summer or winter.[2] The exterior walls also need insulation against conduction of heat by the sun. The following are some of the technical requirements in this code:

(1) Air conditioning – Size of unit; location of air handler (air distributor) and compressor; duct system, its insulation, and size; air filter, combustion air, and air transfer; and temperature control.
(2) Ventilation – Natural ventilation through windows is possible when the building depth is not large, say up to 50'. Buildings with greater depth require mechanical ventilation.
(3) Exhaust – Exhaust air from cloth dryer, kitchen, motors and appliances must be ventilated through ducts. Standards are set to accomplish venting.
(4) Boiler, water heater, fire place, and refrigeration are also regulated for safety and proper functioning.

Fuel Gas Code

This code address design and installation of fuel gas systems and gas-fired appliances to safeguard the public health and safety. Many cities supply liquid petroleum gas (LPG) to consumers by pipelines. LPG is used for cooking, water heater, home heating, furnace, etc. It is combustible. Therefore, minimum regulatory standards are required. This code does not apply to portable LPG canisters and appliances.

(1) LPG piping shall have an operating pressure of 10 psig or less. Pipes shall be protected against physical damage.
(2) Gas-fired appliances shall not be located in a hazardous location such as sleeping room, bathroom, toilet room, closet, surgical room, etc.
(3) Equipments/appliances shall have air for combustion, ventilation, and dilution of fuel gases.
(4) Equipments/appliances shall have clear access space for servicing, replacement, and maintenance.
(5) The piping system shall have pipe sizes specified by the code. Pipe material and joints shall be as specified in the code.
(6) Supply pressure shall be reduced using pressure regulators as required by the appliance.
(7) Piping system shall be provided with shutoff valves.
(8) Every appliance shall discharge the products of combustion to the outdoor by venting systems.

Electrical Code

The purpose of this code is safeguarding of persons and property from electrical hazards. This code is necessary for safety, efficiency, convenience, adequacy for good service, and future expansion of electrical use. Only trained persons should do electrical installations. The code covers:

(1) Installation of electric conductors – load calculation, number of circuits, voltage, wiring, etc.
(2) Installation of conductors and equipment that connect to the supply of electricity.
(3) Installation of other outside conductors and equipment on the premises.
(4) Installations of optical fiber cables.

CODE EDUCATION

There is no formal education in colleges on building codes. The people who are code experts have gained knowledge through own studies, workshops, and on the job training. The codes have become so complex that it deserves formal training to become a building codes professional. An architect may design a beautiful building but the building may not pass building codes. At least one building codes course in architecture and civil engineering is necessary.

INFRASTRUCTURE DEVELOPMENT

The story of infrastructure is the story of human civilization in certain ways. The first human beings were nomadic hunters, wandering from place to place in search of food and water. They were not living in one place long enough to worry about support facilities for human activities such as agriculture fields, wells for water, habitat, privy, etc. But when they began to stay in one place for extended periods to cultivate crops, they needed support facilities or infrastructures. The primitive facilities were the first man made infrastructure. They needed roads and waterways to trade their products. As towns grew in Egypt, China, Mesopotamia, and India, they needed better intercity transportation, water supply, waste disposal, market place, and buildings to support government activities. Romans had built permanent roads, elaborate viaducts and sewers.[3]

What is Infrastructure?

The basic purpose of infrastructure is to support human activities. One definition of infrastructure is the physical facilities that move people, goods, commodities, water, waste, energy and information. As civilization advanced, support facilities also became numerous. The modern city is a vast and complex network of infrastructure. I shall categorize the modern-day infrastructure in the following six groups:

(1) *Primary or functional infrastructure* – Without this, modern life cannot function and economic development cannot take place. Other infrastructures mentioned below are also dependent on this infrastructure. It includes: transportation (roads, waterways, railways, airports, appropriate carriages, and urban transit systems); electricity; water supply; sewer system; drainage; solid waste collection and disposal; and communication (wires, cables, and transmission towers for telephone, television, radio, and internet).

(2) *Economic infrastructure* – The facilities that will promote production, employment, and local tax base. This may include: Industrial parks, commercial parks, business districts, office parks, warehouses, etc.

(3) *Education infrastructure* – Schools, general colleges, vocational institutions, music schools, art schools, technical colleges, institutions for research and higher learning, libraries, etc. Some facilities like planetarium, zoo, botanical garden, and aquarium, are educational and tourist attractions.

(4) *Civic infrastructure* – Cultural, social, and entertainment facilities such as museum, art gallery, public auditoriums, civic center (for conventions, meetings, celebrations, circus, indoor sports events, large cultural events, etc.), stadium, cinemas, social clubs, and large parks (maidans) for public meetings and public events.

(5) *Health infrastructure* – There are three types. Type I: Medical infrastructure – for physical and mental ailments we need hospitals, clinics, doctors' offices, therapist, laboratories, and pharmacies, etc. Type II: Passive recreation infrastructure – open spaces, gardens, landscaped parks, which supply oxygen and fresh air and where people can meet leisurely, walk, run, and have picnic. Type III: Active recreation infrastructure – playgrounds, sports facilities, swimming pools, and gymnasiums, which provide opportunity for exercise and physical rejuvenation.

(6) *Public and government infrastructure* – Government and semi-government office complexes, police offices, fire stations, post and telegraph offices, crematories and cemeteries, etc.

The primary infrastructure is needed in every urban and progressive rural area to be functional and for economic and educational development. How much of the other five groups of infrastructure is needed and can be supported by the local body of administration will depend on the size and will of the local jurisdiction. Metropolitan areas definitely need all six categories of infrastructure.

Inventory

A wish list of infrastructure for city or metropolitan area should be done. Inventory of what is available and what is missing or need reconstruction should be completed. A list of infrastructure provider should be completed. In addition to the municipality, many provider such as the Central Government, the State Government, community organizations, private corporations, and private individuals provide many infrastructures. It is the responsibility of the municipality to provide the primary infrastructure either under its ownership or through privatization.

Coordination

The municipality shall seek help from other infrastructure providers and coordinate their efforts in planning, project preparation, location, and finding land in proper locations. Neighboring municipalities also may have common interest in many infrastructures such as large public parks, civic center, sports center, major roads, water supply, etc. Therefore, these issues must be dealt at inter-governmental level.

Financing Infrastructures

This the most critical issue. The municipality must be very innovative and informative on municipal financing. Very determined leadership is a key factor. In the following chapter budgeting and finance is discussed.

In addition to these, urban renewal must be considered. It is discussed in Chapter 11.

CAPITAL IMPROVEMENT: PROJECTS, PLANNING, PROGRAMMING AND BUDGETING

Capital improvement means construction of roads, water supply, sewer system, drainage, landfills (garbage dumps and covering with darts), parks, playgrounds, electricity, schools, urban renewal, etc. Capital improvement is about providing infrastructures. Capital improvement is the ultimate challenge in making a good city. Providing adequate public facilities and public services is the most important function of a city government. Without this the city will not function. These are also very expensive projects.

Projects should be identified and priorities established based on public need, cost and benefits; make detail plans, cost estimate, and time needed to complete. Program the projects in time sequence; and allocate budget expenditures. The obvious goal is execution of the capital projects.

Capital improvement is more of a political will, courage and wisdom of the city council. The city planners, engineers and financial managers can guide the process of capital improvement. The tax revenue alone is not enough to bear these expenses. Additional funding sources must be explored. Financing of capital projects is discussed in the next chapter.

IMPLEMENTATION POLITICS

Many do not like good men who try to reform the society and do good things. Mahatma Gandhi, Martin Luther King Jr., and Abraham Lincoln were assassinated for the same reason. Baron George Eugene Hussmann, who transformed Paris from slums to a beautiful city in mid-19th century, was criticized. Jagmohan, who cleared most of Delhi's slums, had many enemies. Emperor Napoleon was supporting Hussmann and Mrs. Gandhi patronized Jagmohan so they could succeed. But the legends of these two able administrators live forever.

Many good projects fail implementation because of politics. A project administrator must be aware of oppositions and politics they employ. The administrator must find powerful allies, seek public support, and be tactful. Some probable scenarios are discussed below.

A political party in power decides to: clear slums and resettle them; evict illegal settlers from public land; remove illegal construction; or stop use of incompatible building in violation of the zoning ordinance. An opposition political party may side with the evacuees to protect them in exchange for their votes. They may resort to strikes, processions, vandalism, and even murders to block the decision.

At the end of October 2006, the Delhi Development Authority decided to lock and seal shops for misuse DDA built homes for shops and unauthorized use of shops for automobile workshops, etc. The traders union called for 72-hour closure (*bandh*). There were incidences of arson. As a result, the traders have lost an estimated Rs.200 crore a day.

A city authority decides to move street shops to a mall and make street shops illegal. The purpose is to remove road congestions. The shopkeepers may be happy if they are given better facilities. But the landlords are going to loose money from rents. Therefore, they will protest, take help of politicians, and get the administrator transferred. There are plenty of news reporters and newspapers, which publish untrue stories without investigations to discredit a good administrator or a department.

Jagmohan has given a true description of politics and intimidation he faced during slum clearance and resettlement in Delhi, in his book *Island of Truth*. The following is an extract:

Routine and casual character of our administrative set-up is notorious. As far back as 1905, Lord Curzon, in his famous farewell speech at the Byculla Club, Bombay, described the India bureaucracy as "the most mechanised and lifeless of all form of administration." Notwithstanding the fact that more than 70 years have elapsed when the above remarks were made, the "lifeless" character of our administration has not basically changed; in fact, it has taken a sharper turn towards ineffectiveness. Explanation for this is to be found in our national ethos, in our values, in our tendency to keep a wide gap between what we preach and what we practise.

Every day, we hear journalists, intellectuals, politicians and senior civil servants denouncing the old-fashioned methods and stressing the needs for result-oriented administration. But what happens in actual practice? Whenever anyone tries to break the shackles of routine and impart dynamism, he finds himself in trouble. His firmness is described as ruthlessness, his commitment as personal ambition, and his speed as rashness. And he is soon shown the way out. On the other hand, those who spend their life-time in tying red tapes over the blue flaps of bludgeoning files have smooth sailing. Let me give an example.

In Delhi, large tracts of lands are owned by various departments and ministries of the central government. These lands were under the charge of senior officers of the rank of Joint Secretary or Commissioner, and sizeable staff was engaged for their management. But they were allowed to be illegally occupied by shopkeepers, mechanics, wood merchants, warehouses, etc. Except for pushing papers up and down and holding scores of meeting, no steps were taken for over two decades to retrieve these lands. Consequently, public lands worth crores remained in the hands of racketeers. Cityscapes was uglified. Traffic jams and accidents increased, and execution of development projects inordinately delayed. After years of deliberation, the central government recognized that the DDA was the only agency that could solve the problem and transferred all these lands to it in 1975. By discarding ineffective methods and taking a courageous stand against vested interests, the DDA solved the problem in about a year. The skyline improved. Traffic hazards were reduced and long-pending development projects were executed.

What were the results? What happened to those who took their jobs seriously? Those who tried to be result-oriented, and spent long hours in the field under scorching sun, taking quick decisions and settling cases at the spot, instead of pushing papers in air conditioned offices, find themselves in the dock and are subjected to ridicule on behalf of those who showed nothing but contempt for law and morality. On the other hand, those who considered themselves too refind and sophisticated to soil their hands in the mire of slums, squatters and illegal constructions are leading a comfortable life. (pp. 113-114)

Notes

1. Sanderson, Richard, *Code and Code Administration*, Building Officials Conference of America, Chicago, 1969.
2. Canadian Center for Occupational Health and Safety.
3. David F. Schulz, ITI Executive Director, dschulz@nwu.edu

6

Budgeting and Finance

Budgeting and financing are necessary to implement all planning activities. Local government makes budget and finance decisions. It effects all planning activities. For example: (1) if a local government refuses or unable to come up with money for a sewer system, septic tanks have to be allowed, which threat groundwater contamination; and (2) if potable water supply project is not funded, people will depend on wells, where the groundwater is already contaminated. That is why financing of capital improvement projects is so important. The local governments have the responsibility to provide public services. The main topic of discussion in this chapter is the financing of local government.[1]

Local governments are the smallest unit of governments after central and state. Central government funding policies influence the state government funding and down to the local governments. The funding policy varies from country to country. Certain projects, programs, and services are directly provided by the central government, some others directly by the state, and the rest are provided by the local governments. In India the central government provides funds for national highways, airports, slum clearance, etc., the state government provides funds for schools and colleges, hospitals, state highways, police protection, etc., and the local government provide municipal services.

LOCAL GOVERNMENT REVENUES

The municipalities depend on property taxes, local option taxes, user fee and service charges, governmental grants, and impact and development fee. These revenues are spent on city maintenance and public services.

The property tax is the largest source of revenue. It is the tax on real property on the estimated market value of the property. Generally the value of property assessed for tax purpose is less than the market value. Commercial, office, and industrial properties pay higher tax than residential property. Some municipalities attract industries to create employment by giving property tax reduction for a limited time. The daytime population of cities is much higher than the resident population. People from the surrounding region come to the city for employment, shopping and office business. These visitors create extra need for services but do not pay property tax. Therefore, the shops, restaurants, etc. where the visitors come should be charged higher property tax. Since municipalities are lower in status, they cannot tax properties of state and central government but obligated to provide services. On the other hand municipalities also get grants and aids from the higher governments. The amount of property tax a municipal government collects depends on aggressiveness of taxing and collection methods. It can get very complex and varies from municipality to municipality and state laws.

The local option taxes are selective sales or excise taxes on certain items such as cigarettes, meals, lodging, automobile, appliances, and furniture in addition to the state sales tax. This is a way of shifting part of the tax burden to nonresidents who come to the city. The state remits the local portion of the tax to the appropriate local government. A state law has to allow such local option tax.

User fee and service charges have little difference and some times indistinguishable. User fee is charged to customers when they use a facility. For examples: parking fee, building permit fee, water or sewer connection fee, municipal swimming pool or tennis court fee, garbage pickup fee when occasionally requested, toll on bridges or highways, etc. For continuous services, service charges are based on units used or a flat rate. For road maintenance, street cleaning, garbage collection, and drainage maintenance a flat rate may be charged. For water supply and sanitary sewer, charge is based on liters of water used recorded in water meter. Electricity charge is based on KWH used. All the fee and charges are calculated on operating cost, amortization cost on land and equipments, savings for future replacement cost, and some profit. All these services are called urban services. Ideally the costs of urban services must be recovered from the users.

WHAT ARE CAPITAL IMPROVEMENTS?

The projects or improvements that need to be constructed at heavy capital (or investment) costs are capital improvements. This may include projects such as: (a) water refining facilities and distribution of potable water; (b) sewerage systems and treatment plant; (c) major storm water drainage and disposal; (c) garbage collection, and disposal in land fills or incineration, (d) new city roads and road widening projects, (e) public transportation (f) new public parks and beautification of existing public parks, (g) public playgrounds, (h) parking lots and multistoried garages, (i) urban renewal projects, (j) civic center or auditoriums, (k) community centers, (l) public buildings, (m) preservation of historical sites, (n) conservation of natural resources, (o) fire trucks, garbage trucks, and other major equipment purchases, (p) public transportation, and (q) slum clearance, etc. These are cumulative projects to be done by all municipal departments.

CAPITAL IMPROVEMENT PROGRAM (CIP) OFFICE

Each city should have a CIP office. The states should require it. Each of the projects in the CIP shall have (1) predetermined locations, (2) project plan and engineering design, (3) cost estimates, (4) funding sources available, (5) target date of accomplishment, and (6) a schedule chart of all projects according to priorities. Projects can be short term (5 years or less), medium term (10 years or less) or long-term (longer than 10 years). Capital improvement program is a continuous and ongoing process.

Every municipality should have a finance and accounting branch. There should be a separate CIP office in big cities. This office will have the duties of grant management: to co-ordinate and administer the capital improvement program, to find grants and aids available from governments, international agencies, non-profit organizations and private donors; to write grant applications; provide project details and estimates; follow the terms and conditions of the grants; and proper use and accountability of the funds.

PROJECTS THAT ARE CAPITAL IMPROVEMENTS BUT NOT THE RESPONSIBILITY OF THE MUNICIPALITY

Acquisition of land and construction of roads, drainage, water lines, sewer lines, electric line, and public parks in subdivisions or neighborhoods is not the responsibility of the municipality. The philosophy and strict rule in the United States is "the people who created the need must pay for it". The land developer or the landowners at their own cost must construct these infrastructures according to municipal standards. Otherwise lot sale cannot be permitted and building permit shall not be issued. Once these infrastructures are built according to municipal standards, the municipality shall take over maintenance. This philosophy and rule is not prevalent in India. But it makes good sense. Otherwise, the municipality shall never have money to acquire land, build these infrastructures. Existing taxpayers should not take this burden. The absence of this rule is probably the biggest reason why Indian cities have developed substandard. If this rule is adopted and enforced, the municipalities will be relieved of a big financial burden.

FINANCING THE CAPITAL IMPROVEMENTS

Each capital improvement project costs crores of rupees. They are so expensive that the municipalities will never have enough financial resources of their own. Therefore, the municipalities must constantly look for and compete for any available long-term loans, grants or aids.

1. Government grant or aid – This was the main source before the 74th Constitutional Amendment Act of 1992. Need to find if any project specific grants are available.
2. General tax – The municipalities need to improve general tax collections.
3. Municipal bond – The central government is encouraging to sale municipal bonds to finance capital improvement projects.
4. Donors – There are private donors who will donate land and/or money for small projects such as parks and buildings. However, they would want it in memory of someone. It should be acceptable as long it is helpful to the society and no antisocial element is attached.
5. Single purpose corporation – This is privatization or commercialization of infrastructures. Private corporations produce and distribute electricity; operate public transportation; operate water supply and sewage; and do garbage collection and disposal in many countries. These corporations will operate for profit but private capital will be used and public services will be provided. The municipalities should facilitate the services by regulating the corporations. The Government of India created State Electricity Boards, but they are not commercially viable. The governments also may directly subsidize private corporations for a limited period.
6. International organizations – World Bank, U.S. Agency for International Development (USAID), and Asian Development Bank (ADB) are the major international long-term investors in infrastructure development. They provide infrastructure financing at low interest to viable projects. Some information on them will follow.

   A few of the options for infrastructure financing are being discussed below:

Financing for Urbanization and Shortage of Urban Services in India[2]

Almost 30 percent of India's population or 285 million people lived in cities in 2001. This urban population is expected to increase nine million annually to 405 million by 2021. Urban areas also produce 60 percent of GDP. The urban centers are contributing 90 percent of central government revenue. But, the urban services in India are poor to nonexistent. With the addition of nine million urban populations annually, the urban services will have severe shortages.

The total investment for urban infrastructure projects has been estimated at 28 to 40 billion rupees per annum, but existing funding sources provide only 5 billion rupees. The funding resource required for 2000-2005 for urban infrastructure was estimated at 1.25 trillion rupees for operating expenses and capital improvements. The local governments are weak to respond to this need. Inadequate administrative structure and resources, and inability to attract private sector funds for capital improvements continue to limit necessary urban development.

The urgency is real in India for fast development of infrastructure for economic growth, and better living conditions. The financial burden shifted from government financing to commercialization of infrastructures since 1992. The doors are now open for private and foreign capital for infrastructure development.

Progress of Urban Reforms and Financial Assistance by External Agencies

The 74th Constitutional Amendment Act of 1992 delegated the primary responsibilities of urban affairs (functions, power and financial resources) from state to local governments. Since then, the Government of India has supported decentralization efforts by formulating guidelines for urban development plans in 1996. The central government is promoting improved financial management planning and capital borrowing, and authorizing the use of tax-free municipal bonds for urban infrastructure projects. Now there is a consensus among central government, state governments and external agencies (USAID, World Bank, Asian Development Bank, etc.) for direction of needed reforms. These include long-term systematic changes to Urban Local Bodies (ULBs), financial discipline in municipalities, and long term financing arrangements for infrastructures. Many municipalities in the states like Andhra Pradesh, Tamil Nadu, Uttar Pradesh, Gujarat, and Maharashtra have advanced urban development by increasing local tax revenue, finance slum upgrading, improve staff management, and restructuring operations. The Gujarat Infrastructure Act is the forerunner in state initiative on infrastructure development.

The external agencies provide significant support to Indian urban sector reforms. Since 1989 to 2000 these agencies provided financial assistance, lone-financed investment projects, and technical assistance totaled 132 billion rupees.

Financing by U.S. Agency for International Development (USAID)

It has supported urban sector reforms through the debt market component of the Financial Institutions Reform and Expansion (FIRE D) project. The FIRE D project's goal is to assist municipal, state, and central government in India to develop sustainable urban environmental services (water, sewer, and solid waste) and ensure the poor have access to these services. The FIRE D project works with central, state, and municipal bodies and has supported Indian cities with project development and financing, resource mobilization, decentralization, capacity building and training. FIRE D's accomplishments include:

- Acceptance of the concept of commercial viability in delivery of urban infrastructure services.
- A proven structure is in place for municipalities to access domestic capital markets and finance infrastructure projects by issuing municipal bonds.
- Introduction of financial management and accounting reforms.
- Development of a state-level policy framework for water and sanitation services and a national policy framework for improving solid waste management.
- Sharing lessons learned through a training network, study tours, city managers associations and the dissemination of reports through the internet.

Financing by World Bank (WB)

The World Bank assistance for India has focused on water supply and sanitation (WSS). It has allocated 60 percent of its urban investment funds on WSS. The strategy emphasizes private sector investment in development and delivery.

The capital budget and investment planning is concerned with the creation of long-term assets such as roads, water treatment plants, sewer plants, pipe lines, etc. The capital budget details the local government's long-term capital investment needs. Governments commonly establish a uniform and organized multi-year (5-year) capital investment plan (CIP) to outline the public facilities, infrastructure, and land purchases that the jurisdiction intends to implement during a multi-year period given the availability of funds.

A central element of capital budget and the multi-year capital investment plan is the financial analysis aimed at minimizing the financial effect of investment projects on the local budget, while maximizing the impact or return of the project in addressing the communities needs. The capital budget process is a management tool for guiding the expenditure of public resources over an extended period of time and it represents a commitment by the local government to provide its community with the desired and required level of services. The capital budget process is a multi-step process, which includes the following components.[3]

- *Inventory of Capital Assets*: A municipality must have (a) an up-to-date inventory of existing facilities including the date of construction, cost, and current conditions, and (b) an ongoing program for regularly examining the quality and level of service provided by the infrastructure facility. The inventory and condition of the infrastructure will facilitate the tasks of local government in determining the need for renewal, replacement, expansion, and retirement of current inventory. This will help determining future investment spending. Special capital project analysis will give detail and accurate project expenditures.
- *Development of a Capital Investment Plan*: Decisions to undertake capital investment are motivated by several criteria, including: degree of urgency of the project, benefits derived from the project, cost and financial impact of the project, and acceptability to the local constituency. Establish goals for level and quality of services. This will lead to justification whether infrastructure should be replaced, upgraded/extended, or entirely new investment should be undertaken.
- *Development of a Multi-Year CIP*: Based on preliminary project cost estimates and the time schedule established by technical studies, the initial priority list of projects may have to be re-prioritized. Revise it annually. The multi-year plan establishes the time schedule and costs for all capital investment projects. The benefits of multi-year capital investment plan includes: assisting the jurisdiction in programming scarce financial resources, allowing the jurisdiction the opportunity to select alternative and cost effective solutions, and allowing the jurisdiction to engage in prudent borrowing and other debt policies.
- *Development of the Financial Plan*: The municipality must investigate the financing options and fiscal feasibility of funding the projects. The most critical stage of the capital investment program consists of conducting detailed financial analysis of the municipality's capacity and ability to undertake the investment program. The number of projects a local government can finance generally depends on: the level of recurring future operating expenditures; the cost recovery for individual projects and potential for public investment to be

revenue generating; the availability of cost sharing by different tires of government and adjoining municipalities; and debt structures and investments (debt-carrying capacity).

- *Implication for Recurring Expenditures*: Project expenditures and operating expenditures both are to be considered in a capital budget. Recurring operating expenditures may quickly accelerate. Until this expenditure is under control, it may be inappropriate to engage in additional capital spending. The expenditure of operation and maintenance of the capital infrastructure will significantly influence the decision for undertaking of new capital investment projects.
- *Cost Recovery and Revenue Generating Elements for Capital Projects*: The basic approach to capital investment planning assumes that all projects can rank-ordered for priority. Municipal officials can work down the list until they exhaust the financing resources available. Many investment projects are fully or partially financed from dedicated revenue sources. A municipality's general funds are free to be allocated, as local authorities prefer. The remainder of the capital budget consists of projects financed by specific grants or international funding sources which are restricted to certain purposes. A system of dedicated user fees and benefit-related taxes can enhance the efficiency of local capital allocation. Confronted with pressing community investment demands, local government authorities have option of relaxing the capital budget constraints by raising additional public revenues, borrowing capital funds, or re-allocating funds from the operating budget to investment budget. Revenue mobilization for capital spending should consider: (a) collection of revenues that are due from the existing tax structure, (b) increase user fee to cover the incremental costs of service delivery, and (c) the local government should let the citizens know about the financing of the projects.
- *Implementing the Capital Budget*: In the final implementation stage, final development and final capital budget should be adopted. The multi-year capital investment plan should include the following components: (a) all project cost details including project development costs, construction costs, and financing costs; (b) annual capital cost disbursement schedule, and all principal & interest for debt financing; and (c) costs for project design; future operation and maintenance; and all fees and interest charges needed for successful project development should be transferred from the current operating budget.

At the final stage the completed capital budget should have annual cost and total cost for all projects. The capital budget is an important management tool. It makes the local jurisdiction and the constituency better informed on the capital expenditures. The jurisdiction adopts the capital budget by resolution, but subject to annual revision and authorization.

Financing by the Asian Development Bank (ADB)[4]

ADB is a multilateral development financial institution dedicated to reduce poverty in Asia and the Pacific Islands. It was established in 1966 and owned by 64 member countries. It's headquarter is located in Manila, Philippines and has 19 resident missions in Asia. ADB formulates operational strategies for individual countries, including economic and policy analyses. It undertakes country performance reviews, which provides a basis for policy dialogue with governments of developing countries. ADB develops Country Strategy and Programs, which include identification of individual technical assistance and loan projects, and programs. ADB establishes and maintains relationships with developing member countries governments for overall economic reporting and for loan negotiations.

ADB is in a unique position to support private sector projects with clear development impact in the financial sector or infrastructure sector. ADB's role is to mobilize funding from local and foreign sources. ADB uses equity investments, loans, guarantees, and complementary financing schemes. It offers complex capital market solutions and other innovative approaches to financing challenges, including the emerging structured financial and security market. The Private Sector Finance team of ADB gives expert guidance and financial assistance to private sector projects. ADB offers many opportunities for contractors, consultants, investors, and job applicants.

ADB provides project lending assistance based upon the following considerations:

(a) Economic viability, technical feasibility, and financial soundness;
(b) Effect on development activity in the country concerned;
(c) Contribution to the removal of economic bottleneck;
(d) Capacity of the borrowing country to service additional external debt;
(e) Introduction of new technologies to raise productivity;
(f) Expansion of job opportunities;
(g) Strengthening of institutions according to criteria of good governance;
(h) Integration of environmental and social considerations into ADB projects; and
(i) Statement of ADB operations in 2004.

ADB also has an application rating system with 5-star maximum rating.

Financial Resources: ADB borrows and lends prudently. It (a) maintains adequate net income, liquidity, and reserves; (b) monitors the creditworthiness of borrowers; and (c) requires borrowers to justify thoroughly the economic, financial, and technical viability of their projects for which they seek ADB loans. The financial resources of ADB consist of ordinary capital resources (subscribed capital, reserve and surplus, and borrowed funds) and special funds (mostly contributions of members for ADB's concessional loan and technical assistance programs).

Latest Aid Agreement

It was announced at the Fourth World Water Forum in Mexico City, March 20, 2006, that as a part of world-wide clean water initiative, US-Japan Initiative will collaborate with India. The USAID and Japan Bank for International Development (JBIC) will work with the Ministry of Urban Development, India. They have already started working in partnership to provide water and sewer to slum and poor areas of Bangalore, and will expand to other cities.

Procuring Funds from Financial Institutions

The followings steps are generally required:

Preparation of Outline Plan/Proposal
↓
State Government
↓
Government of India (Planning Commission)
↓
Government of India (Department of Economic Affairs)
↓
Financial Institution (ADB, WB, USAID, or JBIC)
↓
Approval of Project
↓
Detail Project Report
↓
Approval by Financial Institution
↓
Fund Released Through Government

Technical Assistance

All financial institutions provide technical assistance in preparing plans and proposals. Several contributors including members of 3iNetwork (a network of three institutions), produce India Infrastructure Report annually. Oxford University Press, New Delhi, publishes this report. These institutions are: the Infrastructure Development Finance Company, the Indian Institute of Technology, Kanpur, and the Indian Institute of Management, Ahmedabad. The staffs of India Infrastructure Report and those three institutions provide technical assistance and valuable information on all sectors of infrastructure. The Government of India's Ministry of Urban Development, the Planning Commission, and the Department of Economic Affairs provide technical assistance and valuable information. Independent consulting firms, experienced in international financing of infrastructures also provide technical assistance in preparing projects and grant applications. Large cities may still need their own Capital Improvement Program Office.

Notes

1. *Budgeting and Finance*, International City/County Management Association, The Practice of Local Government Planning, Third Edition, 2000.
2. Assessment and Analysis of the Status of Urban Service Delivery & Urban Infrastructure Sector Reform in India, USAID/New Delhi, Draft Final Report, November 2, 2001, TCG International, LLC.
3. World Bank Institute.
4. ADB, on Internet.

7

Planning Law: Legal Basis of Planning

Modern planning laws started developing from the beginning of the 20th century in England and other countries. Now, it is a specialized subject practised by people trained in both urban planning and law. Planning laws are enacted by State Governments in conformance with the constitution of the country and address the following:

(a) Defines the planning functions or intent of planning;

(b) Defines the perimeters of planning;

(c) Provides legal authority to planning agencies to regulate land development;

(d) Provides for constitution of the planning agencies; and

(e) Provides funding provisions.

Without legal authority, planning cannot have legitimacy and power. If a state does not have powerful legislative support and leadership, the state cannot be effective in urban planning. Without legal backing or authorization no one can plan, enforce, or implement the plan. Therefore, it is paramount that the State Government enact enabling legislation. The discussions in this chapter shall include constitutionality, state enabling act, property rights, and the difficulty of public planning on private land.

CONSTITUTIONALITY

The Constitution of India, the supreme law of the land, provides for power, authority and responsibility of municipalities in Article 243W. According to this, the legislature of a state may, by law, endow municipalities power and authority as institutions of self-government as provided in the Twelfth Schedule, which list the following matters:

1. Urban planning including town planning.
2. Regulation of land-use and construction of building.
3. Planning for economic and social development.
4. Roads and buildings.
5. Water supply for domestic, industrial and commercial purpose.
6. Public health, sanitation conservancy and solid waste management.
7. Fire service.
8. Urban forestry, protection of the environment and promotion of ecological aspects.
9. Safeguarding the interests of weaker sections of society, including the handicapped and mentally retarded.
10. Slum improvement and upgradation.
11. Urban poverty alleviation.
12. Provision of urban amenities and facilities such as parks, gardens, playgrounds.
13. Promotion of cultural, educational and aesthetic aspects.
14. Burial and burial grounds, cremations, cremation grounds and electric crematoriums.
15. Cattle pounds; prevention of cruelty to animals.
16. Vital statistics including registration of births and deaths.
17. Public amenities including street lighting, parking lots, bus stops and public conveniences.
18. Regulation of slaughterhouses and tanneries.

Thus, the above matters, including urban planning, become municipal responsibilities. Therefore, the functioning of the planning agency and exercise of rule making power is within the governmental structure of self-government. Governmental authority must be applied for a well-ordered community for public health, public safety, and public welfare.

It is a local government responsibility to prepare the city plan and the citizens should have input in it. Some state governments have assumed the responsibility of preparing city plans, with unfortunate results. State government's role is to review and approve local plans and give expert assistance. There are two options available: (a) The first option is to have an independent and semi-autonomous City Planning Commission comprised of citizens. This will insulate the planner from political influence of the city commissioners. Also, the City Commission does not have enough time to devote on city planning. But the City Planning Commission does not have policy-making authority. (b) The second option is to have a City Planning Department under the City Commission, which has policy-making power. The city planning director is the principal advisor on planning. Planning agency structure is discussed in more detail in Chapter 4.

Socialistic planning exercises certain restraints over private property by police power (limiting use of property with out compensation) and eminent domain (taking private property for public purpose paying just compensation). Landownership does not automatically grant development rights. If the development is harmful to the public, it may be restricted or denied. Any restriction must be constitutional.

STATE ENABLING LEGISLATION

Constitutionally, a state can enact legislation enabling its political subdivisions such as municipalities, districts, regions, or the entire state to prepare and enforce general plans for any of the purposes listed in the Twelfth Schedule of the Constitution. These legislations include: scope of planning; authority to plan; specific methods for its adoption, enforcement and revisions; power and authority to regulate land development; use of police power. The general plan which is also called the master plan, comprehensive plan, or growth management plan is advisory or of a general nature.

Based on the general plan, the zoning ordinance is prepared for enforcement. The enabling act may provide scope of zoning, the procedure for adoption of the ordinance, the composition of the zoning board and its powers and functions, and the method for modifications or rezoning. Every community has the right and responsibility to determine its own character for orderly growth, and it is a valid use of police power. Zoning is used for both conservation and planning.

Probably, the first legislation dealing with planning and building matters was enacted in Sweden, which came into effect in 1874. In early 20th century planning legislations were enacted in the United Kingdom, United States and many other countries. In the later part of the 20th century a variety of planning legislations were enacted covering a variety of planning subjects, some were extensive and some were regarding very specific areas. Some of these are listed below:

Local Government Comprehensive Planning and Land Development Regulation Act

State and Regional Planning Act

State Comprehensive Planning Act

State Environmental Land and Water Management Act

Development of Regional Impact Act

Planning and Building Act, etc.

Writing legislation is an art requiring understanding of the complexity of planning, administrative procedures as well as vision, boldness, foresightedness, and mastery of legal writing. It is advantageous to write different aspects of planning into one law with different parts such as: Part I: State Planning, Part II: Regional Planning, Part II: Municipal Planning, Part IV: Regional Impact, Part V: Environmental Land and Water Management, etc. This will avoid repetition of many provisions, and all related laws are together for reference and coordination. It is wise to study many existing and successful laws of other states and foreign countries for progressive ideas before writing, rewriting, or amending planning laws of a state. The laws need to be tailored according to needs and situation of the state.

PROPERTY RIGHTS WITHIN THE CONTEXT OF SOCIAL PLANNING

Right to property is as sacred as life and liberty. This right is eroding gradually. In 1876 Chief Justice Waite of the U. S. Supreme Court set forth the theory of public interest in private land – in which he had set forth that private land must submit to control by the public for common interest. Private ownership of land is not compatible with socialism and communism. Stalin, Hitler, Castro, and Mao forcefully nationalized the land. Now the United Nations and environmentalists are asserting public interest in private land. The United Nations Conference on Human Settlements (Habitat I), held in Vancouver, May 31-June 11, 1976, articulated the official land policy of the U. N. These should be considered very seriously, because experts in the field from various countries with various political ideologies wrote and endorsed them. The preamble says:[1]

> "Land ...cannot be treated as an ordinary asset, controlled by individuals and subject to the pressures and inefficiencies of the market. Private land ownership is also a principal interest of accumulation and concentration of wealth and therefore contributes to social injustice; if unchecked, it may become a major obstacle in the planning and implementation of development schemes. The provision of decent dwelling and healthy conditions for the people can only be achieved if land is used in the interests of society as a whole. Public control of land use is therefore indispensable...."

Nine pages of specific policy recommendations endorsed by the participating nations follow the preamble. Some of the recommendations are cited below:

A.1(b) All countries should establish as a matter of urgency a national policy on human settlements, embodying the distribution of population...over the national territory.

A.1 (c) (V) Such a policy should be devised to facilitate population redistribution to accord with the availability of resources.

D.1 (a) Public ownership or effective control of land in the public interest is the single most important means of...achieving a more equitable distribution of the benefits of development whilst assuring that environmental impacts are considered.

D.1 (b) Land is a scarce resource whose management should be subject to public surveillance or control in the interest of the nation.

D.1 (d) Government must maintain full jurisdiction and exercise complete sovereignty over such land with a view to freely planning development of human settlements....

D.2 (a) Agricultural land, particularly on the periphery of urban areas, is an important national resource; without public control land is prey to speculation and encroachment.

D.2 (b) Change in the use of land...should be subject to public control and regulation.

D.2 (c) Such control may be exercised through:

(i) Zoning and land-use planning as a basic instrument of land policy in general and of control of land-use changes in particular;

(ii) Direct intervention, e.g., the creation of land reserves and land banks, purchase, compensated expropriation and/or pre-emption, acquisition of development rights, conditioned leasing of public and communal land, formation of public and mixed development enterprises;

(iii) Legal controls, e.g., compulsory registration, changes in administrative boundaries, development building and local permits, assembly and replotting.

D.3 (a) Excessive profits resulting from the increase in land value due to development and change in use are one of the principle causes of the concentration of wealth in private hands. Taxation should not be seen only as a source of revenue for the community but also as a powerful tool to encourage development of desirable locations, to exercise a controlling effect on the land market and to redistribute to the public at large the benefits of the unearned increase in land values.

D.3 (b) The unearned increment resulting from the rise in land values resulting from change in use of land, from public investment or decision or due to general growth of the community must be subject to appropriate recapture by public bodies.

D.4 (a) Public ownership of land cannot be an end in itself; it is justified in so far as it is exercised in favor of the common good rather than to protect the interests of the already privileged.

D.4(b) Public ownership should be used to secure and control areas of urban expansion and protection; and to implement urban and rural land reform process, and supply serviced land at price levels which can secure a socially acceptable pattern of development.

D.5(b) Past patterns of ownership rights should be transformed to match the changing needs of society and be collectively beneficial.

D.5(c)(v) Methods for the separation of landownership rights from development rights, the latter to be entrusted to a public authority.

The 1987 Brundtland Commission (UN Commission on Environment and Development) defined land and land use conflicts as follows: "Land is normally defined as a physical entity in terms of its topography and spatial nature; a broader integrated view also include natural resources: the solid, minerals, water and biota that the land comprises. Expanding human requirements and economic activities are placing ever-increasing pressures on land resources, creating competition and conflicts and resulting in suboptimal use of both land and land resources. It is now essential to resolve these conflicts and move towards more effective and efficient use of land and its natural resources. Opportunities to allocate land to different uses arise in the course of major settlement or development projects or in a sequential fashion as land becomes available on the market. This provides opportunities...to assign protected status for conservation of biological diversity or critical ecological services."

It is therefore clear that as an environmentally conscious society, we should allocate land to the best possible use for an environmentally sustainable community. We need consistent national, state and local policies and legal remedies. Once the land use is allocated, the land owners should have property rights to develop the property within the permissible limits and enjoy absolute right to the property.

DIFFICULTIES OF PUBLIC PLANNING ON PRIVATE LAND

When almost all the land is in private ownership, how can it be dictated that the owners follow a public plan? There are two types of problems the planners and the land planning agency face: land use restrictions and taking away land, and actual physical planning on developable land. The justification of land use restrictions and taking away land is covered in the preceding section on Property Rights Within the Context of Social Planning. The following will focus on practical problems faced:

(a) Land use restrictions and taking land

According to a public plan, some landowners may not be able to build anything on their land and some others may be restricted to lesser development than they would like. The questions are then: (a) Do the landowners have the absolute right to develop their land to any use and to any extent for maximum profit? (b) Does the planning authority have absolute authority over private land? The answers to both questions are NO.

The landowner seeks to develop land to maximize profit. However, the development could be harmful to the neighbors, community, or environment, and it may be expensive to the municipality to provide services and mitigate the harmful effects of the development. Therefore, land use regulations are justified and enforceable under police power. In the case of environmentally sensitive land, no development may be allowed and the land may be taken for public purpose paying the landowner just compensation under the power of eminent domain.

Over the centuries the question of rights to land ownership were raised, and in the 20th century the answer to this question was settled in all democratic countries. The right to use or develop land is now regulated by the doctrine of common good. The public for the common good may enforce land use control/regulation or take the land with reasonable compensation. The local self-governments may use police power and eminent domain to accomplish this objective.

A local government may, when reasonably necessary, acquire an interest in land to achieve the objectives of a state or local Land Development Plan or the objectives of permissible regulation under this code including the following:[2]

(1) To protect or improve environmental values including ecological balance;
(2) To preserve historical or archeological structures or sites;
(3) To minimize potential damage from floods, earthquakes, hurricanes or other natural disasters;
(4) To protect existing scenic or recreational values or to preserve open space; and
(5) To facilitate the future construction of, or the continued usefulness of, needed public facilities.

Land use regulations must be for public good, politically feasible, economically sensible, and must hold up in the court. Article 300A of the Constitution of India provides Right to Property: "Persons not to be deprived of property save by authority of law. – No person shall be deprived of his property save by authority of law."

Refusal of sanction to erect a building does not deprive a person of his property within the meaning of article 300A. He is not deprived of his possession of the property by reason thereof. Inability to construct on account of legal restriction is not a deprivation of right to enjoy. Inability to enjoy according to one's own will are subject to legal restrictions which can never be equated with the deprivation of property. Though however, prevention of user of a land without any legal sanction or freezing of user of land is contemplation of preparation of Land Use and Development Plan without any such provision provided in law is a deprivation within the meaning of article 300A. (Girdhari Lal Soni v. Municipal Commission, Calcutta Municipal Corporation, AIR 2001 Cal 12).[3]

(b) Actual physical planning on developable land

How to physically plan an area with systematic roads, parks, homes, schools, shopping, and amenities? Do we have the freedom of planning? Greater the freedom, better the planning. The freedom of planning depends on the size of land holdings, ownership of land, and the legal mechanism given to the planners.

In the United States physical planning is relatively easier than in India. Large land holdings of hundreds of acres are often concentrated in the hands of few families. When the landowners are ready to develop land into residential subdivisions, office complexes, commercial development, industrial development or a mixture of multiple development classes, the planners deal with few landowners. In large track development there is lot of freedom and flexibility in design. Established subdivision regulations, zoning regulation, building codes, environmental review, development impact analysis, etc., are followed and beautiful schemes emerge.

In India, fragmented land holdings, multiple landownership, and lack of adequate legal remedies are obstacles to systematic development planning. Rural areas have historical land divided into irregularly shaped plots, often is with zigzagged boundaries. When the land developed into an urban setting, old bridle paths and cattle paths are retained as winding small roads. The haphazard plotting of land continues to cause problems for systematic development. Therefore direct intervention is necessary. There are several solutions to this problem for accomplishment of better planning as discussed below. *The best solution is to acquire the entire land, plan, and sell the plotted land with roads and other planning elements included.* European measures taken were very bold and effective. There is no small measure for a big problem. Innovative effective measures are necessary.

1. *Land Development Corporations*: The Garden City Association formed First Garden City Limited, a limited dividend society in 1903 and purchased 4,500 acres of land and developed the city of Letchworth. The company provided streets, water, sewers and other facilities before any construction started. The land value increased and paid stockholders 5 percent dividends as the lots were sold. Any extra profit was kept for the benefit of the whole community. All 32 new towns in United Kingdom had development corporations and followed the same model of buying and developing cities. Law required landowners to sell land to the development corporations. Infrastructure was completed before any building started. Land around London was purchased for the green belt.[4]

2. *Housing Corporations*: Sweden aggressively participated in the supply of housing through private housing corporations beginning in 1904. Stockholm purchased 20,000 acres of land surrounding the city and planned for garden suburbs. Government loans were made available. The city also resettled slum dwellers by means of rent rebates in 1930s. France also had similar programs for industrial workers.
3. *Private Land Pool and Redistribution*: In 1902, a law was passed permitting the city of Frankfurt to pool private property, rearranging it to the city plan, and redistribute such land for redevelopment. The city was authorized to retain 40 percent of the land, without compensation to the owner, for streets, parks, and other public uses. This policy was adopted in numerous German cities to acquire vacant land in the periphery. This was to protect from inevitable speculation of land price and to stop rapid growth. The land was also given to cooperative housing development corporations until 1926, when Hitler came to power. Similar policies were adopted in Austria, Switzerland, Holland, and Denmark.[5]
4. *No Building Permit*: The local government may adopt an ordinance or other legal means prohibiting building permits if urban services such as roads, water, sewer, and electricity are not available. Those services will not be provided until the area or neighborhood is planned and lots are rearranged and plotted. This is the same concept as Private Land Pool and Redistribution.
5. There are other methods such as land banks, formation of public or private development enterprises, assembly and replotting, and housing cooperatives. It is beyond the scope of this book to go into the details of these methods.
6. In India, large-scale land acquisition and planning has been done in Delhi and Navi Mumbai.

HARMFUL LAWS AND PRACTICES: SQUATTERS, RENT CONTROL, EVICTION

There are fair and unfair laws just like people. If a law is unjust it must be changed. The sense of fairness and justice makes the laws change in a democratic country. Everyone wants wealth and happiness but it should be a fair game.

Squatters occupy government, public, and private land. They create slums and unhygienic conditions. Yet the state and city authorities are reluctant to evict them. This creates social, health, crime, economic, urban planning, building code enforcement, and political problems. Some politicians assure their stay in exchange for their votes and others cannot take bold steps to solve this problem and to make sure this does not happen again. The landowners lose property without compensation, and the miserable living conditions continue. The city authorities cannot provide them urban services such as roads, water, electricity, drainage, garbage collection, building permit, etc. when the squatters have no property rights. Yet sale and registration of occupation rights continue among squatters.

Laws must take a stand and enforce what is just. The laws must recognize that taking away property without just compensation is illegal, current squatters shall be rehabilitated at government cost, and squatting shall not be tolerated in the future with violators evicted immediately. Otherwise the continuous streams of squatters will continue. Dispersing the population to other urban areas and creating new urban centers will reduce squatting.

There are rent control acts or ordinances in every major city in India. These regulations protect the tenants at the expense of the property owners. The owner cannot increase rent or evict tenants. The property tax continues to increase, rent remains same, and the owner cannot afford to spend any more money to repair and maintain the property in good condition. The results: (a) the rental housing stock is deteriorating; (b) investment in rental housing is not a viable economic option; (c) There is severe shortage of rental housing in India; and (d) construction industry and employment in construction is suffering. Construction industry is the biggest employer in the United States. In India, there is a huge market for rental property: apartments, commercial property, offices, and industrial facilities. But those will not develop and create employment because of the insecure position of property owners. They may effectively lose the property or may earn less than the interest they would earn keeping the money in a bank. The government is not undertaking any subsidized housing programs but shifting this burden to the private property owners.

There are plenty of cases when the tenants will not pay rent and cannot be evicted. On the other hand, tenants demand lakhs of rupees if they have to vacate the property. Some will never vacate the property and by fraudulent means will register the property in there own name.

The effects of these laws and ordinances are as follows:

(1) Ongoing court battles cost money to landlords and tenants.
(2) The existing stock of rental housing, business, offices, and industrial properties is deteriorating because the property owner cannot recover the money spent on up keep of the property.
(3) There is severe shortage of rental housing, business, offices, and industrial property. These are not profitable and includes the risk of losing property.
(4) Employment in construction, building product manufacturing, and related industries could increase if these laws are amended.
(5) The construction industry loses opportunities for investment and profit.

(6) Constitutional rights are violated. The right not to be deprived of property except by authority of law is no longer a fundamental right, though it is a constitutional right (Bakshi).

(7) Any rent control law puts the burden of providing affordable housing on the owners. Instead, the government can provide affordable housing through subsidized programs, low interest loans to homebuyers, or some other means. Rent control keeps property prices down.

Notes

1. Henry Lamb, "The UN and Property Rights 1997", www.sovereignty.net/p.land/unproprts.htm
2. Fred Bosselman, David Callies, John Banta, *The Taking Issue*, 1973.
3. P.M. Bakshi, *The Constitution of India: With Selective Comments*, Universal Law Publishing Co., Delhi, 2004.
4. Arthur B. Gallion and Simon Eisner, *The Urban Pattern*, D. Van Nostrand Co., 1963, pp. 97-113.
5. Ibid.

8

India's Housing Crisis

The housing crisis in India is frightening. How much decent housing backlog India has and how much more need to be provided in the immediate future and thereafter. Some planners and the Planning Commission of the Five-Year Plans of India are aware of the extent of the problem. The last nine Five-Year Plans of India allocated billions of rupees, and the government enacted much legislation to improve housing for the people. Yet, there are no significant success stories. The housing problem has to be solved at the local level but there are National Housing Policy implications. This chapter is an attempt to apprise the readers of the housing shortage, miserable housing conditions, the difficulties of providing housing, complexities and possible solutions.

THE HOUSING SHORTAGE

About 20 million new housing units are needed today. In addition, there are substandard housing units which need improvements – structural and sanitary. In 2001, 33.4 percent of urban households and 37.3 percent of rural households lived in one room accommodations. It is extremely hard for the lower middle income group to afford to own a home or flat. Rental units are also in severely short supply. The poor section of the society mostly lives in slums and some are homeless, sleeping on pavement. It is a gigantic challenge for the nation to provide adequate housing.

The housing shortage also presents a tremendous opportunity for a construction boom and employment in the housing sector, urban and rural renewal and revitalization, and social and economic well-being for India. Seamless coordination and cooperation is paramount in this effort among financial institutions; enabling legislations; governments at national, state, and local levels; infrastructure providers; and planners, architects, engineers, and contractors at the private levels. India should be motivated by some great examples in the United States. During the great depression in the 1930s U. S. created massive public works projects for mass employment, which created infrastructure and helped the country to go forward. In late 1950s U.S. started interstate freeways, which created employment and made the country mobile. In the 1970s massive projects for low-income housing and subsidized housing for the urban poor started and still continuing.

Table 1

Housing Shortage in India

	Year		
	1991	*1996*	*2001*
Urban	8.23	7.71	6.64
Rural	14.67	13.85	12.76
Total	22.90	21.56	19.40

Figures are in millions of housing units.

Source: National Building Organization, Government of India.

URBAN SLUMS AND SQUATTER SETTLEMENTS

When some foreign visitors describe India as a dirty and stinky country, it hurts the sentiment of the Indians. It is harsh but true if you look at the miserable conditions of the slum dwellers. About 20 percent to 25 percent of India's urban population are slum dwellers. This does not give a pretty picture of India. The slums started spreading in the 1960s along with industrial developments in India. The main concern is human suffering due to unsanitary and crowded housing or lack of housing. The unplanned migration of rural population to metropolitan cities and unbalanced economic developments in the country are the main two reasons for creation of slums.

It is stunning that 54 percent of the population of Greater Mumbai, the great city of India, live in slums. In India's 27 metropolitan cities with population above one million, 17.7 million or 24 percent of people are slum dwellers.

The genesis of slums needs understanding before attempting any solution. Gopal Bhargava gave a good account of the plight of rural immigrants in his book *Development of India's Urban Rural & Regional Planning in 21st Century*. I shall borrow some of his information in the following brief analysis of slums.

Rural areas have not been developed economically. There is not much opportunity for employment or self-employment. Especially landless people or small landowners cannot produce enough to make a living. Devastating draught or flood is always a risk. There are no suitable roads or means of transportation to market their produce. They also do not have electricity and modern conveniences. The same plow from the days of Maharajah Janak is being used to plough the fields. Those who have some education are the first to leave villages for towns. The illiterates also leave the villages for odd jobs in the cities. About one-fourth of the people who come to cities to attend political rallies, do not go back. There is also glamour associated with moving to cities.

Statement 1.2

Total Population, Slum Population and Their Percentage in Municipal Corporations With Population Above One Million-2001

Sl No.	*Name of Million-Plus Municipal Corp.*	*State*	*Total population*	*Total slum population*	*% slum population*
1	*2*	*3*	*4*	*5*	*6*
1	Greater Mumbai	Maharashtra	11,978,450	6,475,440	54.1
2	Delhi	Delhi	9,879,172	1,851,231	18.7
3	Kolkata	West Bengal	4,572,876	1,485,309	32.5
4	Chennai	Tamil Nadu	4,343,645	819,873	18.9
5	Bangalore	Karnataka	4,301,326	430,501	10.0
6	Hyderabad	Andhra Pradesh	3,637,483	626,849	17.2
7	Ahmedabad	Gujarat	3,520,085	473,662	13.5
8	Surat	Gujarat	2,433,835	508,485	20.9
9	Kanpur	Uttar Pradesh	2,551,337	367,980	14.4
10	Pune	Maharashtra	2,538,473	492,179	19.4
11	Jaipur	Rajasthan	2,322,575	368,570	15.9
12	Lucknow	Uttar Pradesh	2,185,927	179,176	8.2
13	Nagpur	Maharashtra	2,052,066	737,219	35.9
14	Indore	Madhya Pradesh	1,474,968	260,975	17.7
15	Bhopal	Madhya Pradesh	1,437,354	125,720	8.7
16	Ludhiana	Punjab	1,398,467	314,904	22.5
17	Patna	Bihar	1,366,444	3,592	0.3
18	Varodara	Gujarat	1,306,227	186,020	14.2
19	Agra	Uttar Pradesh	1,275,134	121,761	9.5
20	Thane	Maharashtra	1,262,551	351,065	27.8
21	Kalyan-Dombivli	Maharashtra	1,193,512	34,860	2.9
22	Varanasi	Uttar Pradesh	1,091,918	137,977	12.6
23	Nashik	Maharashtra	1,077,236	138,797	12.9
24	Meerut	Uttar Pradesh	1,068,772	471,581	44.1
25	Faridabad	Haryana	1,055,938	490,981	46.5
26	Pimpri Chinchwad	Maharashtra	1,012,472	123,957	12.2
27	Howrah	West Bengal	1,007,532	118,286	11.7
	Total		73,345,775	17,696,950	24.1

Source: Census of India 2001

On arrival in a city, migrants will spend a few nights on the railway platform, bus terminal, or even on the streets. After getting acquainted with the city or finding someone from their community, they will move into a slum area or squatter settlement. They live within walking distance, because they cannot afford bus fair, from where they can find a job. They find low paying jobs as domestic servants, street cleaners, washer men, cobblers, coolies, rickshaw pullers, construction workers, etc. After earning some money, some of them become street vendors. If lucky, some of them may find permanent jobs. Some of them get involved in illegal and antisocial activities to make quick money. They send money orders home regularly. It is a necessity for rural unemployed to move to cities for survival, even living in harsh conditions.

Slums in Mumbai

There are two types of slums. One type is dilapidated or un-maintained buildings which are overcrowded. This type of slum emerged as a result of rent control and tenant protection laws. It is of no benefit to the owners to spend money on repairs when they cannot recover the costs by increasing rent or evicting tenants. Municipal taxes increased but the rent proceeds did not. The other type is built by squatters forcefully encroaching government and private vacant land or on land unfit for human settlements such as river banks, drainage canals, marginal railway lands, swamps, road sides, under bridges, and even in public parks. They build with scrap materials such as salvaged gunny bags, tarpaulin, tin sheets, wood planks, pieces from packing boxes, cardboard boxes, etc. There are also some slum lords who build squatter colonies overnight and operate them for profit. Once they are settled, they cannot be removed. There will be bribery, riots, and politicians who will protect them in exchange for votes. These settlements have no paved roads, water supply, latrine, or electricity. Human excreta and garbage are malodorous. It is a health hazard for the inhabitants and other public. Yet the stinking legend and inhuman settlements continue.

The slums in Mumbai are the worst slums in the world with very high density. Mumbai slums are of three kinds. *Chawls* are permanent multi-storied dilapidated buildings. *Patra Chawls* are semi-permanent constructions, both authorized and unauthorized, built with corrugated iron sheets (locally called *patra*). And *zopadpatties* (hutments) built with scrap materials by squatters. In addition there are pavement dwellers. In some areas common toilets are shared at the rate of one toilet per 60 to 100 persons. There is tardiness by the Municipal Corporation in garbage collection. There is no effective law or political will to relocate the slum dwellers.

Kolkata has a long history of slums. During industrialization of Kolkata in 19th century, cheap labor housing was provided legally. The landlords leased out their land to middlemen called *thika* (contract) tenants, who built huts and rented them to laborers. The Thika Tenancy Act was passed. These hut clusters came to be known as *bustees*. The modestly built *bustees* became overcrowded and became slums in confined areas. The landlords and the *thika* tenants were not interested in spending money to improve the conditions of the *bustees*. After the independence of India, refugees poured in Kolkata. An attempt was made to resettle slum dwellers in four story buildings on the outskirts of Kolkata, and make room for construction of buildings for the refugees. Few hundred units were built, but those were not suitable for the slum dwellers because of travel distance and cost of travel. The scheme was abandoned. It was realized that slum clearance was not feasible. West Bengal Slum Areas, (Improvement and Clearance) Act of 1971 was passed. Slums were provided with paved roads, street lighting, water supply, drainage, and latrines. The program benefited 21 lakh of the 30 lakh slum dwellers. The Calcutta Thika Tenancy Act of 1981 transferred the ownership of bustee land from the landowners to the government. Numbers of measures were taken such as financing small scale enterprises, education, and health and nutrition programs. But a new wave of slums came in the form of squatter settlements just like Mumbai.

In Delhi slums are categorized in two classes. The first one is Notified Slum Areas as per Slum Areas (Improvement and Clearance) Act of 1956. Notified slum areas are Chawri, Chandni Chowk, Sadar Bazar, Katras, and others. These areas had permanent but dilapidated structures and overcrowding. The second category of slum is *jhuggi-jhopri* (JJ) clusters, which lack even the basic amenities. Three approaches taken in the Delhi metropolitan area are: (1) relocation of slum dwellers, (2) environmental upgrading by restructuring of layout, and (3) upgrading basic services when the first two options are not possible. Delhi initiated the largest resettlement program in the country, covering 2.5 lakh households with more than 10 lakh people. Lots of 25 sq yards were provided to each JJ slum dwellers. Environmental upgrading was done in four slum settlements with about 800 households. Other slum clusters were covered under upgrading basic services. It is estimated that there are more than 1,080 JJ clusters in Delhi Metropolitan Area. Construction workers who were given temporary shelters near the construction sites, stayed permanently. Expenditure of slum settlements was Rs. 48 crores in the 7th Five-Year Plan, and Rs. 36.25 crores in the 8th Five-Year Plan. The Central Government spent Rs. 866 crores during 1972 and 1996 on environmental improvements of slums. Yet the slum problem has not been solved in Delhi or other cities since new immigrants and migrants continue to arrive.

The politics of slum clearance is worth noting. Slum clearance in Delhi started in 1960s. During emergency rule of Indira Gandhi the slum clearance and resettlement was accelerated under the leadership of Jagmohan, Vice-Chairman of Delhi Development Authority. He directed and accomplished the largest slum clearance program in Asia. Australia and other countries recognized his work as a model. He also received Padma Bhushan honor. But it was not without demonizing him by some politicians, officers, and the press.. "I came in clash with powerful vested interests – land racketeers, speculators, and those who tried to build bases of political and financial power at the cost of the planned development of the city. It is these people who are now engineering all types of false, frivolous and motivated complaints. Some officers, affected jealousy, are playing their own part."[1]

All metropolitan and large cities have slums including Chandigarh, the most modern city in India. New immigrants keep coming. There is no end to formation of new slums in sight. There are Slum Area (Improvement and Clearance) Acts, by the Central Government, and in almost all states and union territories. Delhi has five different legislations on unauthorized construction, slum clearance, and improvement. The Central Government adopted Environmental Improvement of Slum (EIUS) Scheme in 1972. Implementation of these Acts has a very poor record. Whatever has been accomplished is an inadequate and temporary solution. Only a few cities resettled some slum dwellers in permanent buildings. The Acts do not address the issue of legality of illegal occupation of private or public land. Unauthorized constructions and sale and registration of occupied land are going on. All legislations related to slums need to be reviewed for legality, feasibility, implementation and effectiveness.[2]

A balanced economic and physical development in rural areas, small towns, medium towns, and cities under 500,000 in population in every region of the country is the solution. This will relieve the metropolitan cities from slums, chaotic developments, transportation problems, infrastructure problems, management problems, and financial burdens. The metropolitan cities need to be stabilized. This is discussed in more detail in the next chapter.

LOW AND MIDDLE INCOME HOUSING

Types of Housing Needed

Housing is needed for all income groups. Housing choices should include variety of unit sizes and design, different price ranges, in single story and multi-storied buildings, and in different locations (see Housing Element in Chapter 4). Regardless of political ideologies, people need food, cloth, housing, good health, and therefore money to support themselves. Taking this as a goal, our plans, policies, and actions can evolve. Education, good environment, transportation, infrastructure, etc. are ingredients to support this goal.

Rental Housing

The poorest section of the population cannot afford to pay full rent, and therefore need subsidized rental housing. The younger generation, just starting to work, cannot afford to buy homes or flats, therefore rental units should be made available at market rent. The transferees also need rental units or apartments. The lower middle income group also cannot afford to own a flat or home. They may fulfill the dream of owning a home midway through life. Therefore, there is a big rental market, but it has not developed in India. People rent some homeowner's rooms or accommodation which were not designed as full rental units. The renters are in hardship to find a rental place. The scarcity of rental housing has driven the rents high. In European countries more people live in rental apartments than in their own homes.

There are several hurdles in the development of rental apartments: (1) The rent control and tenant eviction laws are in favor of the tenants. These laws have been deterrents in the availability and development of rental housing. The owners cannot increase rent and cannot evict tenants. Some tenants even demand a great deal of money from the owners for vacating. There are locked up units which owners will not rent because of this experience, even though they left home for years to live in another city or abroad. (2) India encourages industrial development, but has not recognized rental housing as an industry. It can produce rental units for profit like any other industry, employ people during construction, management, and maintenance; and it serves the needs for rental customers just like any other industry serving consumers. India is not facilitating its development and growth.

Home Ownership

People aspire to own a home. But it does not come easy. Developed lots are hard to find, legal issues related to the lots are unknown, utilities are not available most of the time, and reliable contractors may not be there. Financing the project is also not easy. Mostly the aspirant has to depend on own savings, provident fund or some kind of loan that is not easily available. The aspirant homeowner has to overcome many problems which can be exhausting and discouraging.

HOUSING PROCESS IN THE UNITED STATES

Housing in the United States is well developed. There are some problems like housing discrimination and politics of development. Some cities allow only high income developments to keep property tax high. Even school teachers cannot afford to live there, so there is shortage of teachers. Workers like lawn maintenance persons, home makers, and hotel worker live 30 or 50 miles away and commute by bus. The process of land development, home construction, home financing, rental apartments, and subsidized housing in the US may be interesting information to India. In the US private land development companies develop land, provide infrastructure, and sell the plots of land. Private contractors build homes and condominiums for sale. Market conditions dictate what, where, and how much they will build. Apartment complexes are built by companies interested in the rental market. The Federal Government's involvement is only facilitating low-income housing and subsidizing rental apartments for the poorest.

Land developers purchase large tracks of land and prepare plan for housing development. The local government reviews the plan for impact on environment, traffic circulation, roads, student load on existing schools, drainage, water supply, sewage disposal, shopping facilities, recreational facilities, etc. Through negotiations the plan is approved or rejected if not acceptable.

The developer must build roads, water lines, sewer lines, electric lines, and provide other facilities as per local government standards at his own cost before he is allowed to sell the lots. The development work is performed by licensed general contractors. The philosophy behind this is the people who create the need must pay, the municipality will not pay. The developers pass on expenses to the land buyers. But the municipality shall take over the maintenance and repair after completion.

Lots are sold to licensed residential contractors (also called home builders) and private individuals. Home builders submit plans and get building permits from the local government. The home builders build according to zoning regulation and in compliance with building codes. The building department inspects the construction about a dozen times: foundation, wall construction, roof construction, electrical wiring, plumbing pipes, sewer pipes, air conditioning ducts and installation of equipments, and final inspections before giving a certificate of occupancy. The certificate of occupancy is issued when the house is complete, complies with building codes and zoning regulations, and is ready for occupancy. Individuals who build their own homes can do so by following the same process. The owners can save money in labor costs if they do the work.

Home builders sell these homes in the open market. Prices of homes vary according to size of home, size of lot, quality of materials, location, and quality of neighborhood. Multi-storied condominiums (called flats in India) are also built for sale. Generally sales are handled by certified and registered real estate agents. Some homeowners sell their homes by themselves. People are very mobile; they change jobs and move to different cities. Therefore, new and used homes are available for purchase. When too many homes are in the market for sale compared to the number of buyers, it is called a buyer's market. That means the buyers are in a position to offer a lower price. When homes are in short supply, it is a seller's market. The sellers can ask for higher prices. The housing market is very competitive.

Long-term residential mortgage loans are available from lending institutions. Low and middle income families depend on this loan to buy their homes. Generally a lender requires a minimum 5 percent of the purchase price as a down payment from the borrower. The borrower must have enough income to make monthly payments (interest, principal, and property tax). Mortgage loans are available for 15 years, 20 years, or 30 years. The mortgage lender also requires the property to be appraised for market value. There are professional and licensed property appraisers.

The interest rate on the mortgage loan varies from time to time. The Discount Rate is the interest rate the Federal Reserve Banks charge depository institutions. In 2001 Federal Reserve monetary policy reduced the discount rate to 1.25 percent, its lowest rate in more than 50 years to stimulate the economy. The residential mortgage rate is higher and it is market-determined. The Federal Home Loan Mortgage Corporation publishes "contract interest rate on commitments for fixed-rate mortgages". The discount rate and the mortgage rate tend to experience similar trends. Conventional mortgage rate came down to below 5 percent in 2001 and went up to above 6 percent in 2006. As a result of low interest rates, home ownership increased, and home construction boomed in US in last five years.

The home buying process is very easy and it has three steps: (1) The buyer and seller will sign a Contract for Sale and Purchase. The contract contains information: location and description of property, price, closing costs, closing date, etc. Generally the seller agrees to pay for: real estate broker's fee, documentary stamp for deed, property survey, and termite inspection. Generally, the buyer agrees to pay for: title insurance, recording fee, and mortgage securing expenses. (2) The buyer applies for a long-term residential mortgage loan. The lending bank requires information on: buyer's assets, liabilities, credit history, and income. If creditworthy, the loan is approved. (3) Real estate law firms and also title companies complete real estate transactions and act as the closing agency. The seller or his agent sends the contract and other documents to the closing agency. The lender also sends the loan package, including a cheque for the loan amount, to the closing agency. The closing agency checks in the court house to ensure that the property has no legal problem and the seller has a clear title to it. On an appointed date the buyer, seller, and the realtors of both parties come to the office of the law firm or title company. The closing lawyer takes signatures of the buyer and the seller on appropriate documents and gives copies to both parties. The lawyer also dispurses money by cheques to the seller, real estate agents' commissions, and keeps money for his fee and court expenses. The lawyer's office files all necessary papers in the court. The title to the property remains with the lender until the buyer pays the full loan amount. The buyer and the seller do not go to the court.

INDIA'S HOUSING EFFORTS

In 1950s India initiated subsidized housing for industrial workers in urban areas. In late 1950s the government directed Life Insurance Corporation of India to provide housing financing to the middle income group. In the Fourth Five-Year Plan beginning in 1969, slum clearance and housing for industrial workers and dock laborers were undertaken. The government spent some money on rural housing. In the Fifth Five-Year Plan beginning in 1974, housing for the landless labourers and weaker portions of the rural community was taken up. Housing Boards provided limited finance to low and middle income groups. In the Sixth Five-Year Plan, low income groups earning less than Rs.700 per month were to be helped, but the families earning Rs.7,700 to Rs.15,000 were also helped instead. In the Seventh Five-Year Plan beginning 1984, the government realized the contribution of the private sector was far greater than public sector in housing. So far the government was emphasizing on public sector, foreign exchange reserves were limited, and more emphasis was given to agricultural production. The Chinese invasion in 1962, wars with Pakistan in 1965 and 1972 drained money from the Five-Year Plans. The Central Government also spent a great deal of money on slum improvements, as discussed earlier, but the problem of slums became overwhelming. Under the circumstances, housing efforts were too little.

The National Housing Policy in 1988 recognized that the role of government should be as initiator rather than home builder. The government should facilitate access to land, material, technology, and finance. This policy is on the right track. This policy was criticized that low income families will be priced out of the open housing market. The government cannot forever support free or subsidized housing. The economic condition of the poor has to be improved. Cooperative Housing

Societies operated in some big cities of some states beginning late 1950s. By 1993 there were 85,000 primary housing cooperatives with 5 million members. All of them were members of National Cooperative Housing Federation, the umbrella organization of the cooperative housing movement in the country. The cooperative sector built 1.4 million housing units and 0.54 million dwellings during 1989-95. In Mumbai, this sector developed housing in 1,500 slum settlements, for 100 to 500 households in each.[3]

The Delhi Development Authority (DDA) was formed in 1957. It was created under the provisions of the Delhi Development Act to promote and secure development of Delhi. DDA undertakes all projects: residential, commercial, industrial, horticulture, institutional, or recreational. It acquired 67,355 acres of land, of which 59,504 acres have been developed, including 30,714 acres for residences. It also acquired 5,051 hectares of land for parks, forest, and playing fields. Housing Development Authorities are operating in other cities and states: Bangalore, Chandigarh, Chennai, Gurgaon, Haryana, Hydarabad, Jaipur, Kolkata, Lucknow, Mumbai, Noida, Pune, Punjab and Visakhapatnam.

Private developers are mostly discouraged in India. In Haryana, however, private developers are welcome. They developed land and built houses in mini city complexes. They are also utilized in satellite towns around Delhi, Ghaziabad, Meerut and Noida. The National Commission on Urbanization (NCU) has pointed out that the elimination of private enterprise from real estate development is one of the major reasons for the current housing shortage. NCU recommended to the government that the role of housing authorities and development authorities should be that of a facilitator and not land developers and home builders themselves.

OBSTACLES IN INDIA'S HOUSING EFFORTS

The major obstacles in housing are as follows:

(1) Developed lots including infrastructure are in extremely short supply and very expensive.

(2) Developable lands are in the hands of small land holders and therefore, difficult to acquire and plan.

(3) India is not encouraging private large scale developers. Only housing development authorities, with bureaucracies and without motivation for cost reduction and profit, are encouraged.

(4) Long-term home mortgage loans are not available at a fair interest rate.

(5) Home construction for sale and rental apartment construction has not developed and been recognized as an industry.

(6) Rental housing is in extremely short supply. Because of unfair rent control laws and tenant eviction difficulties private landlords are hesitant to rent out their property.
(7) Innovative technologies in construction methods and building materials, which can reduce construction costs, have not developed.

Technological Innovations

India needs to focus on three fronts for rapid, durable, and cheaper construction of homes and other buildings. Those are: (a) development of cheaper but durable building materials, (b) new construction methods, and (c) industrialized buildings.

(a) Development of cheaper and more durable building materials

The traditional constructions in India have been; mud plastered walls and threshed roofs, wood framed walls with mud plastered walls and corrugated iron sheets roofs, and brick walls and corrugated iron sheets roofs. The latest is reinforced concrete columns, roofs, and brick walls. Older homes had all wood or all stone constructions. Threshed homes were comfortable because of the insulation value of thresh but threshes are no longer available in large quantities. Stone homes are very expensive. Forests are also exhausted, so wood is not easily available and is expensive. The RCC buildings, which are now widely used, are expensive and very hot to live in because of absorption of heat from the sun which they release at night. So there is a great need and scope for making money by developing new construction materials at reasonable costs such as insulation and hollow concrete blocks, which will solve the heat problems.

Lightweight structural iron members covered with mortar; prefabricated and insulated wall and roof panels; prefabricated and insulated exterior metal doors; prefabricated masonite interior doors; steel framed windows; particle board for counter tops; industrial byproduct flyash can be used as cement substitute; corrugated plastic sheets can be used as wall siding and roofing; PVC plastic moldings; fiberglass and asphalt sheets for roofing; fiberglass and foam home insulations, etc. are some suggestions. Prefabricated building components/materials in mass production are cheaper, faster to build and less labor intensive, and hence cost effective. In the US, a small or medium size home is built in three to four months because of standardization and prefabrication. Besides the building structures, plumbing, electrical, and mechanical (HVAC: heating, ventilation, and air conditioning) equipments, fittings, and materials need innovations. Skills need to be taught to workers either on the job or in local technical institutions.

(b) New construction methods

Construction methods of intensive labor need to be changed to take advantage of machines. It is inhuman, slow, dangerous, and uneconomical to carry a bucket of mixed concrete or other materials to higher floors. Let the heavy jobs be done by cranes and other machines. There will be plenty of work for the skilled, semi skilled and unskilled workers. In large projects in Delhi, automation is being used.

Ideally, the contractors are motivated to use new construction methods and materials to build faster, produce high quality buildings, make a name for the company, get more contracts, and make a good profit. If there are a few principled contractors with this motivation, others will follow and compete. My father's principle was 'make less profit and sell more, rather than sell few at a high profit'.

Some new, but now old in the western world, construction methods are already in use: structural steels and light but strong structural members to build the skeletons of the buildings; wide use of cranes and back hoe; prefabricated components such as hollow floor, roof and wall sections.

(c) Industrialized buildings

Industrialized buildings, also called manufactured buildings, have not been introduced in India. The manufactured building industry in the United States has a huge market demand for it as affordable housing. These buildings are constructed in factories, under huge sheds. Three dimensional buildings are completed in all respects – interior finish, exterior finish, plumbing, and electrical. Completed buildings are then moved to the site on wheels or on flat bed trucks. On site installation requires site preparation, pillar foundation, and connections to water supply, septic tank or sewer, and electricity. The building can be constructed in one or more sections. Highway restrictions are 14' wide, 14' height from the surface of the road, and 50' long. The roof can be folded to reduce height and raised on site. The buildings can be designed for dwelling, commercial use, office, storage, or school. Predominantly it is used for residences in rural areas or in urban areas when the lot size is large enough. Industrialized buildings are built mostly with wood, but galvanized light weight iron studs, metal roof, plastic siding, ¾" plywood floor, and gypsum board covered interior walls are also used. Every building, except storage, is insulated with fiberglass bats. Buildings are built to building code standards and inspected for quality control.

The buildings are produced economically, since the building materials are not wasted, structural members can be supplied precut to the specifications, and workers are used efficiently under a covered roof. Work proceeds in an assembly line. However, construction of the manufacturing facility itself is expensive.

Obviously, manufactured buildings as manufactured in US cannot be introduced in India because of inadequate roads. Smaller buildings and sections like 8'×24' may still be possible to transport and install on foundations with smaller cranes in most places. Sections may be put together on site for bigger homes. It should be economical and affordable if long term home mortgage loans are made available.

Notes

1. Jagmohan, *Island of Truth*, Vikas Publishing House Pvt. Ltd., Delhi, 1978.
2. For more details please see: Gopal Bhargava, *Development of India's Urban Rural & Regional Planning in 21st Century*, Gyan Publishing House, New Delhi, 2001.
3. For more details please see: Gopal Bhargava, *Development of India's Urban Rural & Regional Planning in 21st Century*, Gyan Publishing House, New Delhi, 2001.

9

The Future of Urbanization in India

The problems of cities and their planning in India cannot be solved in isolation from a balanced economic development in villages, small towns, medium towns, regional centers, and prime cities in the country with emphasis on regional planning. The population must be distributed based on economic developments throughout the country. This is the main theme of this chapter.

The urban population in India was about 30 percent in 2001. This population may increase to about 70 percent by the middle of 21st century. This is due to natural increase of population in existing urban centers, small settlements growing to urban centers, and migration from rural to urban areas. Therefore, the country should be prepared to plan this growth. There are certain global and internal factors to support the notion that India is doing better in economic growth, standards of living is improving, and more people are living in urban areas. Economic boom in India has started. Natural growth and neglect of rural population is a big factor in the urbanization process, especially growth of slums. Six reasons to suggest a balanced development, which may lead to development policies in India, is being discussed below.

ECONOMIC BOOM IN INDIA IS REAL

There are many factors leading to economic boom in India.

(1) The western world is looking for cheaper labor market to provide goods and services at affordable cost to its own people. The companies are outsourcing their service centers to India and many other countries for low cost and high

profit. India is leading in information technology. Computer works, telephone answering services, preparation of transcripts for medical and court records from the United States and United Kingdom are now done in India. India has the advantage of English language compared to China and other countries. Manufactured goods such as garments, furniture, shoes, electronic goods, and a whole assortment of goods can be produced cheaper in India than in the western world. Therefore, the economic opportunities are shifting to Asia. For example, Rock Port shoes manufactured in Italy was sold in USA for over $100 a pair in 1990, was over $80 in 1997 when manufactured in Brazil, and now for $65 when manufactured in China. The company is competing in price, and making more profit.

(2) India has the largest untapped consumer market of over one billion people. Industrialists from India and abroad are interested in producing consumer products in India, market in India and export to other countries at competitive price.

(3) India has about one million young workers in the labor market who are uneducated and unemployed. They are now regarded as assets and not burdens. India is improving its industrial and research infrastructures and poised to compete with western industrial nations. India's brainpower and educational institutions are catching up with advance western education. Investments in technical education have started paying off dividends.

(4) India has plenty of natural resources yet to be exploited such as iron ore, coal and bauxite in the central part of the country. Commercial exploitation will bring employment in factories to unskilled and semiskilled worker by millions.

(5) Jaswant Singh, India's Finance Minister declared on 26 February, 2004 in Guwahati, that India's foreign exchange reserve was $106 billion, and now it is over $300 billion, which is an impressive amount for India. India now has the means to buy foreign machineries and technology.

In spite of these encouraging signs there are problems. "India remains a difficult place to do business, several multinationals have been placing big bets on India in hope of taking advantage of this shifting global dynamic. – Plenty of obstacles remain, however, notably India's weak infrastructure. China invests $7 on roads, ports, electricity and other backbones of modern economy for every dollar spent by India – and it shows. Ports are struggling to handle rising exports, blackouts are frequent and dirt roads are common even in Bangalore, the center of the country's sophisticated computer industry. Pervasive corruption has slowed many efforts to fix these problems. India's labor laws, little changed since they were enacted just after independence in 1947, also continue to discourage companies from hiring workers, by making it difficult to lay off employees even if a company's fortunes sour or the economy slows."[1]

U.S. news media gives a rosy picture of India's future growth, but also give a bleak picture of India's infrastructure, which are still inadequate. The Government of India is aware of inadequacy of infrastructure but slow in developing. India is improving its transportation and communication systems, which are ingredients to development. The East-West and North-South corridors and other road projects are bold steps, which will improve mobility throughout the country and remove the disadvantages of remote areas. Good roads, electricity, water supply, sewer, community facilities, sea ports, air ports, and developed land must be made available to the industries easily and quickly.

The economic development will occur in some land space. The question is how India prepares herself for this development for at least next half century. India's Balanced Development and Regional Urban Development Policy is discussed at the end of this chapter.

WISDOM OF THE FATHER

The wisdoms of Mahatma Gandhi, the Father of the Nation, and A.P.J. Abdul Kalam, India's current President are relevant. Mahatma Gandhi said: "India lives in villages, only when villages advance, India will advance." He also said: "Instead of graceful hamlets dotting the land, we have dung heaps. The approach to many villages is not a refreshing experience. Often one would like to shut one's eyes and stuff one's nose; such is the surrounding dirt and offending smell." He advised to take the jobs to the people and not taking the people to the jobs and uproot the people. We did not understand the implications or did not listen to his advice. But, we have come to realization. Prosperity and progress have not reached two-thirds of India's population.

President Kalam on the occasion of inaugurating Mysore IT.com in December 2002 made a plea to create a "knowledge society" that is world's envy. He stressed that technological innovations would create wealth in addition to knowledge. He also stressed on a reverse flow of population from urban to rural areas.

The consequences are: (a) Industrial and economic developments are confined to about 100 cities, based on influential political power. (b) Rural areas, small and medium towns remained undeveloped and neglected. (c) The technically educated and skilled worker from all over India moved to these economically developed cities. An endless stream of educated and uneducated people from the rural areas moved to economically developed urban areas for any odd jobs. (d) The heavy immigration overpowered the resources of the big cities. The cities became very congested and slums grew. The health and quality of life in terms of fresh air, potable water, sanitation, housing, and transportation seriously diminished. (e) Diminished cultural heritage, decreased link with the ancestral families, and the remote areas were left without educated people, better facilities, and employment opportunities. These are social consequences.

President Kalam's suggestion also leads to creation of new cities. Please refer to property rights within the context of social planning in Chapter 7.

THE BRITISH EXPERIENCE

In Chapter 1, under Development of Modern Cities, British new towns were discussed in length. In 1944 the Greater London population was 8 million. The 1944 plan directed by Professor Patrick Abercrombie had triple purpose – reduction of population from congested central London, to provide better housing in satellite towns outside the greenbelt around London, and discourage urban sprawl. Welwyn, the second garden city designed by Ebenezer Howard was built in 1919 outside the greenbelt. Seven more garden cities were built between 1946 and 1950 outside the greenbelt. All the eight cities are in commuting distance of 30 to 40 Km. from central London. Satellite towns were also built around regional centers Glasgow, Edinburgh, Durham, and Newport.

This plan also moved industries to the outer ring of London. Some employment opportunities were also created in these towns. "This theme was consistent with the enlightened tradition of planning in England, but it demanded courageous conviction and bold decisions".[2]

THE CENTRAL PLACE THEORY

The Central Place Theory was formulated by Walter Christaller, a German geographer, in 1933. August Losch, a German economist, also formulated this theory further in 1940. In 1954 Christaller's work was published in English by C. Baskin of the University of Virginia. The same year W.H. Woglom and W.F. Stolper, New Haven, published LÖsch's work as *The Economics of Location*. In 1956 Brian J. L. Berry, University of Washington, write *Geographic Aspect of the Size and Arrangement of Urban Centers*. Since then dozens of scholars have advanced this theory by using different hypothesis and mathematical models. In Regional Science, two major classical theories *Input-Output Theory* by Leontief and *Central Place Theory* by Christaller merged.[3]

"The Central Place Theory is a geographical theory that seeks to explain the size and spacing of human settlements. It rests on the notion that centralization is a natural principle of order and that human settlements follow it. Created by Walter Christaller, the theory suggests that there are laws determining the number, size and distribution of towns. He was interested only in their functions as markets, thus excluding specialist towns such as mining settlements."[4]

Christaller developed this theory based on southern Germany's homogeneous human settlement pattern. Nonetheless, this theory laid the foundation for fundamental principles in marketing goods and services, economic development and employment, transportation network, and administrative network even in non-homogeneous human settlements.

A.K. Philbrick distinguished between seven broad categories (orders) of functions, each of which occur in geographic space. The first-order category is consumer, a unit of household; the second-order category is retail trade; third-order is wholesale trade; fourth-order is transshipment; fifth-order is exchange; sixth-order is control; and the seventh-order is leadership. Each one of them performs economic functions of different hierarchy. As theorized by Philbrick, the seventh-order city will have four sixth-order cities, 16 fifth-order cities, 64 fourth-order cities, 256 third-order towns, and 1024 second-order village settlements. The lower-order settlements increase four times. Each one of them has a hinterland or tributary area. Higher ranking order's hinterland includes lower ranking categories. The second-order settlements all other higher-order settlements are central places to their respective hinterlands.[5]

Minimum population sizes are essential for each hierarchy of the settlements for economic viability. Maximum distances between the settlements may vary. Lower order goods and services such as groceries, bakeries, newspaper, etc. are nondurable and people are not ready to go far. People may go little further for medium order goods such as cloth, small tools, utensils, bank, post office, police station, doctors' office, etc. For higher order and durable goods such as jewellery, building construction material, furniture, wholesale goods, or household appliances, lower level courts, government field offices, etc. people may go even further distances. All of these settlements are within a commuting distance from villages. The highest-order settlements are further apart and provide speciality goods and services such as automobile sale and services, luxury goods, building appliances, offices, hospitals, institutions of higher learning, higher courts, etc. and still can be at distances within a day commute. The existing roads and mode of transportation available and economic conditions of the people are important factors in spacing and size of the hierarchy of settlements.

The Central Place Theory is ideal for application in regional planning and state land planning. The central places can be developed deliberately either by creating towns on virgin land or with planned expansion of existing towns. This theory is a key to balanced economic development. The network of central places with connecting transportation systems works like the nerve system in a human body. It works both ways from the highest rank city to the village level for distribution of goods and services and for marketing local products such as agricultural produces, forest products, and arts and crafts. Need to remember that central place theory cannot be applied as a perfect geometrical model as theorized. The essence of the theory is still valid to distribute different hierarchies of cities.

THE REALITY OF METROPOLIS AND MEGALOPOLIS

Huge cities called metropolis or megalopolis are created by agglomerations and urban sprawl. These places are exciting for most people, noisy and disturbing for some others. It is a great urban space for activism: a hot spot for political rallies and labor unions; lovers of sports; entertainments; business ventures; employment opportunities; individual freedom of expressions; intellectual pursuits in science, technology, literature, arts, music, drama, and education; and unfortunately an anonymous hiding space for organized criminals. Always they find some people to join them and their causes flourish.

On the other hand some people suffer. There is a social and economic cost to metropolitan living: (a) Land price and housing is very expensive in metropolitan areas. Most people cannot afford to own a home and rental housing is expensive yet not available. Therefore, low income people live in slums. Skyscrapers rise due to high land price. (b) There is 'urban fatigue' due to urban frictions. Everywhere you go, there is congestion, competition for space, and physical bodily friction while walking, riding bus or train, shopping, or going to cinemas in the hot and humid conditions. Even driving a car is not easy – it is slow, dangerous, expensive due to very high petroleum cost, lack of parking spaces, and high parking fee. The urban fatigue sets in on journey to and from work and after work, and left with no energy to do anything constructive or recreational at the end of the day. (c) Elderly and weak people cannot venture to go out as they cannot fight permanent congestion. They are confined to homes. (d) Mega cities are also difficult to protect against terrorist attacks. Terrorists have plenty of hiding room.

It is a mammoth task to provide services such as electricity, millions of gallons of water every day, hundreds of miles of sewers, huge sewage disposal plants, remove millions of tons of garbage a day, disease control to prevent epidemics, police and fire protection, and construction and maintenance of roads. Because of non availability and high cost of land, the service providers are bound to go tunneling hundreds of feet below ground level. Underground electric lines, telephone lines, water lines, sewer lines, and subways become necessary and hence very expensive. It is an engineering and funding challenge. The following are few examples of massive works and huge expenditures.

There are many secrets beneath the city of New York. There are more than 32 miles of tunnels for utility lines, 230 miles of subway tracks, 22 tunnels, about

10,000 miles of gas mains and steam pipes, thousands of miles of cables and pipes, and 750,000 manholes.[6] All metropolitan cities in the world have similar large scale infrastructures.

The Metro Railway, Kolkata started in 1972 and by 1995 a 16.45 km route from Dum Dum to Tollygunge was completed at a cost of Rs.1,706 crores. The extension from Tollygunge to Garia, a distance of 8.45 km is under construction at an estimated cost of Rs.696 crores. The total cost of construction is Rs. 2,402 crores for 24.9 km, or Rs. 96.5 crores per km. Underground route is 15 km and the rest is elevated or on surface. It is expected to carry more than 58 million passengers annually. Fares are Rs. 4 for 1-5 km, Rs. 6 for 5-10 km, and Rs.8 for over 10 km.[7] It has significantly reduced traffic congestions and pollution from buses, cars, and taxies on the roads but at a very high cost and long hours of commuting.

The Metro Rail Transport System (MRTS) study completed in 1990, recommended a route of 198.5 km underground, elevated and surface corridor for Delhi metro. The construction was started in October 1998 by Delhi Metro Rail Corporation Ltd. The first phase, which is completed in March 2006, comprises three lines. Line No.1: Shahdara-Tis Hazari-Barwada (28 km); Line No.2: Delhi University-Central Secretariat (11 km); and Line No.3: Barakhamba-Connaught Place-Dwarka (23.16 km). The estimated construction cost for a total of 62.16 km. tracks was Rs.10,570 crores or Rs170 crores per km. This does not include annual operation and maintenance costs. The construction of remaining 136.34 km track may cost another Rs. 23,184 crores. Population of Delhi metropolitan areas increased to 13 million in 2001. Number of registered motor vehicles in the year 2000 increased to 3,423,000 in Delhi, and 3,670,000 in Bangalore, Chennai, and Mumbai combined. Some of these passenger automobiles will not be used due to better and quicker mass transit. It is expected that the number of buses will be reduced by 2,500 on Delhi roads. This will reduce congestion and pollution.

There are 27 metropolitan cities in India in 2001 with population of one million to 13 million. It will cost India heavily to provide mass transportation, roads, water supply, sewer and other infrastructures. India should not spend millions of crores of rupees only on the metropolitan cities and neglect the rest of the country.

No city should be allowed to grow into a mega city as it is expensive and difficult to manage. The negative consequences are many as discussed in this section.

INDUSTRIAL AGGLOMERATION IS NO LONGER NECESSARY

In 21st century it is no longer necessary to bring all industries to the same location. Components parts for automobiles, aircrafts, electronic machines and appliances, etc. are now manufactured at different places and transported to other cities or countries for assembly. Similarly, with the advent of computer and information technology, duties can be performed at home, another place, or another country. No physical contacts among workers are necessary in some office works. Therefore, there is no justification to have large cities for agglomeration.

PLAN FOR DECONGESTION OF METROPOLITAN CITIES, CONTROL CONGESTION IN GROWING CITIES, AND BUILD NEW CITIES

There is nothing gained by overcrowding (Raymond Unwin). Every city has its optimum size. Excess population should be moved to new communities by planning intervention and by creating counter magnet settlements. The following strategies should be employed:

1. The development of alternative growth-poles in regions.
2. Creation of satellite towns within commuting distance.
3. Independent new towns having employment and housing.
4. Creation of a parallel or twin towns by distinct separation.[8]

The growth-pole strategy has proved to be successful in Great Britain. Satellite towns are being created around major cities within commuting distance of 30 to 45 minute. Satellite towns maintain strong ties with the major city but deflect population pressure on the main city. Independent new towns created away from the other cities must provide complete range of urban activities and services. Employment opportunity and a lively town center are very important. Twin cities are a low priority option. They are physically separate but pose similar problems of congestion, compete for same water source, jobs, entertainment, and other urban services.

Tamil Nadu is the only state where regional balanced development has taken place. Regional Centers: Coimbatore, Madurai and Tiruchi have developed as counter magnets to Chennai. Education, health facilities, trade and commerce, and transportation facilities have developed in these regional centers. People like to live in these centers rather than in congested Chennai. There are about 24 sub-regional towns in Tamil Nadu.

INDIA'S BALANCED DEVELOPMENT AND REGIONAL URBAN DEVELOPMENT POLICY

All six reasons discussed above, converge to one conclusion: India must have balanced economic and population distribution throughout the country. This will provide the entire population access to markets and employment opportunities with minimal displacements from traditional homes. Planner Henry Wright prepared the 1926

Figure 9.1
Satellite Towns

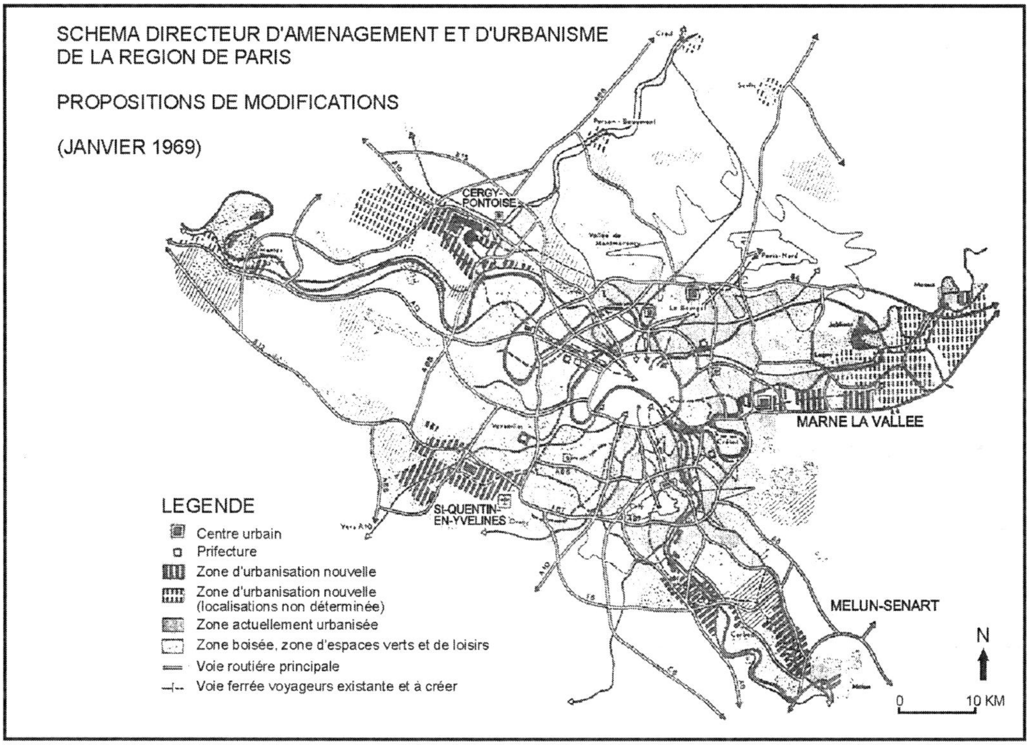

Paris Regional Master Plan, 1969, locating five satellite towns.

regional plan for New York State and suggested a balanced distribution of population and industry by the creation of new towns.

India needs national urban growth policies (a) to restrict and discourage further expansion of existing metropolitan areas and cities over 500,000 populations, (b) to create counter magnet cities where industrial and other employment facilities are provided with sufficient develop land and infrastructure, (c) to stabilize large cities by urban renewal and depopulation, and (d) to create urban growth centers as percentral place theory, creating new towns and planning existing towns, distributed regionally in every state. This will meet the aspirations of Mahatma Gandhi and President Kalam, and regional planning principle of balanced development. The Great Britain successfully created new towns to distribute urban growth regionally and restricted further growth of London more than sixty years ago.

The Planning Commission, and the Town and Country Planning Organization, Ministry of Urban Development, Government of India should review success and

Figure 9.2
Concepts for Satellite Town

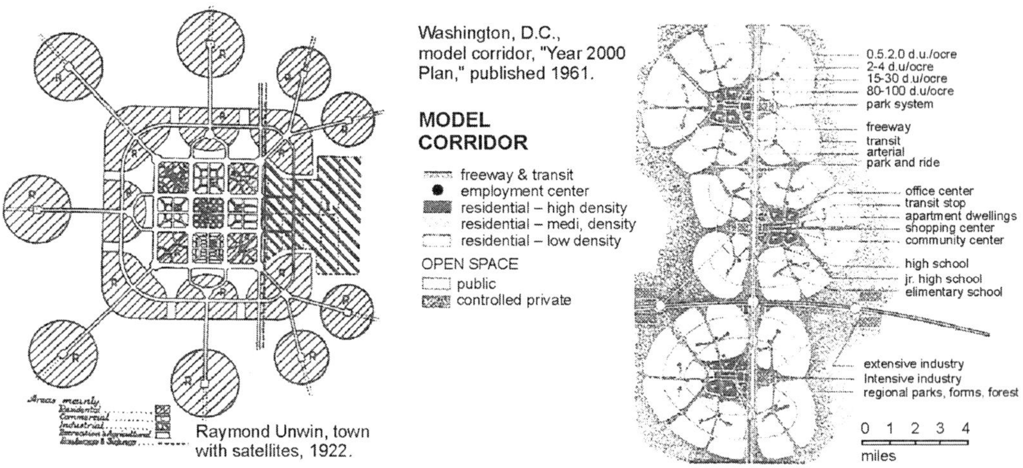

Source: Ervin Y. Galantay, *New Towns: Antiquity to the Present.*

failure of the current efforts in economic development and distribution in the country.

State and Regional Planning

India has been formally divided into 15 macro regions, but no actual regional planning is done. It is urgent that all 15 macro regions should be planned for distribution of various sizes of cities and for economic developments. Every state should have state land use planning considering environmental concerns, preservation of forests and wetlands, transportation, and land uses of various categories. Within each state micro region should be formed and planned.

Satellite Cities in the Making

Mukesh Ambani, India's most influential businessman, is planning to build new satellite cities outside Mumbai and Delhi.[9] This is a bold private project and expected to be like British New Towns, self-sufficient and well planned. These projects, when successful, will inspire other new towns in the country, encourage private developers, show how to overcome hurdles, and be more profitable and faster in development in private sector.

Notes

1. Keith Bradsher, *The New York Times*, September 1, 2006.
2. Gallion and Eisner
3. Sonis
4. Wikimedia Foundation, Inc. http://wikipedia.org/wiki/Central_Place_Theory
5. Walter Isard, P222-227
6. Bob Sacha, http://www.atlasmagazine.com/photo/sacha6/
7. http://www.calcuttayellowpages.com/metrorail.html
8. Ervin Y. Galantay, *New Towns: Antiquity to the Present*.
9. Ron Moreau and Sudip Mazumder, *News Week*, September 18, 2006.

10

An Evaluation of Guwahati Master Plan: A Sad Story of Missed Opportunities

This chapter is an overall evaluation of planning efforts in Guwahati. During my stay in Guwahati from 1967 to 1969 as an Assistant Town Planner of the Government of Assam, I experienced many frustrations. The opportunities to plan and improve Guwahati were not taken seriously. As a result Guwahati is an unplanned city. This experience has led me to write this sad story.

GUWAHATI'S PLANNING HISTORY

Urbanization in Assam and particularly the growth of Guwahati to a metropolitan size is a new phenomenon. Assam is one of the last frontiers in India where large urbanization began. The government and the citizens did not have the experience to handle the rapid unanticipated growth. Enacted in 1959 by the State Assembly, the Assam Town and Country Planning Act's pioneering efforts to plan Guwahati signaled an attempt to prepare the city for its upcoming growth. But the Act was very weak in its provisions for planning guidance and implementation mechanisms. The Act created the Town Planning Organization (TPO), Government of Assam prepared the Guwahati Master Plan and Zoning Regulation, and it was approved by the Governor on March 24, 1965 and notified and published in the Assam Gazette on April 30, 1965. The Guwahati Development Authority (GDA) was created by the Government of Assam in order to administer the Master Plan. However, the GDA failed miserably in the planning effort. The Guwahati Metropolitan Development Authority (GMDA) replaced the GDA in 1987.

Figure 10.1
Map of Guwahati City

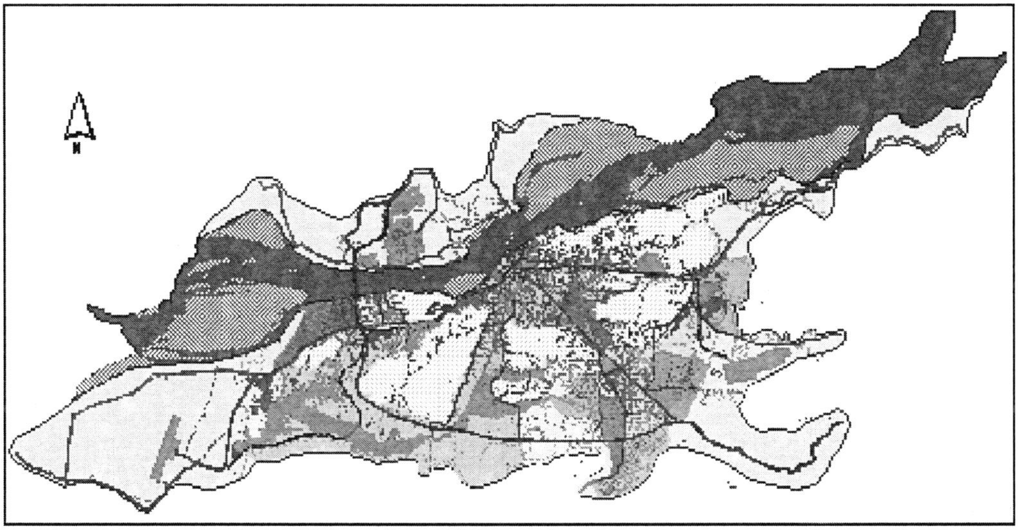

Source: EN-GEO Consulting and Research Centre, Guwahati.

When the Master Plan was published, the population of Guwahati proper was about 120,000 and its area was about 25 sq. kms. The Master Plan area included vast open land around the city with paddy fields, wetlands, hills, and a few small villages. This was the greatest opportunity to think big and plan the existing area and every extended new development. The GDA not only missed the opportunity, it created bad precedents.

Qualified engineers and an architect town planner were employed. However, the GDA's priority was issuing no-objection certificates on land divisions without considering planning. Then the GDA instated the bad precedent of issuing building permits on 12'and 16' wide roads, now called lanes. Though the master plan specified minimum road widths of 100' for arterial roads, 65' for major roads, and 40' for internal and secondary roads, the GDA violated these specifications. By issuing building permits on only 12' wide roads, the GDA returned to road widths of medieval cities in which roads were for pedestrians only. Thus, Old Guwahati has wider roads than newer developments.

Additionally, zoning was not enforced. Land use occupancies, specified by zoning regulations, were ignored. The GDA permitted any land use on any land. Anybody could build any building without complying to land use specified by zoning regulations, provided the applicant submitted an affidavit stating that the building would be demolished when asked by an authority. Thousands of affidavits were accepted by the GDA. Who is now going to enforce the affidavits if the files still exist? There are minimal off-street parking space requirements in the zoning regulation, but they were never enforced. Development Schemes (detailed prerequisite plans for development), once the backbone of the Assam Town and Country Planning Act, were never prepared.

Thus the master plan resulted in little planning. Land division permit and building permit acquisition became a trap for bribery. The GDA missed these opportunities to make the city better and hundreds of crores of rupees will be needed to correct these mistakes. This is a Herculean task. Today, the GMDA is not doing much better, finding it difficult to break away from the bad precedence already established. It is still working under the same weak planning law. The enforcement itself became a source of corruption.

GROWTH OF GUWAHATI

I have seen Guwahati since 1946 when my father treated me with my first ice cream at Fanci Bazar. The city bus route and its length is a simple and good indicator of urban growth. The city bus route in 1946 was from Pandu Ghat to Fanci Bazar jail, approximately 10 kms. Later it extended to Barowari, Guwahati Club, Silpukhuri, Chandmari, and Noonmati, spanning approximately 20 kms. Now there are city buses going in all directions, covering as much as 100 kms with bus routes. Both Guwahati's municipal population and area grew rapidly. In 1951, Guwahati's population was 43,615 and area was 7.68 sq. kms, 1961 population was 100,707 and area 14 sq. kms, 1971 population 253,851 and area 216 sq. kms. In 1971 the master plan area population was 292,029 and area 262 kms. The 2001 population of Guwahati Municipal Corporation was 809,895; and in Guwahati Metropolitan Area were 890,773. The population is projected to increase to 2,173,900 by 2025 if the current trend of growth is allowed. The map in Figure 10.1 shows that there is not much developable land left. Some developments continue to destroy environmentally sensitive lands.

Some new developments increased population moderately, such as establishment of Guwahati University in 1948, Assam Engineering College in 1955, Guwahati Oil Refinery in 1963, and IIT Guwahati in 1995. Government departments like Flood Control, Public Works Roads and Buildings, and others offices moved from Shillong to Guwahati in the 1960s. The relocation of the Assam Capital from Shillong to Guwahati in 1970 had the biggest impact on the development of Guwahati. It became a necessity to some and source of pride to others to have a home in Guwahati. The importance of Guwahati became real as it developed into a center of trade, commerce, education, medical treatment, transportation hub, and politics for the North-East Region of India.

However, along with tremendous urban growth, some anti-social elements have emerged: (1) Land agents (*matir dalal*), a new class of profiteers, arose. Some of them are selling the same piece of land more than once and making exorbitant profits without investing any money. They have still not been regulated as real estate agents. (2) Groups of people began to actively take land. Those who do not have money to purchase land occupy private or public land and build huts overnight. Some even take houses and land by registering them in their own names through bribery. It is alleged that some police department and judicial department personnel are also involved in the scams. Bhaben Saikia depicted exploitation of poor and simple-minded people for land grabbing in his cinema *Itihas*. (3) The number of property dispute cases increased in the courts. Some people connected with the court are reaping massive profits. The longer cases are prolonged, the more money is to be made from both the plaintiffs and defendants. Even judges and politicians are involved in the scams. (4) Some politicians harvested votes by handing out permanent settlements to occupiers of government land, which could have been used for parks and green spaces or other public purposes. (5) Certain organized groups extracted payment from the occupiers of government land so that they might remian on the land without the threat of official eviction. (6) In the late 1980s false bill culture known as 60 percent-40 percent sharing, submitting bills without doing work and getting paid, began and continues to thrive. (7) Corruption money found an easy outlet in buying land and constructing buildings. There is a correlation between the level of corruption and construction boom. The cost of construction skyrocketed. (8) There is no one to stop the cutting of hills to fill wetlands for development. This is creating havoc by increasing erosion of the destroyed hills and filling up drains with silt, eventually flooding a large part of the city. While hundreds of homes get flooded with polluted water, water-born diseases spread, and animal habitats and green hills are lost forever. (9) Finally, the number of automobiles also increased suddenly, most of them purchased with easy money and easily available loans.

VEHICULAR TRAFFIC IN GUWAHATI

Guwahati is in Kamrup district. Kamrup district's available data is as follows:

Motor Vehicles in Kamrup District

Total number of registered motor vehicles			148,488	– as of December 31, 1995
			217,792	– as of March 31, 2000
			330,696	– as of March 31, 2006
Motor vehicles registered in one year – 33,755 April 1, 2005 to March 31, 2006				
This includes	1,408	heavy trucks	17,380	motorcycles
	1,203	three wheelers (goods)	1,573	scooters
	250	auto rickshaws	10,369	cars
	246	buses of all categories	1,326	all other types of vehicles
Total number of registered motor vehicles – 330,696 as of March 31, 2006				
This includes	40,777	heavy trucks	79,122	motorcycles
	6,859	three wheelers (goods)	79,371	scooters
	9,012	auto rickshaws	76,152	cars
	5,808	buses of all categories	33,595	all other types of vehicles
Accident vehicles examined by M.V.I. 385 in 2001-2002; 1,116 in 2005-2006				

Source: Pranab Kumar Baruah, Kamrup District Transport Officer.

There is no statistical information on motor vehicles plying in Guwahati but registered outside Kamrup district. The roads are already congested with vehicles. The vehicles are moving at a crawling speed. This burns more fuel and takes three times more time to reach a destination than five years ago. If the automobile registration increases at this rate annually, the city will be at a stand still and will not function. Drastic steps are needed to alleviate the current and future problems.

The public blames the municipality for not solving these problems. The antisocial elements have created anarchy. Such a social environment makes it difficult to accomplish many positive things. Enforcement of master plan provisions, especially those involving building codes, has become impossible. Governance of the state is absent.

Rapid developments were allowed without subdivision or sector planning and without making provisions for wider roads, additional water supply, sewer system, drainage, and community facilities. The GDA did not take up any development scheme as authorized in the Assam Town and Country Planning Act. The public is buying lands in Guwahati irrespective of planning or no planning or quality of land. Land price is doubling every 4 to 5 years.

GUWAHATI'S FUTURE

In Guwahati everyone talks about miserable urban conditions, some write about it, and some people dream of transforming Guwahati into a world-class city. But no one seems to know what to do and how to improve Guwahati. There is a process available (planning, programming, budgeting, and implementation) to accomplish the goal of a better Guwahati. Given public understanding of the process and willingness to improve, the quality of urban life in Guwahati can be improved.

The planning thoughts, process and planning law in Assam have not advanced since 1959, when the Assam Town and Country Planning Act were passed. It remained stagnant and isolated from the rest of the world. A lot of water has passed through the mighty Brahmaputra since, and so has the evolution of planning. But Assam remained unaffected. Assam needs to go with the flow of modernization.

Guwahati today is a city with nearly a million people with many problems. Streets are narrow and supersaturated with automobiles and pedestrians. During working hours traffic moves at the speed of 3 to 4 km/hr. Cars waste precious petroleum (Rs.50 per liter) and pollute the air. Drivers get tired and irritated and have accidents. Narrow roads are made even narrower by pot holes, open drains, street vendors, building materials dumped on road sides, parked vehicles, road construction work, or water and mud puddles. Broken or nonexistent drain covers & footpaths have led to the death and injury of pedestrians. Competition and conflict between road traffic and street side business further aggravate the congestion. It is virtually impossible for an ambulance, a fire truck, or a police vehicle to attend an emergency situation.

Natural drains, water retention ponds and marsh lands are filled with earth. Hills are dug for earth filling. Half an inch rainfall is enough to wash the earth from the hills and block the drains and flood streets and homes. Often flooding brings traffic to a stand still. Flooding is also a health hazard since the rainwater mixed with contaminated drain and septic tank waste water runs through homes, shops and streets.

Modern life is impossible without roads, electricity, water, and sewer. If every family or business has to invest money to have a backup electric generator, own source of water supply, own septic tank, and private method of garbage disposal, what service is the municipality providing? These amenities and services could be privatized if government at any level will not take responsibility.

Historically, cities become concerned when their problems become chronic and attention is given to solutions. Guwahati Master Plan was adopted in 1963, but no one took the planning effort seriously. The State Government, Guwahati Development Authority, and the public did not give serious attention. Now that the city is congested and chaotic, there is some consciousness about the problems and solutions must follow.

The general public must take initiative for Guwahati city planning, rather than entirely depending on state and municipal government. The city belongs to the public, it is their urban space to live, work, and raise families in the pursuit of happiness. Therefore, it is imperative that the public participate in the development process of Guwahati. Public must have their input, cooperation and effort in building the city.

PUBLIC RESPONSIBILITIES

The public also needs to take responsibility and initiative in the development of their own beautiful city. But they did not do their part. Now, the people are complaining about congestion, poor drainage, flooding, inadequate urban services, etc. and blaming the state and municipal authorities. For many of the problems the public is directly or indirectly responsible. Numerous people encroach upon road right of way and neighbors' land, and will not give land for widening their own road. They want only more land and would like to build more than they are permitted, or even where they are forbidden to build. Many of them would not even pay municipal taxes regularly to support municipal services. Even if they pay taxes, it is not enough to pay for land acquisition and road widening costs, and construction of water supply, sewer, drainage, and electricity. Then the money has to come from the government by depriving funding to rural areas or other towns. How much the state and municipal budget can pay. Where is public contribution amount to Guwahati Municipal Corporation? GMC's annual income is Rs.1.2 crores and expenditure Rs.25 crores.

The general public needs to participate and understand the planning process and financing the improvements in their community. They need to organize themselves to solve community problems, and keep pressure on their elected representatives. Intelligent public participation is an obligatory civic duty.

MY CITY PLANNING ORDEAL

We are all familiar with the ideas that bureaucracy is slow and frustrating, corruption prevalent, and indifference and inefficiency are for the weak of heart and mind. From a distance, with youthful enthusiasm and lack of baggage, we think we will be different, that we will make a difference. This was my perspective as a young officer when I began two years of service in planning in Assam. It is my hope and intention that readers have chosen this book with the desire to do something helpful for this society. I offer the following personal experiences as guides to the challenges ahead. Nearly forty years later, I still have not given up.

After graduating in architecture and city planning, I started my first job as assistant town planner with the Town Planning Organization (TPO), Government of Assam, my home state, in August 1967. I was associated with preparation of master plans for Silchar and Tezpur. Data on land, demography, economic situations, etc. were collected but no credible inferences were made to impact planning decisions.

I used some of my architectural training to design market places for Palashbari and Aizal to assist the municipalities. Rebels had burned down the Aizal market. The government sent S.M. Hoque (Acting Director) and me to Aizal to survey and prepare a site plan and buildings for the market, without any instructions on financial limitations. Later the proposal was deemed too expensive. The travel to Aizal from Silchar made me realize why the Mizos rebelled. To travel less than 150 miles by road used to take three days. We had to take a military helicopter.

Prafulla Saikia, Executive Officer of Guwahati Municipal Corporation (GMC), encouraged me to prepare a plan for Fanci Bazar vegetable market, near the jail. I prepared a four story building plan in which the ground floor will have grocery and vegetable shops; the first floor will have lightweight shops such as cloths, stationery, pharmacy, barber, eye glasses, and other services. The 2nd and 3rd floors would have offices for rent. Parking and public toilets were also designed. The project would have created a clean environment and generated sizable revenue. *The Statesman*, Calcutta published a one-page article on this project with the perspective view I drew. No newspaper in Assam gave any coverage. My boss commented that he had not seen any two-storied shopping center in the United States and therefore it was not feasible. Maybe I was ahead of the times. Now I see two-storied shopping centers in all big cities in the U.S. Saikia was transferred and enthusiasm for the project died down.

On my visit to Guwahati in 1999, architect Upen Kakati told me "Das we are following your dream of Fanci Bazar market. I took your idea and it is under construction." It gave me satisfaction. But the project is still unfinished.

In 1968, I drew up a redevelopment plan for Gandhi Basti defining roads 30' wide, parks, and a primary school when about 70 percent of the area was undeveloped. This was an excellent development scheme authorized in Chapter IV of the Town Planning Act. The GDA, the TPO and the GMC were not interested implementing the scheme. It needed only detail planning, convincing landowners in support of a better development, and implementation. It could have been a model for development in Guwahati.

In 1968 Dharmnanda Das, Chief Secretary, asked the Town Planning Director and the Chief Engineer of Guwahati Development Authority to see him with cadastral map of Guwahati. I represented TPO and Shanta Choudhury represented GDA. Secretary Das instructed us to show a site in Guwahati where the temporary Assam Capital can be moved. Dispur was our selection based on: Dispur is above the highest flood level of Brahmaputra, it has good road connections from the National Highway and Assam Trunk Road, nearness to Guwahati for housing and other infrastructures, and the land was wide and open. We rejected Chandrapur because of high cost of construction in the difficult terrain, a long distance from the airport, and infrastructure was not there. My handwritten report was submitted. Such an important decision on the location of Assam's capital was made within an hour. It became a permanent capital instead of temporary.

The decision was entirely political. It was already decided to move the capital to Guwahati; only the location in Guwahati was not decided. Once the temporary capital was moved, land interests of politicians and high-level officers settled in, it became impossible to move to a new location and build a new capital city like Chandigarh.

I was appointed Town Planner to GDA effective 6th March 1969. I was asked to work morning hours in GDA and afternoon hours in the TPO. I observed many problems at the GDA, including:

1. GDA issued land division permits and no objection certificates for land sale, and building permits with 12' wide roads. It took affidavits to the effect that the landowner will give land for road widening when necessary. Landowners also built permanent compound walls; compounding the problems. The GDA went back to the Medieval Age. Now, everyone knows the consequences.
2. Building permits were granted in violation of zoning, again taking affidavits to tear down the building when required to comply with the land use zone.
3. GDA did not do any Development Scheme as authorized by the Assam Town and Country Planning Act in Chapter IV. Did not make detailed road schemes, or zoning area delineation based on cadastral maps, which is prerequisite in the implementation and enforcement of the master plan.
4. There was no office discipline among staff, such as absence from office without notice, staff not available for discussion in a staff meeting, missing files, and ignoring office order. Non-technical persons were appointed to do technical jobs.
5. There were verbal complaints of bribery, inefficiency, and unprofessional acts and behaviors.

I had a mission to accomplish – to improve all the above. Time was short – 10 to 12 noon. So I normally stayed longer to 1:00 or 1:30 pm. Soon I realized I was alone in this mission. GDA Staff was uncooperative. Rumors struck my ears of imminent physical threats.

I had verbal insults. One Sunday a person came to bribe me for a residential permit in an industrial zone next to the refinery. I refused the bribe but assured him of looking into the application. Next day I looked at the file. Residences were permitted in that area of industrial zone. I did not see any reason to deny his permit. So I permitted.

During this period I developed a cordial relationship with Ramani Deka, municipal engineer. I served notices on spot at illegal construction sites and Deka had them demolished immediately. If this precedent were continued, illegal constructions would have totally stopped.

A decisive day came. I was suspected that because of the opportunity to take bribe I was spending more time in GDA. I was stunned and drafted a resignation letter immediately. On insistence of a senior colleague, I did not submit it but made determination to leave TPO on my earliest opportunity. I was confident that I can earn Rs.360 a month by drawing building plans, which was my monthly salary. I left India for USA on the independence day of India in 1969. That day also signified my personal independence.

Before I left, I submitted a six-page letter to the Chairman, GDA stating draw backs and lack of progress in implementation of the Master Plan. In brief I made the following points:

1. The Master Plan was not translated on cadastral map showing land use zones and proposed roads. So exact locations of those by dug numbers was impossible and created controversies.
2. GDA has not prepared detailed road schemes and prescribed street lines per Sections 22, 23, and 24 of the Town Planning Act. Building permits are being given without knowing prescribed street lines and development control.
3. The staff of the Technical Branch was idle since there was no construction work. They could have been utilized to prepare road schemes. Many of the building inspectors were non-technical persons.
4. In a meeting on 28 May, 1969, attended by the Director of TPO, Executive Officer of Guwahati Municipality, The Chairman of GDA, and myself it was decided to conduct a land survey and prepare road schemes. The staff from the Building Branch was not made available and the scheme did not start.
5. GDA did not use prescribed forms for land sale permit and building permit. The Director of TPO submitted drafts (which I prepared) to the Chairman of GDA, which he approved but never used.
6. On several occasions files were missing and timely action could not be taken. I also suggested procedures to manage files. This was also not used.
7. The staff attendance in the office was a mystery. At the time of need they cannot be located. My suggested procedure for improvement was ignored.
8. Guwahati Master Plan included Guwahati, North Guwahati, Kamakhya, and Barjar. But building permit control was not there for North Guwahati, Kamakhya, and Barjar.

I also made seven suggestions to improve GDA and five suggestions to amend the Town and Country Planning Act. This letter was copied to the Director TPO and the Under Secretary, Town and Country Planning Department. As usual it had no impact.

Over time, I made a number of suggestions and attempts to form a dialogue with the planners and government in Assam. In June 1979 I wrote a twelve page letter to a planner in the TPO, explaining the planning process in the State of Florida, concept of comprehensive planning, policy planning, planning tools, etc. I commented that town planning in Assam is a very simplistic approach to a very complex problem and that is why town planning failed miserably in Assam. Obviously this letter did not make any difference.

In January 1982, on my visit to Assam, I invited planners to join a discussion on present trends in planning. The venue was Dr. Binoy Das's home. Only one person besides Das had shown up.

In August 1983, I wrote a seventeen-page paper to TPO, named "Problems and Prospects of Town Planning in Assam". This paper pointed out current unplanned growth; lack of political power behind plan implementation; lack of responsible authority (state, municipality, or citizens); lack of clear concept of planning, zoning, building code, development schemes, etc. This paper also discussed basic steps of the planning process, comprehensive planning elements, need for public participation, implementation strategies, planning tools, a new tool I suggested, and housing strategies.

In the summer of 1986, I visited Honorable Prafulla Mahanta, Chief Minister. I talked to him about town planning and offered to give free technical support. He asked Jiten Sarma, Under Secretary to take me to the Chief Secretary and the Town Planning Minister. I had a onetime discussion. There was no follow up or any invitation for technical help.

In January 1987, I wrote a letter to Honorable Prafulla Mahanta, CM expressing my interest on improvement of town planning in Assam and capital site selection. I copied the letter to the Chief Secretary, Town Planning Minister, and Dinesh Goswami, MP. I received a response only from Goswami stating that he will discuss the matter with the Chief Minister. That was the end of that issue.

On 19th March 1987, I wrote a letter to the Program Director, Doordarshan, Guwahati asking him if he would be interested in televising a presentation on "Problems and Prospects of Town Planning in Assam". The presentation was intended to be educational to general public, planners, legislators and journalists. A preliminary outline was attached. I suggested it could be a joint presentation with Doordarshan staff. I never received any response.

In 1999 I expressed my desire to meet the Architects Association in Guwahati for an informal discussion. It was arranged and about 12 architects attended. We had a general discussion on architecture and Guwahati urban planning. I suggested that practicing architects are in a good position to speak and exert pressure for better urban planning in Guwahati. Some of them supported the idea, but the president of the association, who was the senior most, was negative. His opinion was that it is not possible to change the process of planning in Guwahati.

Since 1967, we have lost 40 years of planning. I have advocated for the improvement of planning in Assam with little or no result.

THE ASSAM TOWN AND COUNTRY PLANNING ACT, 1959 (PLEASE SEE APPENDIX)

This Act appears to have been drafted based on English planning laws but was never updated with new planning trends. Many things have changed since 1950s. Please refer to Chapter 2: Development of Modern Urban Planning. The Act should be rewritten to facilitate modern planning concepts, planning mechanisms, and plan implementation mechanisms.

Though 'country' planning is in the title of the act, there is nothing about country planning in the act. Great Britain passed the Ribbon Development Act of 1935 to regulate development along roads. But no such measure has been taken in Assam. People have settled along roads and highways, accidents happen frequently, and have cut down the speed of automobiles.

The Act has 90 Sections, but only one Section is devoted to contents of the Master plan and one section to implementation of plan.

Section 11: Contents of Master Plan and Zoning Regulations – The Master Plan to be prepared as defined under section 9, may include:

(a) A general land-use plan for residential, commercial, recreational and public and semi-public purposes;

(b) Zoning plan;

(c) Transportation plan including roads, railways, canals etc.;

(d) Public utilities plan;

(e) A report giving relevant data and information in respect of proposals in the Plan and any other things which the State Government may deem necessary.

Section 12: Implementation of the Plan – After adoption of the plan and zoning regulation they shall be sent by the State Government for implementation to the Authority constituted under section 8A.

This is the core of planning and implementation in the planning law. Yet it is too simplistic and open handed. The Act simply stated in the preamble to provide developments on sound planning principles. Sound planning principles, which might have implied planning tools, and implementation mechanisms were absent. The Act must specify what the requirements are in planning. It must state required planning elements, implementation mechanisms, procedures, enforcement responsibilities, etc. The Act was amended many times in the administrative parts but the technical part of actual planning was never amended. The Act gives more emphasis to administrative requirements. The biggest fault of the Act is, it vested too much discretionary power in the development authorities, which means they may do something or nothing at all. Development authorities decided to do nothing at all. There are no definite guide-lines. Oversight power to Town Planning Organization was not given.

The Act has a good provision, Chapter IV: Development Scheme. This could have been refined, but application of this provision as it is would have resulted in orderly development of Guwahati and other towns. Under this provision an area potential for development shall be declared a development scheme area and roads, lots, and community facilities are planned. Development of land shall not be allowed until the scheme is completed. Unfortunately the GDA or the GMDA never employed this tool.

The Act has given authority only to the state government for planning. Planning by local governments and consultants are excluded. Consensus building with citizens and government agencies is ignored.

Financing Improvements

In Chapter 6: Budgeting and Financing has been discussed. The Asian Development Bank was willing to fund capital improvement projects in Guwahati up to about Rs. 500 crores at low interest on a long-term basis. This would have improved Guwahati and created employment to thousands. But detailed project reports need to be acceptable and the state government must guarantee completion and financial liability. This did not happen.

It is also alleged that the costs of the projects were inflated to keep a margin for misuse. The international lending agencies are aware of corruption, so they scrutinize projects very carefully. Creditworthiness is the bottom line.

Dilemma of High Rise Buildings

The GMDA is permitting high-rise flats on three kathas (8,640 sq. ft.) of land or more. There are now more than 75 flat developers in Guwahati. If this continues population, traffic, and businesses will increase at least three times in next ten years. One can walk faster than riding a car in Guwahati. It took me an hour and a half to go from Chandmari to Courthouse, a distance of 4 km. Guwahati is already supersaturated. Water supply, sewer, drainage, and electricity are severely limited and unreliable. It is not wise to allow such super high density. This also has increased land prices to unaffordable levels of course some land owners are making windfall profits.

For horizontal growth land is limited. So people want vertical growth. If vertical growth is to be permitted, it should follow the Transfer of Development Rights technique as discussed in Chapter 3. Floor Area Ratio should be optimum, unchanged, and enforced strictly. Buildings should be limited in 3 stories with some exceptions to those with low coverage of ground space.

There are limitations on horizontal and vertical growth. (1) Infrastructure and facilities have a designed limit beyond which capacity to serve the population will diminish. (2) Fire departments have height limits for public protection. (3) Need provisions for more schools, open spaces, shops, and other amenities of population density increases. With out increasing these provisions allowing flats to be built is a serious mistake. GMDA is requiring only car parking. For such high-density amenities such as lawn, community hall, convenience shops, laundry service etc. should be required. Swimming pool and tennis courts may be additional facilities to attract flat buyers.

Limits of Growth

In Chapter 9, reality of metropolis, central place theory, and satellite cities has been discussed. It is time to limit growth in Guwahati and instead develop satellite towns in the concept of garden cities. It is also time to stop leapfrog developments. The developments along highways are making fast driving dangerous. A Ribbon Development Act must be passed immediately.

Public Apathy

When I talk to friends about improving Guwahati, almost always I get a negative response "what can we do now, Guwahati has already developed the way it is, and it is over; it is not practical to do anything". My articles "Solutions to Drainage Problems in Guwahati" and "Managing Floods with Conservation of Flood Water in Lakes and Wetlands" were published in the *Assam Tribune* in 2005 in Sunday sections. The public is not concerned. The largest part of the problem seems to be public apathy. The citizens do not believe that there is hope, better methods of planning and implementation, and that funding sources are available. If the patient does not believe in recovery, we have a bigger problem. The non-believers have to endure the pain for a long time. They need willingness to improve our living environment. The recent widening of G.N. Bordoloi road from Guwahati Club to Chandmari is an example that if there is a will good things are possible. An activist group for a better Guwahati, if formed, may help the situation.

It is true that extensive development in Guwahati is almost complete. But there are many more developments coming up and much more planning and preparation needs to be made: (a) Developments will continue beyond and around current developments to a megalopolis unless controlled. Hence the peripheral areas need to be regulated. Satellite towns, also called dormitory towns, will grow around Guwahati and the number of commuters to Guwahati will increase. (b) Even though extensive development is almost complete, intensive developments have started. High-rise buildings are coming up which will make the city even more congested. The current criterion of allowing the high-rise buildings in Guwahati is inadequate. (c) Improvement plans and projects are absolutely needed for roads, water supply, sewer system, and community facilities. Without wider roads and express-ways the city will become even more inaccessible. There is no end to road widening. Hence private automobiles must be discouraged by creating a mass transit system which is easily available and cheaper. Plans for commuter trains, subways, and buses need to be made. (d) These are very expensive propositions, but it will be more expensive and more difficult if we wait. (e) Guwahati is never going to solve traffic problems until shopping is separated from roads. Shopping malls of various sizes with parking facilities, separated from roads is the prudent solution. Property front shops opening to the roads should be stopped. For any commercial use the entire plot of land must be used having shop openings within the plot of land.

The economic boom in India has started. India is on the verge of becoming one of the world's largest economic powers. This will trigger higher employment and higher salary, and it will lead to higher rate of urbanization and higher land value. Hence, it will be more expensive later to acquire land for roads and other infrastructure. It is urgent that we act immediately.

11

Urban Renewal and Infrastructure Improvement

In architecture and urban planning everything has to have a specific space designed for it thoughtfully. The things and space needed are numerous which covers from birth to death in the life cycle – from maternity hospital to crematorium/burial ground and in between. We desire a functional and beautiful city. A functional city will come from well-developed infrastructure and well-organized urban space, and a beautiful city will emerge from landscaping every plot of land and public space. Guwahati has a beautiful surrounding with low hills and the great Brahmaputra. Assam's land is very fertile, climate is hot and humid, perfect for tropical plants and vegetations. It is up to the will of the citizens to make Guwahati a functional and beautiful place. They need to contribute their share for the cause. The governments alone cannot do it.

WHAT IS URBAN RENEWAL

Every city grows through changes and developments as the time passes. The changes can be organic as it happens without planning interference or by planning default. Guwahati has master plan but developed by planning default. Old Guwahati had better plan and wide roads. Therefore, even new developments need renewal. The changes are desirable with deliberate planning efforts. Changes through conscious planning efforts by urban renewal process and urban design are being emphasized here.

Urban renewal becomes inevitable as a city grows, matures, becomes old, undergoes physical decay, creates slums and environmental problems; cripples movements due to congetion; and becomes unfit for residential or business use. All urban land goes through a cycle of land use changes: new construction, decay, expansion, relocation, modernization, reuse of land to the most economic value, and social changes.

Overtime the existing land use can become incompatible to the surrounding land use. For examples: (1) the commercial area expands into residential area and becomes noisy, congested, and frequented by strangers and no longer peaceful. The area's cohesive neighborly environment is lost and it is no longer suitable to raise children. By slow process commercial areas will take over the residential areas if not checked. The residents will move out. (2) A jail or prison built long time ago, like Fanci Bazar Jail, is now in the middle of the city. It had deteriorated and is obsolete. It is prudent to move it to outskirts and build a modern facility with prisoner reform in mind. (3) Factories in the middle of a city needing modernization must be moved to the outskirts in an industrial area. (4) An old civil hospital in the middle of a city may be expanded and modernized somewhere else. (5) Schools and colleges located on busy streets produce more traffic and are detrimental to the students. These institutions can be expanded and modernized in safer and peaceful locations. (6) The residential quarters for Government or company employee, now deteriorating, may be reconstructed on the same site or relocated to another site. (7) Numerous buildings and land uses nonconforming to the current zoning regulations can be objectionable to the surrounding environment. (8) Outdated water supply and sewer plant may be moved. Older infrastructures deteriorates and becomes inadequate for modern demand and uses.

Urban renewal and urban design is desirable and can be financially feasible. (1) Most of the old buildings were built single or double story but now occupying valuable lands. These buildings have less floor space and not producing sufficient income. The landowners can sale the high income potential land at much higher price and relocate themselves to less expensive and spacious lots. Or they may modernize with high-rise buildings, with parking and landscaping. (2) The city may acquire private dilapidated buildings and plan parks and parking garages, under a city beautification program. A city may exchange land for this purpose. A branch of municipal government should be created as urban renewal and city beautification is a continuous process..

FANCI BAZAR JAIL SITE RENEWAL AND URBAN DESIGN

In this context we shall examine how the Fanci Bazar jail site can be best used to revitalize, beautify, bring new urban form, and preserve some history in Guwahati. It

Figure 11.1

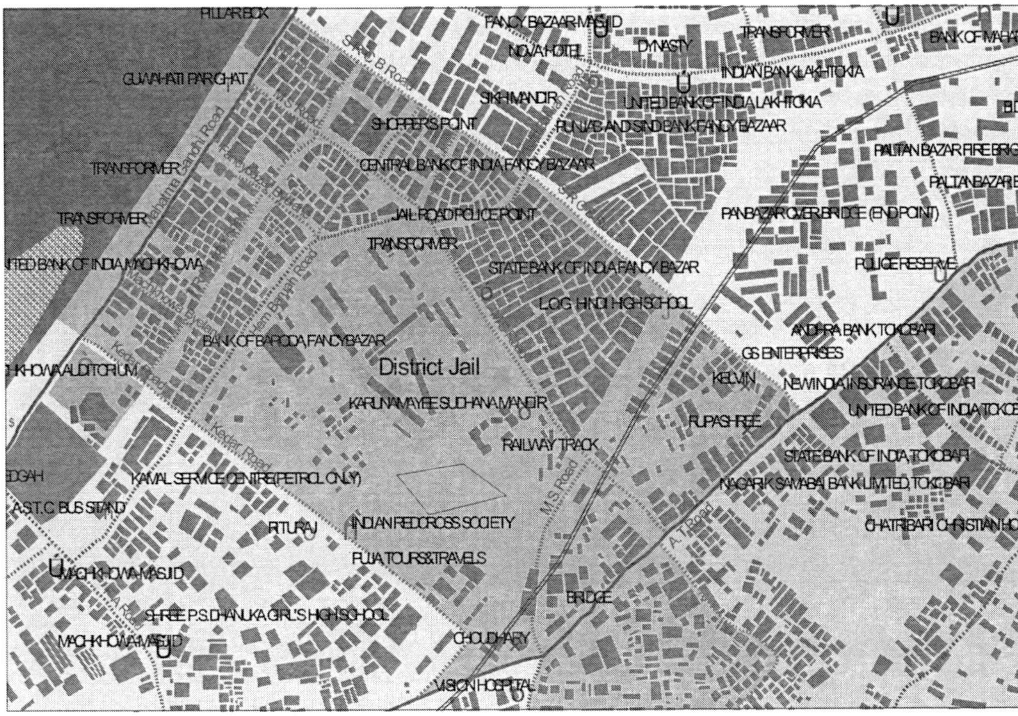

Source: EN-GEO Consultancy and Research Centre, Guwahati

can be put to financially profitable uses. The Government of Assam has already decided to move the old jail from Fanci Bazar to Lokhra in the out skirts of Guwahati.

The site is in the center of Guwahati, closer to the Brahmaputra River. The area of the site is about 11 hectares. Lot dimensions are approximately 396 m, 213 m, 122 m, 274 m and 213 m. It has roads on three sides and railroad on the southeast. The site of Fanci Bazar Jail and surroundings is leveled and above the highest flood level of the river. The State Government of Assam owns the site. The land is of highest value in the city. It is desirable for up scale commercial use and corporate offices. The site also has historic value since many famous leaders of the Indian Independence Movement were jailed here. In the 19th century one freedom fighter was hanged there and hence the name Fanci Bazar came.

All alternatives should include historic preservation of a part of the jail wall and the cells where freedom fighters were imprisoned. All alternatives should include landscaping.

Alternative 1: Ideally the whole site can be made a public park with car parking. This would provide a breathing space in the middle of congested developments. Since the land is of highest value, this option may not be acceptable to the government.

Alternative 2: The site can be planned with modern design for a high scale shopping center, high-rise buildings for corporate office buildings, hotels, and condominiums. This will produce maximum revenue. Lots may be auctioned to the highest bidders. Zoning restrictions such as permitted land use, height restrictions, lot coverage, lot setbacks, and parking should be predetermined.

Alternative 3: Alternatives 1 and 2 may be compromised and a sequential renewal plan can be devised. One part of the site can be built for up scale shopping center, hotels, and corporate offices. In the rest of the site other shops and residential condominiums may be constructed and leased or sold to the property owners of adjacent blocks between the jail and Brahmaputra River. The property owners of these blocks may exchange the property for new accommodations in the jail site buildings on value basis. The blocks thus vacated can be redeveloped with parks and buildings with urban design keeping buildings with good conditions. Thus block-by-block the entire Fanci Bazar area can be revitalized. Public parks, multi-level parking garages, public toilets, garbage bins, etc. must be provided in all developed projects.

In this urban renewal process, negotiations between the government and the landowners are most important. The property owners must get the relocated property of equal or greater value than the properties they are vacating from. The other option is to outright purchase properties block by block and give preference to the property owners to purchase properties in a redeveloped block. Utmost caution must be taken against fraud, bribery and corruptions.

Impacts of the Project

The jail area development is going to be a magnet project attracting business and customers. Several miles surrounding the project will have impact of high traffic and congestion. A technical study should be done to assess the traffic impacted roads. An impact mitigation plan must be prepared and implemented before the super magnet is opened.

It will also create tremendous demand for electricity, communication lines, water, drainage, sewage, solid waste collection and disposal, car parking and pedestrian walkways. The burden of traffic control, security, and cleaning crew will increase accordingly.

The demand and value of the neighboring properties will increase. A development levy may be assessed on the properties in the vicinity and the proceeds may be used to improve the streets.

Overall if this project is successful, it will be a great example to follow in other parts of Guwahati such as Pan Bazar, Ujan Bazar, Chandmari, Dispur, Paltan Bazar,

Maligaon, etc. and in other cities of India. Therefore, the authority in charge of this project also has the moral obligation to be successful and exemplary.

RIVERSIDE DEVELOPMENT

Guwahati is on the bank of Brahmaputra River. There are beautiful spots all along the river. Many riverside parks can be developed. The most beautiful sites which are accessible to general public are: from Bhubaneswari Temple on the top of Kamakhya Hills, river beach next to Fanci Bazar, and Umananda from Kachari ghat to Latasil field. It can be extended for miles up to Chandrapur.

Area around Bhubaneswari Temple should be developed at different terrace levels, with stairs and guardrails. It has to be landscaped, with garden structures, picnic sheds, public toilets, and drinking water facilities. Car parking also has to be provided. Plumeria (*gulanci*) trees with beautiful flowers and fragrance is native to Kamakhya Hill. The streets of Waikiki beach, Honolulu, Hawaii are adorned with these trees and were taken from India, which must be from Assam. Tourists will appreciate lines of *gulanci*.

The river beach and bank from Kamakhya to Fatasil field could be developed into a beautiful public park. Residence of the Chief Justice and other Government structures occupying very large lots may be used for park facilities. Retaining wall should be built in certain parts of the beach next to the road and develop a landscaped public park with garden sheds, bandstands, stalls, toilets, drinkable water, restaurants and car parking. There should be access to the sandy beach and boats.

Restoration and recreational development projects should be taken up for Deepor Beel, Chola Beel, Silsako Beel, Tepar Beel, Basistha River, Bharalu River, and wetlands in and around metropolitan area. Currently all hills are under attack by squatters and land fillers. Legal and illegal occupation of these natural resources is a real threat. Animal habitats should be protected and recreational parks should be developed.

GOVERNMENT OWNED LANDS AND PROPERTIES

All government owned land and property should be evaluated for conservation, demolition, putting to higher value uses, appropriateness of location, and relocation. Urban renewal of government properties could bring efficiency, and beautify the city. Old structures were built spaciously and now occupying very valuable lands. Land selling proceeds may produce enough money to relocate functions and construct new facilities.

RENEWAL OF EXISTING DEVELOPMENTS

Old developments should be corrected and new developments should follow careful planning.

Guwahati is a city of chaos. It is interesting to notice how absence of urban planning can adversely effect the sociology of the citizens. The city is a goldmine to sale things at very high profit and get rich quickly by illegal means. This has led to land buying fringy and construction at exorbitant price. Number of automobile, motorcycle, buses, auto rickshaws, and other vehicles have increased tremendously. The city is rapidly growing beyond the capacity of the authorities to handle the situations. Construction moratorium may be considered until detail planning in completed. Thoughtful planning can modify social behaviors.

Figure 11.2 illustrates one part of the city of Guwahati, section by section the entire city should be reviewed for improvement and urban renewal. Even new developments are not well planned and need improvements.

After the Master Plan was adopted in 1960s narrow roads 3.7 m to 4.7 m wide were allowed. These are now called lanes or golies. In fact permanent settlements were granted on the right of way of many wide roads, which existed before the master plan. The Zoo Road, G.S. Road, and Gopinath Bordoloi Road have been made

Figure 11.2

Source: EN-GEO Consultancy and Research Centre, Guwahati

two lanes in each direction with a barrier in between. But parked cars, auto, carts, garbage dumps, building materials, hawkers, city buses, etc, occupy the left lane. There are no right turn lanes. Any traffic trying to take right turn has to wait and block the right lane until the vehicle can take right turn. Moreover, every one tries to get ahead by forcing his way. Pedestrians also cross the roads all the time. But there are no pedestrian crossing designed. There is no public urinal. By necessity they urinate on the roadside. Imagine how long it will take to drive your dear one to hospital or an ambulance to arrive hospital in case of emergency. It is dangerous to drive or to walk. It creates unhygienic condition, mental tension, and slows down traffic to crawl. For how many years one can take this tension. It affects mental health and temperament.

Public transportation is poor. Buses are packed. Rickshaws are the only affordable option but dangerous to ride and it creates traffic problems. Taxis and auto rickshaws demand very high fare.

Street shopping enhances this problem further. Shops are permitted in front of residences and offices in violation of zoning principle of segregation of land use. Since there are no organized parking spaces "no parking rule" is not enforceable. The property owners make Rs.4,000 or more per month for a small stall abutting the street in addition to *pugry* money. Most shopkeepers make Rs.20,000 and up a month. Even a vegetable seller will pay Rs. 2,000 per month for an open space 2.4 m × 2.4 m and will make Rs.8,000 or more per month, keeping the shop open from 4 pm to 9 pm. Plenty of money is being made at the expense of public health and safety. Some people go to the busy streets for socializing and some others find a perfect place for pick pocketing or planting a bomb. Some police make money for traffic violations. In case of an accident, the vehicle will be taken away to a Police Station and the vehicle owner will be at the mercy of the police and subject to bribe. He has to spend lot of money and time to get the vehicle back. Therefore, accidents are not reported. Both parties will settle accidents on the spot. It can be a very aggravating experience.

Residential areas have 3.7 m or 4.7 m wide roads called lanes with open drains, and potholes on the roads have reduced the effective road width. Two cars cannot pass; pedestrians have to stand on someones driveway to let a car pass. Emergency vehicles and garbage trucks cannot even enter those lanes. Only few houses have green space. Most of them maximized ground coverage. Some do not have car parking space in the premises, and therefore, park on the narrow lanes. There is no park and playgrounds for physical activities. Social contacts are less because of lack of community facilities. Limitations of physical and mental expressions has produced a lethargic and sick society.

The following are suggestions for social change and urban renewal: Big problems need drastic solutions. The basic financing principle is "those who create a need must pay for it". The shops, offices, and residents have created the need for parking and wider roads, therefore, they must pay for it. At least they must give land without compensation for road widening. For multi-level parking garages in business areas, the business owners or property owners must contribute to the cost of construction and land acquisition. After construction, the Municipal Corporation should have the obligation of maintenances or lease out. Guwahati's traffic problems cannot be solved until the shops are removed from all roadsides and shops are moved to confined shopping centers.

Shops and Streets

1. The number of shops and shopping space are severely in short supply. Organized shopping centers must be developed. The property owners can make more money in commercial land use than any other land use. This will work as counter magnets to street shopping.
2. Streets are no place for shopping. It interferes with the traffic and it is unhygienic. Existing shops should be relocated in off the road large shopping centers with parking, public toilets, garbage collection facilities, and protective gates for safety against vandalism and other attacks. Measures should be taken such that property owners cannot rent out thus vacated shops.
3. Small shopping centers may be allowed provided the entire lot is for shopping with parking facilities, public toilets, and garbage collection facility. No stall should be allowed on street frontage of property.
4. Neighborhood convenient shopping centers at distances of half a kilometer from each other should be encouraged without shop front opening to the streets and built on the entire lot.
5. Existing shopping streets may be allowed to continue provided streets are closed for traffic during shopping hours, designated parking spaces and sanitary facilities are made available, with lighting and landscaping.
6. Off the street taxi and auto parking stands should be constructed every km. apart.
7. One or two wide lanes with a barrier from the left driving lane should be made for city buses.
8. In established commercial areas such as Fanci Bazar, Pan Bazar, Plaltan Bazar, etc., four level parking garages without lifts or five or more level parking garages with lifts should be constructed with the money raised from storeowners.

For residential area renewal, the following are suggestions:

1. Each residential neighborhood should be examined individually for road widths, stormwater drainage, green space for play and recreation, community facilities, schools, convenient shopping, library, post office, water supply, sewer, and electricity needs. These should be provided with active participation and donation of lands by public where it is applicable.
2. First priority should be widening of roads. The neighborhoods where public agree to donate land for roads without compensation, should be taken first for road widening projects. Minor thorough fare roads or lanes should have minimum 9.1 m and roads with dead ends shall have minimum 7.3 m width. Incentive may be given to tear down existing walls and rebuild walls along roads without cost to the property owner and with project money.
3. Make detail improvement plans for each residential area with the help of GIS maps. Make cost estimates, find funding source, and execute. Once one or two areas are thus improved, other areas will follow.
4. Slum clearance and settlement of slum dwellers may be taken at the same time.
5. Incompatible land uses should be removed and resettled in compatible areas.
6. Projects should be taken to resettle and evict settlers from hills and government land. Hills must be restored as recreational areas for the public, to preserve ecology, and encourage beautification.

POOR INFRASTRUCTURE

Road conditions are already described above.

1. Water Supply – Potable water is extremely scarce. Municipal water supply is irregular. Sometime water is supplied for an hour or two. Most of the time there is no water for several days. In the outskirts there is no municipal water supply. Most people spend Rs. 1 lakh or more to install a deep tubewell. Some digshallow wells and get contaminated water. Others depend on neighbors for water. Water from deep tubewells has iron and not fit for drinking and washing clothe. Water trucks sale drinking water of unknown quality. Every family boils water for drinking. Overhead water tanks and water pumps are everywhere. People spend thousands of rupees for their own water supply and yet do not get potable water. Not enough water to flush toilets.

   People are ready to pay high water connection fee and fee on water uses. The great Brahmaputra River is there to provide abundant water. Hilltops can facilitate water plants and water supply by gravity force. There are specialists to design and construct water supply plants. Funding sources are also available. Yet there is no leadership and will power to start a water plant.

2. Sanitary Waste – Everybody has septic tank but no drain field. Septic tank and bathroom waste water go to open drains. Therefore, Guwahati smells foul. During storm polluted water floods road, homes and business.
3. Stormwater Drainage – discussed in Chapter 12.
4. Electricity – It is again very unreliable. Power shuts off every day several times. People who can afford depend on inverters, or generator. Each inverter costs more than Rs. 9,000. Those who cannot afford use kerosene lamps or candles. Industries, hospitals, and students suffer the most. The consumption is increasing but the State Electricity Board is unable to supply it.

GOOD NEWS GUWAHATI!

The Central Government awarded a grant-in-aid of Rs. 3,174 crores under the Jawaharlal Nehru National Urban Renewal Mission to Guwahati in August 2006. The Infrastructure Development Corporation of Assam Ltd. (IDCA) has been formed to do the development works in Guwahati. IDCA is a joint venture of Guwahati Metropolitan Development Authority (GMDA) and Infrastructure Leasing and Financial Services Ltd (ILFS). The IDCA is taking up the following projects for the entire GMDA Area.

1. Water, sewage, and drainage
2. River front beautification
3. City roads development
4. Mass traffic transportation
5. Solid waste management, and
6. Urban renewal and slum clearance.

According to IDCA, bids are invited from international firms for preparation of detail project reports. On approval of project reports, the Government of India will release the money. International firms also will do execution of projects. It is expected that excellent quality work will be done and the money will be well spent without corruption and wastage.

It is a great news for Guwahati, the primary city of the northeastern states of India, that some infrastructures improvements are coming. It is expected that Guwahati will see some improvements by the year 2010.

12

Solutions to Drainage Problems in Guwahati

Chronic flooding during monsoon is one of the most talked about hot issues besides traffic congestion, potable water scarcity, and power shortage in Guwahati and other cities in India. Drainage problem poses a serious health issue in addition to property damage and inconvenience. Rainwater runoff, getting mixed with contaminated water from drains, service latrines and septic tank effluents, flood homes and streets. This spreads waterborne diseases. There has been lack of foresightedness and inaction by authorities having jurisdiction over development. Most of the new settlers in Guwahati are in a land exploitation mission and are insensitive to drainage needs. Virtually unregulated encroachment of urban sprawl into the traditional wetlands appears to be the primary cause of this chaotic mess of inadequate drainage. A scientific understanding of the problem and formulation of solutions would not be too difficult engineering feats. However, the past mistakes are going to cost hundreds of crores of rupees of public fund.

UNDERSTANDING THE DRAINAGE PROBLEMS

The State of Assam is known for very heavy rainfall. Average annual rainfall in Assam is 73.4" or 1864 millimeters. The monsoon season is from May to September, and the dry season is from December to February. Average annual rainfall in Guwahati is 71.6" or 1819 millimeters. During the peak of the wet season in June and July, Guwahati receives an average of 13.4" or 340 millimeters of rainfall each month. This is a tremendous amount of water to drain. In the early days, the presence of the vast expanses of wetlands around the city served as the sponge to absorb storm runoff, and the sloughs provided the pathways for conveying flood waters to the nearest river. In addition, the wetland vegetations like water hyacinth acted as filter for pollutants, and provided important habitat to aquatic wildlife.

The robust urbanization during the past four decades and associated landfill of wetlands, sloughs and reservoirs have led to virtual disappearance of all flood water retaining areas. The deforestation and uncontrolled land cut of the hills resulted in clogging of the natural drainage system by mud washed from hills. The hills in and around Guwahati further aggravate the drainage problem by swiftly rolling down the rainwater to the plains. Flooding is not confined to low lying areas only. Localized flooding occurs on high lands along Gopinath Bordoloi Road, Zoo Road, A.T. Road, etc. because water has no place to go.

In undeveloped land under the climatic conditions of Assam, rainwater in excess of 40 percent is evaporated and absorbed by plants and vegetation (evapo-transpiration), about 25 percent goes into shallow ground, about 25 percent infiltrate deeper into ground, and 10 percent become surface runoff and collect in natural reservoirs. As places become urbanized, the buildings, roads, driveways, parking lots and many other things are built. The natural ground becomes increasingly impervious for water. When the impervious surface increase to 75 percent or more of the ground area (Guwahati has exceeded this percentage), these ratios change to approximately: 30 percent evapo-transpiration, 10 percent to shallow infiltration, 5 percent to deep infiltration, and 55 percent become surface runoff. As the surface runoff increased from 10 percent to 55 percent, the effective equivalence of drainage and reservoirs should have been expanded 5.5 times from the 1960 level of natural drainage and reservoirs when there were no significant drainage problems. Instead, the existing drainage and reservoirs have shrunk in Guwahati.

The topographic features of low lying areas have also contributed to another drainage menace. We should not forget that about 9 square miles of Guwahati along Bharalu river basin is below the annual peak flood stages of the river Brahmaputra. Therefore, during the periods when the mighty Brahmaputra is in spate, its high tail water conditions do not facilitate urban drainage by gravity flow. The Bahini River becomes Bharalu River after crossing Assam Trunk Road and pours more water to the Bharalu river basin. Bahini can be diverted to Basista river near Dispur.

Even the Basista area, which is at higher elevation, gets waist deep flood water. The Basista River and the Bahini River, which originated in Khasi Hills, are not controlled and floods the Basista area. A beautiful lake may be built along Assam and Khasi Hills boarder to retain flood water and make a recreational park.

STORMWATER MANAGEMENT PLAN

A comprehensive stormwater management plan must be devised. Professional civil engineers are well-qualified and should be consulted on quantification of storm runoff and design of conveyance and disposal facilities. A stormwater management plan for Guwahati must include wetland preservation. Several measures discussed here must be taken into consideration. Adversity can be turned into unique opportunity. Drainage solutions can be incorporated into an overall beautification plan for Guwahati. Some unique solutions are suggested here.

Regulatory control

The primary focus of a sound stormwater management master plan for Guwahati should begin with the establishment of a regulatory framework to curb the wanton encroachment onto the wetlands. The building permit systems for residential, commercial or industrial land developments can rely on a simple principle: the volume and rate of post-land development runoff from a site should not exceed the site's pre-development volume and rate of runoff. The additions of the impervious areas increased volume of runoff water create the need for water retention on site by structural measures. Strict zoning regulations are needed (a) to stop construction in wetlands, and (b) to reduce lot coverage by buildings and pavements. Lot-coverage must be reduced in undeveloped lots such that more open land around buildings are available for water infiltration into the ground. The realm of regulatory control of land development in the wetland corridors can also be extended to river floodplains. Land filling encroachment in the floodplain squeezes the flow way, and can cause significant backwater effects on the riparian areas upstream. Guwahati and the State can certainly benefit from such a regulatory control.

Contain stormwater from the hills and develop lakes and recreational parks

Dams cum roads around all hills in and around Guwahati should be built to contain stormwater from the hills and create lakes at the foothills, between or below dams and hills. The lakes and land around should be planned as recreational parks. Playgrounds, picnic spots, hiking trails, car parking, tree plantation and landscaping should be developed. This will reduce or eliminate surface water runoff and flooding downhill. This will also help the process of evapo-transpiration and air purification. When this concept is accomplished, Chandmari, Pub-Sarania, Gandhi Basti, and Silpukhuri will see immediate benefits. Mud wash and flooding will be tremendously eliminated. Same benefits will occur around all other hills.

All hills must be preserved at its natural state as public parks and no human settlements should be permitted. The lakes can be as beautiful as Ward Lake in Shillong, Meghalaya, or Haflong Lake. From the Kamla Nehru Park (formerly Hanging Garden) on Malabar Hill, Mumbai, you get a wonderful view of the Arabian Sea, Marine Drive and Mumbai City. The Brindavan Gardens in the Krishnarajasagar near Mysore is one of the most fabulous gardens in the world, compared to the gardens of Versailles in France. Guwahati can have many romantic hill top gardens and parks like Kamla Nehru Park and Brindavan Gardens overlooking the majestic Brahmaputra, and the city. Parks can be developed on ten hills: Nilachal (Kamakhya) Hill, Kharghuli Hill, Sarania Hill, Narengi Hill, Japorighog Hill, Narakasur Hill, Sonaighuli Hill, Fatasil Hill, Silapahar Hill, and Agiathori Hill. In Poban Park, Bangalore and Comatee Bag, Barodra local artists sing and play bands in Saturdays and Sundays free of any charge. These parks will enhance local culture, tourist attraction, and provide much needed recreational facilities for the citizens away from the congested city.

Preserve wetland and develop canals, lakes, and recreational parks

The remaining wetlands in and around the city can be acquired under public ownership for development of drainage canals and lakes for retention of stormwater. These water retention and conveyance facilities can be aesthetically pleasing elements of regional recreational parks, and preserved habitat for fish and wildlife. Wetlands replenish ground water table, biodegrade pollutants, nurture plants and aquatic life, and purify air. It will help solving drainage problem. Guwahati can be transformed to a lustrous place to live with the settings of green hills, green wetlands, reflecting waters of the lakes and canals, and recreational parks. Other added benefits are: beautification by landscaping and reduction of mental stress by attending to the plants and vegetation. Such a scheme is possible and desirable for which the citizens of Guwahati will be proud of. I am not aware of such examples of canal and lakeside developments in India. I hope Guwahati becomes the first proud city to have such unique drainage solution with city beautification.

Bharalu River basin, Deepor Beel, and other water logged areas in and around Guwahati should be included in this scheme. Some people think that channeling Guwahati's drainage water to Deepor Beel and then to Kukurmuta and Brahmaputra River is a solution. The drainage water contains pollutants, which will cause environmental damage to Deepor Beel. The drainage canal must be separated from Deepor Beel in such event.

Deepor Beel is a magnificent raw diamond waiting to be cut. It must be restored for natural habitats, as a beautiful recreational park, water sports and fishery. All developments in the Beel corridors should be regulated with strict control, or dealt with a moratorium until environmental consequences of land development are thoroughly examined. A Deepor Beel beautification plan should be finalized. For inspiration, some excellent examples of wetland developments are narrated below:

The Grand Canal and gondolas of Venice, Italy attract tourists from all over the world. The city of Venice existed since 6th century but beginning the 14th century, Venice ruled the world in maritime trade and commerce. The merchants became rich, powerful, and famous. They could afford best building materials such as rare African marbles, solid gold mosaics, emeralds, rubies and best architecture for their buildings. Venice is an island in the Adriatic Sea, almost attached to the mainland. The Grand Canal and its 46 side canals form the major system of transportation in Venice. *New Yorker* magazine humorist Robert Benchley wrote: "Streets Full of Water. Please Advice". The Grand Canal is 228' to 120' wide and 9' average depth. On both sides of the canal there are 200 palaces and 10 churches constructed with Gothic and Moorish architectural elements. The Grand Canal is a necklace of architectural gems. Venice is a living museum of the past. Venice was depicted in famous paintings and literatures. William Shakespeare, Mark Twain, Lord Byron, Robert Browning, Henry James, Ernest Hemmingway, and others included Venice in their famous writings. Mark Twain described the Grand Canal and the gondola as "free and graceful as a serpent in its glide" and the "gentlest, pleasantest locomotive we have ever known." Henry James called the Grand canal "best of all noble waterways". The activities in the canals are exciting: water bus called *vaporetto*, fruit and vegetable boats, religious processions by boats, carnival pageants, dinner boats, party boats, gondola wedding barges, restaurants, celebration of some event, fishermen back from the Adriatic Sea, and sea gulls screaming above. The area around Rialto Bridge remained as the financial district as was portrayed in Merchant of Venice by William Shakespeare.

This idea of canal landscape has undergone further refinements in the United States. Abbot Kinney, a wealthy tobacco merchant and a world traveler, dreamed of a 'Venice in America' in the 1890's. He acquired marshland west of Los Angeles, California. His vision was to develop a canal and have housing, amusement park, hotels and restaurants, yacht racing, swimming pool, amphitheater, etc. He hired a surveyor for canal network, which are 70 feet wide and about 16 miles long. He also hired a landscape architect, architects, and a town planner in 1904. He was ready to construct buildings and sale lots. The grand opening was on 4th of July 1905. Initially there was disbelief and opposition to this project but it turned out to a booming development with expensive homes and good business. The Grand Canal in Venice, Italy has very little green space. Kinney's development integrated buildings with landscape, restaurants, entertainments, and high quality homes. It became a lively place full of excitements.

San Antonio River in San Antonio, Texas, runs through the Alamo, a historic site. The river is narrow, about the size of Bharalu River in Guwahati. Both sides of the river are beautifully landscaped integrating expensive homes and business. Tourist attractions like boat rides, river walk, restaurants and gift shops are provided. After a visit to the Alamo Museum, every tourist goes to the riverside for a pleasant experience.

The State of Florida is full of wetlands and coastal marshes. However, the growth management laws of Florida regulate stormwater runoff control in hundreds of housing and commercial development projects by incorporating canals, man-made lakes and newly created wetlands, preserving the natural landscape to a great extent.

None of the above examples can be duplicated. But these examples can inspire us to do something fantastic. This is an example of how adversity can be turned into unique opportunity. We need the will and endeavor.

Stormwater retention ponds and lakes

During heavy rains localized flooding and flooding downstream is common. The excess runoff generated by the reduction of natural storage areas must be compensated by adding stormwater retention ponds and/or small lakes. When a pond or lake is full, water can run into the drainage system. This attenuates the peak volume of storm runoff to be carried through the drainage system and makes the drainage economical.

There are added benefits: (a) The first flush of rain washes away pollution from the air and land surface. This polluted water is settled and refined to a certain degree in the ponds and lakes before being entered into the drainage system and disposed off to a larger lake or a river. (b) Ponds and lakes are landscaped to beautify with shrubs, flowers, fountain, ducks, fish and walk. It provides space for daily walk and exercise. Certain kinds of fish eats mosquito larva and keep mosquito under control. (c) Water front properties are desirable and can increase property value substantially.

In existing developed areas where localized flooding is a problem, digging ponds or small lake is a viable solution. Land need to be acquired in a suitable location for this purpose. New developments must be required to build retention ponds within the development. Size of pond is determined by the volume of runoff of a design storm event and water percolation capacity of soil based on the characteristics of the changed land use of the new development.

In the United States the implementation of the above practices are promulgated by strict land development codes. Any land development schemes such as: residential subdivisions, commercial and industrial developments, are required to submit drainage study and stormwater management plan. In Florida, new developments must provide water quality retention treatment for the first inch of runoff, and accommodate on-site retention of the runoff volume of a three-day duration storm of 25-year return period. Environmentally sensitive wetlands are prohibited from development or development is limited with certain conditions. In most states, unavoidable destruction of wetlands is to be mitigated by the creation of an equivalent area of new wetland off-site.

Underground drainage system

The existing drains under footpaths are inefficient, dangerous to pedestrians, difficult and expensive to maintain, unhygienic, and ugly. The open drains are often places for garbage disposal, foul smelling, ill maintained, and harmful to public health and safety. The absence of good drainage and sanitary sewer are the biggest factors in reducing the quality of urban living in Guwahati.

In existing developments, construction of large concrete or iron drains under ground seems to be the practical solution. Only one citywide connected underground drainage system is neither feasible nor practical considering the terrain. There should be several systems at different parts of the city. Since spaces for above ground reservoirs are not feasible in the city, stormwater can be collected in under ground concrete tanks, treated to certain degree, and disposed to stormwater lakes or rivers by pumping. The city of Chicago has a large underground tunnel and reservoir of this type for storage and treatment of stormwater before being discharged to Lake Michigan. Public Parks or parking garages can be built over underground tanks.

A sluice gate and a small pumping facility exist at Bharalumukh to drain out stormwater from Bharalu River. The capacity of this facility need to be increased and many more pumping stations should be installed at other suitable locations. This may be a less expensive solution than digging canal to Kukurmuta.

Large-scale pumping is possible. For example: a part of Boston City, Cambridge, and neighboring towns are below the tidal water level of the Atlantic Ocean. The Charles River, which runs between Boston and Cambridge, was once connected to the Atlantic Ocean. A dam was built to stop the tidal wave, and water from the river is pumped out regularly to the ocean such that these cities are not flooded. The elevation of the city of New Orleans is below the tidal stages of the Mississippi River. Massive pumping of stormwater and dikes have been the only solutions for the major portion of New Orleans. However, hurricane Katrina devastated New Orleans in 2004 and caused billions of dollars of property damage.

Figure 12.1

Hill Development for Recreation

As depicted in the figure, stormwater can be collected at the bottom of the hill to prevent flooding down the hill. It can be made as an excellent recreational facility for the public.

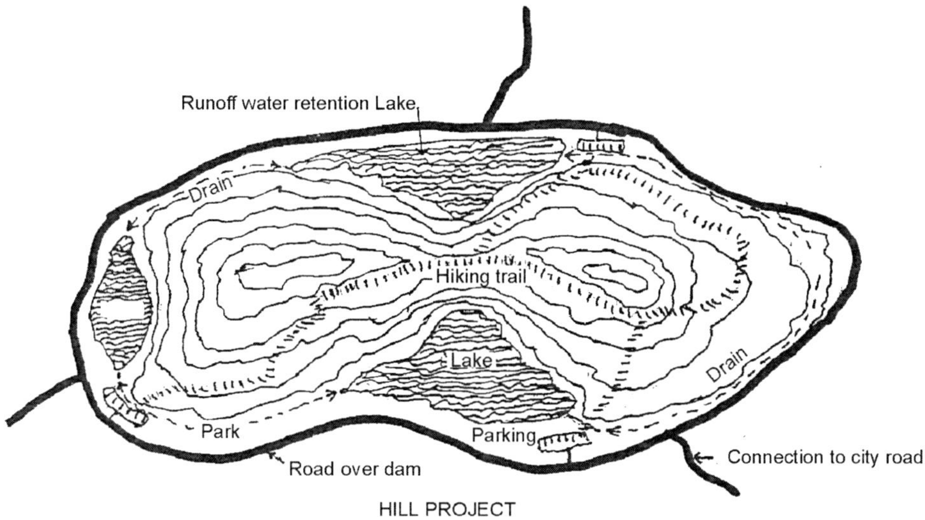

Figure 12.2

Wetland Development

Wetlands should be preserved through intelligent environmental design. It should be used for recreational purpose and with limited residential and commercial development.

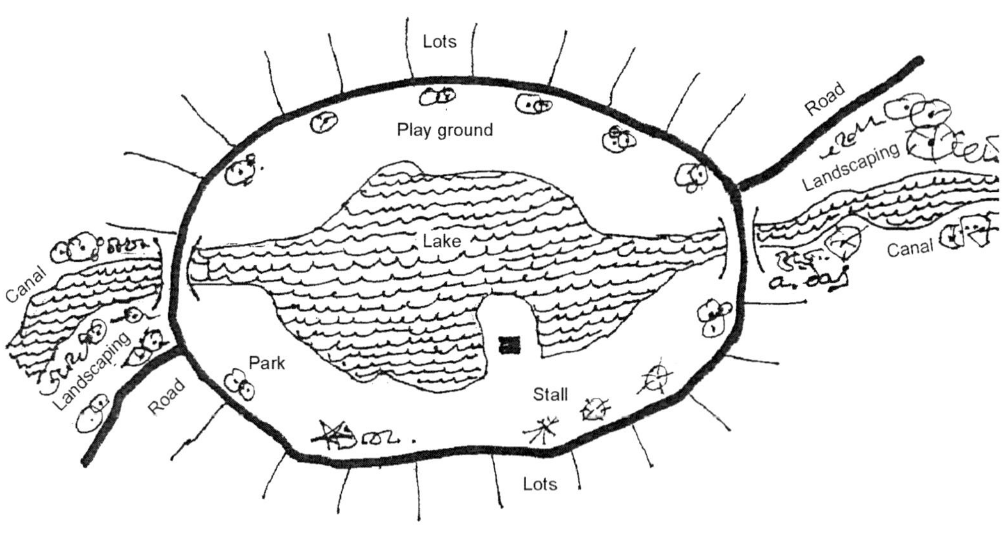

Source: Developed by author.

Public education and awareness

Last, but not the least, greater public awareness to precautionary measures against public health and safety hazards of drainage problems should be an integral part of a sound stormwater management program. Stormwater control measures can start at home. Regular cleaning of the roof drains and gutters; proper care of the yard drain connections to the storm sewers are fundamental homeowner responsibilities. And above all some common civic sense of the general citizenry devoid of our litter-bug habits, just not using the storm drain as the garbage dumping ground, would go a long way in alleviating this public health and safety menace.

> Do not plunder the treasures endowed by nature,
> Do not mutilate the hills,
> Do not fill up wetland,
> Do not destroy the habitat of the wild creature.
> Nature is sacred. Nature will rebut.
> Nature will make us pay for our greed.
> Preserve nature with tender loving care.

13

Managing Floods with Conservation of Flood Water in Lakes and Wetlands

Assam has attempted to control flood water since the 1950s, spending thousands of crores of rupees. The flood control strategy has been to drain, not conserve flood water. The current strategy of flood control involves the systematic construction of embankments along the tributaries to contain flood water within the riverbanks. The Brahmaputra and its tributaries are one of the most silt producing river system in the world. Containment of flood waters within the river channels results in virtual raising of the riverbeds and reduction of the flood conveyance capacities. The embankments are not designed with adequate seepage protection measures and susceptible to breach frequently. I suggest a flood water conservation strategy. Assam must accept the fact that it is a high rainfall (*jalatan*) area and any planning must consider flood mitigation and not flood prevention. Flooding is a reality in Assam and we must learn to utilize and manage this seeming catastrophe.

We know the nature of water. (A) It flows in gravity. (B) It is life giver in gentle state. (C) It is a destroyer when in fury. Recognize the violence of nature. We cannot fight against gravity. We desire the life giving quality. All we can strive for is to reduce the fury. So our strategy should be to reduce the fury and not to eliminate flood.

CURRENT STRATEGY: FLOOD CONTROL BY DRAINING FLOOD WATER

The ancient Chinese built levees to raise the banks of the Huang He (Yellow River) on the supposition that the confined river would then deepen its channel to contain

the maximum flow. The result, however, was a rising of the riverbed because the sedimentary deposits of alluvial soil, previously distributed over the entire flood plain during annual flooding, was confined to the river bottom. In 4000 years the level rose as high as 70 feet above the surrounding plain. The Yellow River then broke the levees, killing millions of people. Economic loss in the 1998 floods in China amounted to US$ 32 billion.

Floods in the Mississippi valley have demonstrated that levees alone do not provide sufficient protection against flooding. The great flood of 1993, overflowed the banks of the Mississippi river, Missouri river, and tributaries, damaging levees, dams, and waterways, inundating 8 million acres of land, and damaging 12 million acres of cropland. Total damage in this flood was estimated at US$12-16 billion. The U.S. also spends millions of dollars annually dredging the rivers.

Similar flood control failure stories are available from all over the world. The Brahmaputra is one of the great rivers in the world and its story of failure is also as great as Yellow River and the Mississippi. In Assam the flood control effort is responsible for drying out lakes (*beels*) and converting the lakes to agricultural land, settling millions of people on this land, giving employment to hundreds of engineers and thousands of laborers from out of the state, and reducing the devastation of floods in many villages. These large projects also presented an opportunity for corruption of Assam's meager state funds.

The negative side of this strategy has been loss of cultural heritage, ecological disaster, shortage of fish, loss of livelihood for fishermen, and loss of public funds without producing any permanent solution. The price we are paying for an unwise flood control program is yet to be determined in terms of economic and permanent damage to the environment and ecology. The flood control projects in Assam failed in several different ways:

(1) *Technical overlook*: The futile efforts to contain flood waters within the embankments have led to the loss of the riverrine floodplains, and allowed silt and

sediment to raise the riverbeds. Thus, water carrying capacity of the rivers is reduced, channel configurations changed, and Mother Nature has eroded land on both sides of the river to make more room for flowing water. Flood fury increased and created havoc, and broke embankments. Sedimentary yield of the River Brahmaputra is second highest in the world next to the Yellow River in China. The sediment factor was overlooked. The flood control measures failed.

(2) *Loss of cultural heritage*: My grandfather told stories of hunting deer. During flood times they used to hunt deer by throwing banana plants from boats to the deer's antlers to keep them from moving or escaping. In 1950s and 1960s, huge fish were available in Assamese lakes. When a man carried fish hanging from his *banka* (a bamboo stick) the tails touched the ground. *Kaoi* fish were palm sized. Mallard ducks, whisling teals (Sarali ducks), cranes, adjutant storks (*bartokola or hargila)*, and other birds were plentiful. Early in the morning *barali, chitol, naora*, turtles and many other varieties of fish were caught by spear fishing in the beels. Lotuses and lilies were also gathered. People learned how to boat and swim in the flood water. Fish was also caught by nets, fishing hooks, *pola, jakoi, chepa* (fish traps) and by draining water from ponds in primitive way.

However the fishermen have lost their trade as the *beels* shoal or dry out. The farmers cannot plant rice in silt covered fertile land. The birds no longer sing. The lotus does not bloom. The cranes do not nest because the tall trees and fish are gone. Bells ringing from the necks of water buffaloes are no longer heard. You cannot rent a boat to visit your sister across the lake. Newcomers are now settled on land recovered by drying out the lake. This cultural heritage is now gone. Villages look grim. Cannot recognize the village or the lake.

(3) *Ecological disaster*: The fields are now dry except in the rainy season. Fields are no longer suitable for *baodhan* (rice grown in wetlands), a variety of rice crop grown during monsoon season. Assam had plentiful fish but it is fast disappearing. *Garua*, the giant fish weighing about 300 pounds, is now extremely rare in the Brahmaputra River. Birds and flowers from lakes and rivers disappeared. Assam used to have about 200 varieties of fish but some are now extinct or severely threatened due to loss of habitat and unrestricted fishing during the breeding season. The wetlands are destroyed. There are rules prohibiting fishing during breeding season but rules are not enforced.

The adjutant stork is the largest wetland bird species on earth. They completely disappeared in Myanmar, Vietnam, and Sundarban and are becoming extinct in Assam as well. According to Dr. P. K. Saikia, Reader of Animal Ecology and Wildlife Biology, Guwahati University, there were about 140 adjutant stork nests in Assam with the largest group of 40 nests found in Doulasal, Nalbari District. Due to lack of food, the storks scavenge from garbage dumps and get sick. Storks eat as much as 15 to 20 pounds of fish each day, can fish only in shallow water, and nest on tall trees like *Kadam, Simalu* and *Satiana*. The disappearance of wetland and tall trees are making the storks disappear as well.

Am I the next to be extinct?

Another eye sore is the encroachment of Kajiranga Sanctuary by human settlement. It was very unwise to settle a village between the National Highway and Kajiranga animal and fish sanctuary and the occupiers must be resettled elsewhere.

(4) *Economic loss*: Besides thousands of crores of rupees on flood control projects, the government has lost crores by auctioning fishing rights in lakes, and several thousand fishermen lost their livelihoods. Assam's annual demand for fish is 273,000 tonnes, but production is 165,000 tonnes according to the State Fishery Department.[1] The remaining 108,000 metric tonnes or about 40 percent are supplied by Andhra Pradesh, Kolkata, Kanpur, and other place outside Assam. The price of fish in Guwahati is Rs.70 to Rs.250 per kilogram depending on the variety and size. Assuming an average suppliers price of Rs.40 per kilogram, Assam spends Rs. 432 crores per year to buy fish from outside the state. If all that fish was produced in Assam, the local economy would have been better off by Rs. 432 crores per year.

Where did they go from our lakes?

FLOOD WATER CONSERVATION STRATEGY: AN ALTERNATE SOLUTION

The basic method of flood control by construction of levees or embankments is not adequate. The following methods have been used in different countries in the last half a century. These methods are yet to be used in Assam.

1. Floodplain restoration and removal of structures is providing a partial solution in many countries. In Florida, U.S. for example, the once channelized Kissimmee River has been reverted to the original river of meanders, oxbows with enhanced floodplain storage and a rebounding ecology.
2. Lakes and wetlands are reclaimed and restored by digging deeper and using reservoirs of flood water. A recent study in the USA estimated that 0.4 hectares of wetland could store over 6,000 cubic meters of flood water. Vegetation also absorbs water and slows down the flow of water. The aquifers are recharged from the lakes and wetlands.
3. Giant dams are constructed in hilly terrain to store flood water and released during the dry season. Hydroelectric power plants are also built.
4. Floodways or artificial channels (*Jans* in Assam) are built to divert flood water.
5. Reforestation, soil conservation, fishery, and agro forestry are other methods of flood control.

MANAGE WATERSHEDS AND RESTORE LAKES

Lakes and watersheds can be re-engineered and vegetation should be allowed to grow. Each lake and watershed should have at least one inlet and one outlet from the nearest river. Flowing water is very important for vitality of the lake or watershed. Banks should be raised with a gentle grade. At highest flood level, the inlet(s) and outlet(s) should be closed to retain the water and the water used for irrigating the fields during the dry season. To maintain oxygen supply in the water and enhance beauty, fountains may be installed. Otherwise lakes and watersheds will turn into eutrophic or dead water bodies.

Lakes should have at least three zones. A littoral zone or area of shallow water for wading birds such as mallard ducks, cranes, and adjutant storks, which cannot fish in deep water. A sanctuary and nursery zone where fishing is prohibited should be created. Laying barbwire rolls or other means shall protect this zone. The rest of the lake may be open for fishing. There may be other zones for raising water buffalos (like *bathans*) and vegetable farms.

Lakes should be made SAROBARS by enhancing the beauty. The banks of the lakes should be planted with trees like *Kadam, Simalu, Satiana, Gulanchi, Bokul,*

Figure 13.1
Sarobar Concept of Flood Management

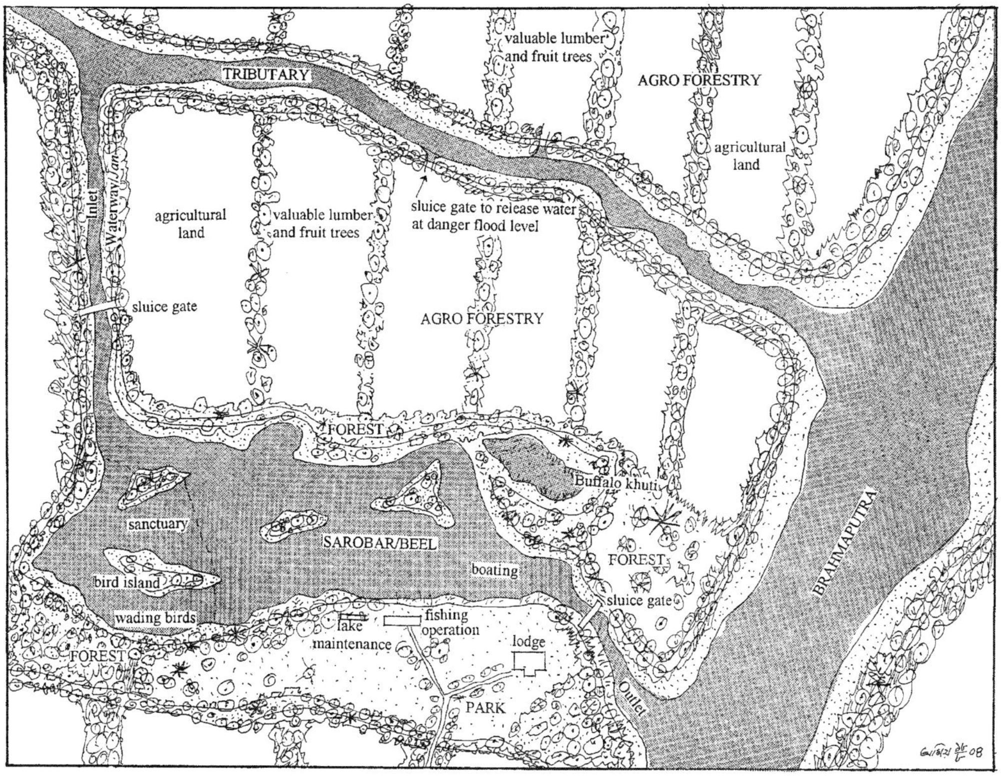

Not to Scale

etc.; the bank can be made a managed forest with wildlife; lotuses and lilies should be in the water; and planted islands for birds to nest should be created. Beautiful gardens, picnic spots, fishing facilities, boating, and lodges will increase tourism and add to the economy. Sarobar Concept of Flood Management is depicted in Figure 13.1.

FORESIGHT, WISDOM AND DETERMINATION

The Assam Legislative Assembly, concerned citizens, and citizens affected by any action of the legislature must be formed with foresight, wisdom, and determination in our flood management program. We must consider the following in our decision-making:

1. The land and resources are limited and must be used wisely for the benefit of present and future generations. Ecological and environmental concerns are real.
2. Human greed for land must be limited.

3. Agricultural employment is declining and will continue to decline as other employment opportunities open up. Mechanized agriculture will require less people and increase the production of fields; extensive agriculture will turn into intensive agriculture. It is therefore more important to have environmentally acceptable fields than vast fields with less productivity.
4. A balance of ecology and environment with human settlement is the desired development we strive for.

Having these understandings the modernized flood control methods should be implemented. The following steps must be taken.

1. A flood management plan must be devised based on modern understanding of the problems and solutions.
2. Land use regulations must be established to protect wetlands, rivers and lakes. It is unwise economically to give settlements in wetlands and then spend crores of rupees to repair or build homes the people loose every year. Human settlements should be allowed only in higher grounds above 50 year flood level. State Government should own Wetlands, rivers and lakes.
3. All schools and colleges should be designed and constructed on high grounds equipped with water, kitchen, toilet and bathing facilities which shall be used as emergency shelters during flood or any other emergency.

POTENTIAL ECONOMIC EFFECTS OF A FLOOD MANAGEMENT PROGRAM

The lake revitalization program has the potential to solve flood problems, increase employment opportunities, help the local economy, and attract tourists. Assam shall be able to export fish to other states and abroad. Currently fish demanded by Southeast Asian immigrants to the United States, are being imported from Bangladesh, Myanmar, and Thailand. Assam can grab a share of it.

In short, flood water is a gift and harnessing its power has great economic potential, perhaps even more than agriculture.

Let us make Assam the most beautiful state on earth with economic wellbeing, environmentally safe, and people consciousness. It can be done and let us make it happen.

Note

1. Sentinel, June 16, 2004.

Appendix

APPENDIX A:
THE ASSAM TOWN AND COUNTRY PLANNING ACT, 1959
ASSAM ACT II OF 1960
Received the assent of the President of India 6th February, 1960
Published in the Assam Gazette 17th February, 1960
As amended upto 1st of May 1985
(Compiled and formatted by Amiya Kumar Das, as no complete act with amendments and additions is available.)

CONTENTS

4. Resignation of non-official members.
5. Term of office.
6. Commencement of the term of office of non-official members.
7. Removal of non-official members.
8. Filing of casual vacancies.

Chapter IIA: Constitution of the Development Authority (November 1962 insertion)

8A. Constitution of the Authority
8B. Composition of the Authority
8C. Term of office and conditions of service of the Chairman and members of the Authority
8D. Functions and powers of the Authority
8E. Meeting of the Authority
8EE. Power of Chairman
8F. Temporary Association of persons with the Authority for particular purposes
8G. Staff of the Authority

Chapter III: Master Plan

9. Preparation of Master Plan.
10. Publication of the Master Plan.
11. Contents of the plan.
12. Implementation of the plan
13. Restrictions of use of land and buildings thereon after publication.
13A. Prohibition of registration in certain cases
14. Power of the State Government to modify the plan and regulation.

Chapter IV: Development Scheme

15. Preparation of the Development Scheme.
16. Publication of the Development Scheme.
17. Implementation of the Development Scheme.
18. Scope of the Development Scheme.
19. Amendments and alterations of the Development Scheme.

20. Power to revoke the Development Scheme.
21. Power the Authority to impose restrictions.

Chapter V: Streets and Lands Subdivisions

22. Width of public streets.
23. Power to prescribe street line.
24. Setting back buildings to the prescribed street line.
25. Acquisition of land within the line of street.
26. Acquisition of the remaining part of building and land after their portions within a Prescribed line of the street are acquired.
27. Subdivision of private land.
28. Plans accompanying notice.
29. Sanction with or without modification or refusal.
30. Layout not according to plan.

30A. Power to stop development

30B. Power of demolition of building

31. Penalty for violation.

Chapter VI: Acquisition of Land

32. Power of State Government to acquire land.
33. Proceeding for acquisition of land.
34. Disposing of land.
35. Provision of private negotiation before compulsory acquisition.
36. Payment to owner by adjustment.

Chapter VII: Compensation and Betterment

37. Right to compensation.
38. No right to compensation.
39. Power of Government to exclude compensation in certain cases.
40. Right of owner to require authority to acquire or purchase land.
41. Levy of betterment fee.
42. Appeal.

Chapter VIII: Appeals and Appellate Authority

43. Appointment of Appellate Authority.
44. Duties of the Appellate Authority.
45. Procedure of working of the Appellate Authority.
46. Right to appeal by recognized agent.
47. Protection of action taken under this Act.

Chapter IX: Finance

48. Development of fund.
49. Power to borrow.
50. Grant advance and loan.

50A. Levy of fees

50B. Resumption of site or building

50C. Audit of account of the Authority

Chapter X: Legal Proceedings

51. Penalty for breach of the provisions of the Master Plan or Scheme.
52. Power to execute works on failure to comply with notice.
53. Right of occupier to execute works in default of owner.
54. Procedure upon opposition to execution by occupier.
55. Recovery of cost of work by the occupier.
56. Penalty for obstructing contractor or removing marks.
57. Officers under the Act to be public servants.
58. Authority for prosecution.
59. Power of authority to institute proceedings, etc. and to take legal advice.

59A. Power to recover dues as an area of land revenue.

60. Bar to suits and prosecutions in certain cases.
61. Punishmcnt for malicious abuse of powers.
62. Registration of documents plans or map in connection with scheme.
63. Orders under the Act not to be questioned in any court.
64. Effect of orders inconsistent with other enactments.

Chapter XI: Miscellaneous Provisions

65. Service of notice.
66. Method of giving public notice.
67. Formal defects in assessments and demands.
68. Power and duties of police in respect of offences and assistance to Authorities.
69. Decision of disputes between Authorities.
70. Power to enter into land for inspection, etc.
71. Mode of proof of records of the Authority.
72. Power of Authority to make agreements.
73. Power of the State Government to make rules.
74. Power of the Authority to make byelaws.
75. Supersession of the Authority.

APPENDIX B:
THE ASSAM TOWN AND COUNTRY PLANNING ACT, 1959

An Act to provide for the development of the towns countrysides of the State of Assam

Preamble

Whereas it is expedient to provide for the development of the towns and the country sides of the state of Assam on sound planning principles with the object of securing proper sanitary conditions, to conserve and promote the public health, safety and general welfare of the people living therein;

It is hereby enacted in the Tenth Year of the Republic of India as follows:

CHAPTER I: PRELIMINARY

1. Short title, extent and commencement.
   (1) This Act may be called the Assam Town and Country Planning Act, 1959.
   (2) It shall extend to the whole of Assam excluding the Autonomous Districts:
   Provided that if any District Council desires that all or any of the provisions of this Act should apply to the Autonomous District concerned, a notification may be issued to that effect and this Act shall then extent to that Autonomous District subject to such exceptions or modifications as may be specified in the notification.
2. Definitions – In this Act, unless there is anything repugnant in the subject or context:
   (1) "Authority" shall mean the Local or Regional Authority by the State Government for the purpose of administering the Act. Unless otherwise appointed by the State Government, the Authority in the case of Municipal Areas shall be taken to mean the Municipal Board for the area constituted under the Assam Municipal Act, 1956(Assam Act XV of 1957).
   (2) "Advisory Council" means the Town and Country Planning Advisory Council constituted under Section 3 of this Act.
   (3) "Betterment Fee" means the fee prescribed in respect of an increase in the value of land resulting from the execution of a Development Scheme.
   (4) "Building" means any construction for whatsoever purpose and of whatsoever materials constructed and every part thereof, whether used as human habitat or not and includes plinth walls, chimney, drainage work, fixed platforms, verandah, balcony, cornice or projection, or part of a

building on anything affixed thereto or any walls, earth bank, fence or other construction enclosing or delimiting or intended to enclose or delimit any and or space.

(5) "Building Industrial" means a building which is wholly or predominantly as a warehouse, factory, distillery, iron foundry and all other buildings put to or be put to any use permitted in the zone by an authorized scheme applicable thereto.

(6) "Director" means Director of Town and Country Planning or any other officer appointed by the State Government.

(7) "Development" means the carrying out of building, engineering, mining or other operations in on or over the land or making of any material change in the use of any buildings or of land:

Provided that the following operations or use of land shall not be deemed for the purposes of this act to mean development of the land, that is to say

(a) the carrying out of works for the maintenance, improvement or other alteration of any buildings being works which affect only the interior of the building or which do not materially affect the use and the external appearance of the building;

(b) the carrying out by a local authority of any works required for the maintenance or improvement of road being works carried out on land within the boundaries of the road;

(c) the carrying out by any local authority any works for the purposes of inspecting, repairing or renewing any sewers, main pipes, cables or other apparatus, including the breaking open of any street or other land for that purpose;

(8) "Factory" means a place to which the provisions of the Indian Factories Act of 1934 or any amendment thereof shall apply.

(9) "Industrial Concern" means a commercial body e.g. Factory, workshop and a mill or any concern of similar nature where materials are manufactured, repaired, altered or processed.

(10) "Master Plan" means a plan as defined under section 9 and shall comprised of items (a) to (e) of section 11.

(11) "Occupier" includes any person paying or liable to pay rent or any portion of the rent of the land or building in respect of which the work is due or compensation or premium on account of the occupation of such land and building and also a rent free tenant.

(12) "Open Space" means any land whether enclosed or not on which not more than one-twentieth part is covered with buildings and whole of the

reminder has been laid out as a public garden or used for purposes of recreation or lies waste and unoccupied.

(13) "Prescribed" means prescribed by rules made under this Act.

(14) "Reconstituted plot" means a plot which is in any way altered by the making of a Development Scheme.

(15) "Road" means and includes any highway, street, lane, pathway, alley, passageway, carriage way, footway, square, bridge, whether private or public, whether thoroughfare or not, whether existing or proposed in any scheme and includes all bunds, channels, ditches, drains, culverts, sidewalks and traffic islands.

(16) "Scheme" means a development scheme and includes a plan or plans together with the descriptive matter if any relating to such a scheme.

(17) "Administrator" means an officer appointed by the State Government as such under proviso to subsection (1) of Section 8A of this Act to perform the functions and exercise the powers of the Development Authority as provided under Section 8A of this Act. (1985 Amendment)

(18) "Estate Officer" means a person appointed by the State Government as such to perform the functions of the Estate Officer. (1985 Amendment)

(19) "Transferee" means a person including a firm or other body of individuals, whether incorporated or not to whom a site or building is transferred in any manner whatsoever and includes his successors and assigns. (1985 Amendment)

CHAPTER II: CONSTITUTION OF THE ADVISORY COUNCIL

3. Constitution of the Town and Country Planning Advisory Council

(1) The State Government may constitute, by a notification in the Official Gazette, the Council consisting of the following members to advise the Government on matters referred to it:

(i)	Minister-in-charge of Town and Country Planning.	Chairman
(ii)	Director of the Town and Country Planning Department	Secretary
(iii)	Secretary, Town and Country Planning Department	Member
(iv)	Secretary, P.W.D. or his nominee *(1985 Amendment)*	Member
(v)	Secretary, Flood Control or his nominee *(1985 Amendment)*	Member
(vi)	Secretary, Health and Family Welfare Department or his nominee *(1985 Amend.)*	Member
(vii)	Secretary, Local Self-Government or his nominee	Member

(viii) Secretary, Finance Department or his nominee — Member

(ix) Secretary, Revenue Department or his nominee — Member

(x) Six other non-official members half of whom shall be elected by the Assembly Member and the rest shall be nominated by the State Government.

(xi) Such member of representatives of Local Authorities falling within the area as may be covered by the Master Plan not exceeding two as may be co-opted by the Council by notification, published in the Official Gazette.

(2) Five of the members attending any meeting of the Council shall form the quorum for the purpose of transacting the business of that meeting of the Council.

(3) All members of the Council including the co-opted members shall have one vote each and the Chairman shall have a casting vote in case of equality of division, in addition to his own vote.

(4) Nothing done by the Council on its meeting shall be held to be invalid because of any vacancy in the seats of the nominated or elected members or the absence of any of the members for any reason whatsoever.

(5) The Chairman shall preside over the meetings of the Advisory Council and in his absence the members present shall elect one among themselves to be the president for that particular meeting.

4. Resignation of non-official members – Any non-official member may at any time resign his office, provided that his resignation shall not take effect until accepted by the State Government.

5. Term of office – The term of office of any non-official member shall ordinary be three years: Provided that in case of the members representing the Legislature or Local Authorities, their terms of office shall terminate as soon as they cease to be members of such Legislature or Local Authority as the case may be.

6. Commencement of the term of office of non-official members:

(1) The term of office of non-official members shall commence on such date as may be notified in this behalf by the State Government.

(2) A person ceasing to be member by reason of the expiry of his term of office as described in section 5, shall be eligible for re-nomination or re-election.

7. Removal of non-official member – The State Government may remove from the Council any member who:

(a) refuse to act, or becomes incapable of acting or absents himself from three consecutive meetings of the Council and is unable to explain such absence to the satisfaction of the Council; or

(b) has to flagrantly abused in any manner his position as a member of the Council as to render his continuance detrimental to the public interest:

Provided that when the State Government proposes to take action under the foregoing provisions of this section, an opportunity of explanation shall be given to the member concerned and when such action is taken, the reasons thereof shall be placed or recorded.

8. Filling of casual vacancies

(1) When the place of a member nominated by the State Government becomes vacant by his resignation, removal or death, the State Government shall appoint a person to fill the vacancy.

(2) When the place of a member elected or co-opted becomes vacant, he shall be elected or co-opted by the Legislature or the Council as the case may be.

(3) The term of office of a member nominated or elected or co-opted, as the case may be, under sub-section (1) and (2) shall be the reminder of the term of office of the member in whose place he has been nominated or elected or co-opted.

CHAPTER IIA: CONSTITUTION OF THE DEVELOPMENT AUTHORITY (Inserted by Amendment 24 November, 1962)

8A. Constitution of the Authority

(1) The State Government may, by notification in the Official Gazette, constitute for the purpose of this Act, an Authority to be called "The —— Development Authority" (hereinafter referred to as the Authority) with justification over such area as may be specified in the said notification.

Provided that if the State Government is of opinion that in the exigencies of public service it is necessary to do so it may, instead of constituting the Authority, appoint an Administrator to exercise all the powers of the Development Authority under this Act. (*May 1, 1985 Amendment*)

The Administrator so appointed shall be deemed to be the Development Authority constituted under this Act and shall hold office during the pleasure of the Governor. *(May 1, 1985 Amendment)*

(2) The Authority shall be a body corporate having perpetual succession and a common seal with power to acquire, hold and dispose of properties both moveable and immoveable and to enter into any agreement and shall by the said name sue and be sued.

8B. Composition of the Authority

(1) The Authority shall consist of the following members, namely:

(a) A Chairman to be appointed by the State Government;

(b) Engineer-in-chief of the Authority to be appointed by the State Government;

(c) Town Planning Officer of the Authority to be appointed by the State Government who shall be the Member-Secretary of the Authority; *(May 1, 1985 Amendment)*

(d) Finance Officer to be appointed by the State Government;

(e) Deputy Commissioner or Sub-divisional Officer, as the case may be;

(f) Chairman or Chairmen of the local Authority or Authorities covered by the Master Plan;

(g) One member representing Commerce and Industry (Private Sector) to be nominated by the State Government;

(h) One member representing the Railways, to be nominated by the State Government;

(i) One member representing Industry (Public Sector) to be nominated by the State Government;

(j) One person each from the local authorities covered by Master Plan to be elected by the members at a meeting from amongst them.

(k) Director, Town and Country Planning Department or his nominee; *(May 1, 1985 Insertion)*

(l) Chief Engineer, P.W.D. (Roads and Buildings) or his nominee; *(May 1, 1985 Insertion)*

(m) Chief Public Health Engineer or his nominee; *(May 1, 1985 Insertion)*

(n) Local Member or Members of the Assam Legislative Assembly covered by the Master Plan Area. *(May 1, 1985 Insertion)*

(2) Notification of members – The name of the members elected and appointed shall be published in the Official Gazette.

(3) Disqualification for election or appointment as member – A person shall be disqualified for appointment, nomination or election as a member, if he

(a) has been convicted of any offence involving moral turpitude;

(b) is an applicant to be adjudicated as a bankrupt or insolvent or is an uncertificated bankrupt or undischarged insolvent;

(c) holds any office of profit under the Authority except those mentioned in clauses (a),(b),(c) and (d) of sub-section (1);

(d) has directly or indirectly, by himself or by any partner, any share or interest, in any contract or employment with by, or on behalf of, the Authority; or

(e) is a Director, or a Secretary, Manager or other salaried Officer of any incorporated company which has any share or interest in any contract or employment, with, by, or on behalf of the Authority.

(4) Removal of members – The State Government may remove from the Authority any member including the Chairman who

(a) refuses to act or becomes incapable of acting or absents himself from three consecutive meetings of the Authority and is unable to explain such absence to the satisfaction of the Authority;

(b) has so flagrantly abused in any manner his position as a member of the Authority as to render his continuance detrimental to the public interest; provided that when the State Government proposes to take any action under any of the above provisions, an opportunity shall be given to the member concerned should not be taken against him;

(c) ceases to be a member of the local authority from which he was elected;

(5) A member removed under clauses (a) and (b) of sub-section (4) all not to be eligible for re-appointment or re-election, as the case may be.

8C. Term of office and conditions of service of the Chairman and members of the Authority

(1) The term of office and conditions of service of the Chairman and members of the Authority shall be such as may be prescribed and they shall be entitled to receive such salaries and allowances as may be fixed by the State Government.

(2) The Chairman or any member may resign his membership of the Authority by giving notice in writing to the State Government and on the resignation being accepted by the State Government, he shall cease to be a member of the Authority.

(3) Any vacancy created by resignation or removal shall be filled by fresh appointment or nomination by the State Government, or by election, as the case may be.

8D. Functions and power of the Authority – Subject to the provisions of this Act, rules and directions of the State Government, the functions of the Authority shall be to promote and secure the development of the area according to the Master Plan and for that purpose it may carry out or cause to be carried out surveys of the area and to prepare report or reports of such survey, and to perform any other function which is supplemental incidental or consequential to any of the functions aforesaid or which may be prescribed.

8E. Meeting of the Authority

(1) Each Authority shall subject to the provisions of sub-sections (2) and (3) observe such procedure in regard to the transaction of business at its meeting, as may be prescribed by by-laws to be framed under section 74 of this Act.

(2) The Chairman or in his absence any member chosen by the members from amongst themselves, shall preside at a particular meeting of the Authority.

(3) All questions of the meeting of the Authority shall be decided a majority of the votes of the members present and voting and in the case of an equality of votes, the person presiding shall have a second or casting vote.

(4) Nothing done by the Authority in its meeting shall be held to be invalid because of any vacancy in the seats of the appointed, nominated or elected members or the absence of any of the members for any reason whatever.

(5) Minutes shall be kept of the names of the members present and of the proceedings at each meeting in a book to be kept for this purpose, which shall be signed at the next ensuing meeting by the person presiding at such meeting and shall be open to inspection by any member during office hours.

8EE. Power of chairman – The Chairman shall, for the transaction of the business connected with this Act, or for the purpose of making any order authorized thereby, exercise all the powers vested by this Act in the Authority: *(insertion 3rd December, 1964)* Provided that the Chairman shall not act in opposition to, or in contravention of any order of the Authority at a meeting, or exercise any power, which is directed to be exercised by the Authority at a meeting.

8F. Temporary association of person with the Authority for particular purposes

(1) The Authority may associate with itself in such manner and for such purposes as may be prescribed by rules any person whose assistance or advice it may desire in performing any of its functions under this Act.

(2) Any person associated with it by the Authority under sub-section (1) for any purpose shall have a right to take part in the discussions of the Authority relevant to that purpose but shall not have a right to vote at a meeting and shall not be a member for any other purpose.

8G. Staff of the Authority

(1) Subject to such control and restrictions as may be prescribed by rules, the Authority may appoint such number of officers and employees as may be necessary for the efficient performance of its functions and may determine their designations and grades.

(2) The officers and employees of the Authority shall be entitled to receive such salaries and allowances, if any, as may be fixed by the Authority and shall be governed by such terms and conditions of service as may be determined by rules and regulations made in this behalf.

8H. The Authority may delegate all or any of its power under this Act to any officer, subject such conditions, if any, as may be specified by the Authority. *(insertion 1st of May, 1985)*

CHAPTER III: MASTER PLAN

9. Preparation of Master Plan – A Master Plan hereinafter referred to as "Plan" in this Act for the development of any area within the State which the State Government may consider necessary, shall be drawn up by the Director in consultation with the local authority/authorities concerned and submitted to the State Government for examination and approval.

10. Publication of the Master Plan

    (1) On receiving the Plan and the Zoning Regulation from the Director, the State Government shall have them, as soon as may be, published in the Official Gazette, in some local news paper and in the locality in the manner prescribed and deemed to be required for wide and sufficient publicity in the locality inviting public opinion and objection, if any, to be submitted within a period not more than two months.

    (2) After considering all objections, suggestions and representations that may have been received, and after getting the advise of the Council, the State Government shall have the plan finally prepared by the Director and adopt the plan.

11. Contents of Master Plan and Zoning Regulations – The Master Plan to be prepared as defined under section 9, may include:

    (a) A general land-use plan for residential, commercial, industrial, recreational and public and semi-public purposes;

    (b) Zoning plan;

    (c) Transportation plan including roads, railways, canals etc.;

    (d) Public utilities plan;

    (e) A report giving relevant data and information in respect of proposals in the Plan and any other things which the State Government may deem necessary.

12. Implementation of the Plan – After adoption of the plan and zoning regulation they shall be sent by the State Government for implementation to the Authority constituted under section 8A.

13. Restriction of use of land and buildings thereon after publication
    (1) The plan as adopted by the State Government shall be published as prescribed in Section 10, and after such publication no person shall use any land, sub-divide any land by transfer, by way of gift shall, partition or any other manner the whole or any part of the land or set up any new structure on any land covered by the plan or change the existing structure of any building or use of any building or land within the area except with the permission of the Authority on a written application submitted for that purpose and on payment of such fees as may be prescribed by by-laws framed by the Authority in this behalf. *(May 1, 1985 Amendment)*.
    (2) Each such application shall be accompanied by a plan drawn to scale showing the actual dimension of the parcel of the land and the building to be built upon it, the site and the position of the building to be erected and in case of alteration in the use of structure of the building or land, the nature and the extent of such alteration.
    (3) The Authority may also call for such other information, as it may deem necessary to examine the application.
    (4) The Authority shall not refuse the permission except on the ground of contravention of proposal contained in the Plan or the Regulations and unless the permission has been refused within a period of one month from receipt of the application or such other information as may be called for by the Authority under sub-section (3), it shall be presumed that the permission has been given.

13A. Prohibition of registration in certain cases: Where any deed or document required to be registered under the Indian Registration Act, 1908 (Act No. XVI of 1908), purports to subdivide any land covered by the Plan, no registering officer shall register any such document unless the party presenting the deed or document for registration produces a No Objection Certificate from the Authority to the effect that the Authority has no objection to the registration of such deed or document.

14. Power of the State Government to modify the Plan and the Zoning Regulation: The State Government may review the Plan and the Zoning Regulations, from time to time, in such manner and in such procedure as followed for the preparation and approval of the original plan and the Regulations.

CHAPTER IV: DEVELOPMENT SCHEME

15. Preparation of Development Scheme:
    (1) After the commencement of the Act, the Authority may, by notification in the Official Gazette, declare any area to be a scheme area and shall

thereafter prepare a scheme. Where no Authority has been constituted, the State Government may, by notification in the Official Gazette, declare any area to be a scheme area and the Director shall thereafter prepare a scheme.

(2) Not withstanding anything contained in sub-section (1), the State Government may, after making such enquiry as they may deem necessary by notification in the Official Gazette, direct any local authority to prepare, publish and submit for their sanction before an appointed date a scheme under this section for an area specified in such notification.

(3) While preparing the scheme, the Authority, the Director or the local authority, as the case may be, shall issue a notice inviting the names of all the claimants of any interest on any land or building within the area under the scheme to be submitted within a period not more than one month.

(4) Save as provided in this Act, the Authority, Director or local authority shall not undertake or carry out any development of land in any area which is not a scheme area.

(5) After the commencement of this Act, no development of land shall be undertaken or carried out in the scheme area by any person or body of persons except in the manner prescribed under section 13 of this Act.

16. Publication of the Development Scheme:

(1) The Authority, the Director or the local authority, as the case may be, shall have the scheme and the report and the names of all the claimants published in the manner prescribed under sub-section (1) of Section 10 and have a copy of them served on all persons who preferred claims under sub-section (3) of Section 15, inviting objections to be filled within a period not more than two months.

(2) After the expiry of the aforesaid period, the Authority, the Director or the local authority, as the case may be, shall examine the scheme in the light of such objection giving sufficient opportunity for hearing to all such interested persons who have filed objections and demanded a hearing in the manner prescribed, and shall approve or refuse to approve or approve with such modifications as it may deem necessary, for the implementation of the scheme and for imposing for that purpose reasonable restrictions in the use of land and building within the area.

(3) After the Authority, the Director or the local authority, as the case may be, has adopted the scheme, it shall be forwarded to the State Government for its approval and sanction, if so required under any rule prescribed, otherwise the scheme will come into force from the date the scheme is adopted.

17. Implementation of the Development Scheme: No person shall within any area where a scheme has come into force erect or proceed with any building or work or remove or alter or make addition or make any substantial repair to a building or a part of it, a compound wall or any drainage work or remove any earth or change the use of any land or building except on permission of the authority on application submitted for the purpose. Unless the permission has been refused within one month from the date of receipt of the application it shall be presumed that the permission has been given.
18. Scope of the Development Scheme:
    (1) A scheme may be made in accordance with the provisions of the Act in respect of any land which is:
        (a) in the course of development,
        (b) likely to be used for building purpose, or
        (c) already built upon

        Explanation: The expression "Land likely to be used for building purposes" shall include any land likely to be used as, or for the purpose of providing open space, roads, streets, parks, pleasure or recreational grounds, parking spaces or for the purpose of executing any work upon or under the land incidental to a scheme, whether in the nature of a building work or not.
    (2) Such scheme may make provisions for any of the following matters:
        (a) the laying out or re-laying out of land either vacant or already built upon;
        (b) the filling up or reclamation of low-lying swamp or unhealthy areas or leveling up of land;
        (c) lay out of new streets or roads, construction, diversion, extension, alteration, improvement and stopping up streets, road and communications;
        (d) the construction alteration and removal of buildings, bridges and other structures;
        (e) the allotment of reservation of land for roads, open spaces, gardens, recreation grounds, schools, markets, industrial and commercial activities, green belt and dairies, transport facilities and public purpose of all kinds;
        (f) drainage inclusive sewerage, surface or sub-soil drainage and sewage disposal;
        (g) lighting;
        (h) water supply;

(i) the preservation of objects of historical importance or natural beauty and of buildings actually used for religious purpose;

(j) the imposition of conditions and restrictions in regard to the open space to be maintained about buildings, the percentage of building area for a plot, the number, height and character of buildings allowed in specified areas, the purposes to which buildings or specified areas may or may not be appropriate, the subdivision of plots, the discontinuance of objectionable uses of land in any area in reasonable periods, parking space and loading and unloading space for any building and the size of projections and advertisement signs;

(k) the suspension, so far as may be necessary for the proper carrying out of the scheme, of any rule, bye-law, regulation, notification or order made or issued under any Act of the State Legislature or any of the Acts which the State Legislature is competent to amend;

(l) such other matter not inconsistent with the objects of this Act.

(3) The draft scheme shall contain the following particulars:

(a) the area, ownership and tenure of each original plot;

(b) the land allotted or reserved under clause (e) of sub-section (2) of Section 13 with a general indication of the uses to which such land is to be put and the terms and conditions subjects to which such land is to be put to such cases;

(c) the extent to which it is proposed to alter the boundaries of original plots;

(d) as estimate of the net cost of the scheme;

(e) a full description of all details of the scheme under such clause of sub-section (2) of Section 18, as may be applicable;

(f) the laying out or re-laying out of land either vacant or already built upon;

(g) the filling up or reclamation of low-lying swamp or unhealthy areas or leveling up of land; and

(h) any other prescribed particulars.

(4) In the scheme the site size and shape of every reconstituted plot shall be determined, so far as may be, to render it suitable for building purposes and where the plot is already built upon, to ensure that the building as far as possible, complies with the provisions of the scheme as regards spaces.

(5) In order to render original plots more suitable for building purposes the scheme may contain proposals:

(a) to form a reconstituted plot by the alteration of the boundaries of an original plot;

(b) to provide with the consent of the owner that two or more original plots each of which is held in one ownership in severalty or in joint ownership, shall thereafter, with or without alteration of boundaries be held in ownership in common as a reconstituted plot.

(6) The scheme shall include all such provisions as the Authority may think necessary for carrying out the objects of the Act including the following matters:

(a) the laying out or re-laying out of land, either vacant or already built upon;

(b) the filling up or reclamation of low-lying swamp or unhealthy areas or leveling up of land;

(c) lay out of new streets or roads, construction diversion, extension, alteration, improvement and stopping up of streets, roads and communications;

(d) the construction, alterations and removal of building, bridges and other structures;

(e) the allotment of reservation of land for roads, open spaces, gardens, recreation grounds, schools, markets, industrial and commercial activities, green belts and dairies, transport facilities and public purposes of all other kinds;

(f) drainage inclusive of sewerage, surface or sub-soil drainage and sewage disposal;

(g) lighting;

(h) water supply;

(i) the preservation of objects of historical importance or natural beauty and of buildings actually used for religious purposes.

19. Amendments and alterations of the Development Scheme:

(1) If after the final scheme has come into force, the Authority considers that that the scheme is defective on account of an error or irregularities or for any other reason, it shall refer to the State Government to modify or withdraw the scheme and to publish the modified or withdrawn scheme in the manner prescribed in sub-section (1) of Section 10.

(2) The modification of the scheme shall state every amendment proposed to be made in the scheme and if any such amendment relates to matter specified in any or all of the clauses (a) to (l) of sub-section (2) of Section

18, the modification shall also contain such other particulars as may be found necessary by the Authority.

(3) The variation shall be open to inspection by the public at the office of the Local Body or Bodies as prescribed, covering the area during office hours.

(4) Within one month of the date of publication of the modification, any person affected thereby may communicate in writing his objection to the Authority.

(5) After receiving the objection under sub-section (4) above, the Authority may, after making such enquiry as it may think fit, approve the proposed modification with or without any further modification thereof.

(6) Such modification shall take effect as if it were incorporated in the scheme from the date of its modification.

(7) The Authority shall thereafter submit the modified scheme to the State Government for sanction. The modified scheme shall be published after sanction as prescribed in sub-section (1) of Section 10.

20. Power to revoke the Development Scheme:

(1) Notwithstanding anything contained in Section 19, a scheme may at any time be modified or revoked by a subsequent scheme made, published and sanctioned in accordance with this Act.

(2) The State Government, at its own initiative or on the application of the Authority may at any time, by a notification in the Official Gazette revoke a scheme, if it is satisfied under the special circumstance of the case the scheme shall be revoked:

Provided that where revocation or modification is ordered by Government after people partially or wholly implemented a scheme, compensation should be paid for the necessary alterations in the manner prescribed.

21. Power of the Authority to impose restrictions: For the purpose of the Master Plan, the Land-use and Zoning Regulation and the Scheme, the Authority may impose reasonable restrictions on the use of the land and building including the regulating of the open space to be maintained around the building or buildings, the percentage of the plot area to be covered by building or buildings, the number of building or buildings on each plot, height and character of building or buildings allowed in specific areas, the purpose for which building or buildings of specified areas may or may not be used, the subdivision of plots, parking space and loading and unloading space for any building and the sizes of projections and such other matters not inconsistent with the objects of this Act.

CHAPTER V: STREETS AND LAND SUBDIVISIONS

22. Width of public streets:
    (1) The Authority shall, from time to time with the sanction of the State Government specify the minimum width of different classes of public streets according to the nature of the traffic likely to be carried there, the localities in which they are situated, the heights up to which buildings abutting thereon may be erected and other similar considerations.
    (2) The width of a new public street shall not be less than that prescribed in subsection (1), or that shown on the Master Plan for the class to which it belongs in areas for which Master Plan has been prepared.
23. Power to prescribe street line: The Authority may prescribe a line on one or both sides of any public street, provided a public notice of the proposal has been issued by the Authority in the prescribed manner. No person shall construct or reconstruct any portion of any building on land within the prescribed new street line.
24. Setting back buildings to the prescribed street line:
    (1) If any building or any part of a building on a public street is within such line of the street, the Authority may require such building to be set back to the prescribed line, whenever it is proposed:
        (a) to re-build such building or to take down such building,
        (b) to remove, reconstruct or make any addition to or structural alteration in any portion of such building which is within the regular line of the street.
    (2) When any building or any part thereof within the prescribed line of the street falls down or is burnt down or is taken down, under the provisions of this Act or otherwise, the Authority may at once take possession of the portion of land within the prescribed line of the street previously occupied by the said building and if necessary, clear the same.
    (3) Land acquired under the foregoing sub-sections shall henceforward be deemed to be a part of the public street.
25. Acquisition of land within the line of street: If any private land whether open or enclosed lies, within the prescribed line of a public street and is not occupied by a building or, if a platform, verandah, steps, compound wall, hedge, or fence or other structure, is within the line of such street the Authority may, after giving the owner of the land or building a notice of the intention to do so, take possession of the said land with its enclosing wall, hedge or fence, if any, or the said platform, verandah, steps or such other structure as aforesaid or of the

portion of the said platform, verandah, steps or other such structure as aforesaid which is within the prescribed line of the street.

26. Acquisition of the remaining part of building and land after their portions within a prescribed line of the street are acquired: If a building or land is partly within the prescribed line of a public street and if the Authority is satisfied that the land remaining after the exclusion of the portion within the said line will not be suitable or fit for construction of independent building, the Authority shall acquire the remaining portion of the land if so desired by the owner.

27. Subdivision of private land:

    (1) Every person who intends to sub-divide any plot of land within the Master Plan Area shall give notice to the Authority of his said intention and such notice shall be accompanied by the plans and statements in triplicate.

    (2) All plans for subdivision of land shall be in accordance with the standards prescribed by the State Government.

28. Plans accompanying notice: A layout plan drawn to a suitable scale and containing the following information shall accompany the notice given under Section 27:

    (a) The location of the land,

    (b) The boundaries of the proposed land shown on the map, and sufficient description to define the same,

    (c) Name and address of the owner of the land,

    (d) Location, name and present width of the adjacent roads and lanes,

    (e) The major physical characteristics of the land proposed to be sub-divided, including topography, the approximate location and width of any water course and location of any areas subject to inundation or flood,

    (f) The complete layout of the proposed subdivision showing the location and widths of all the proposed streets, dimensions and uses of all the plots,

    (g) The locations of all drains, sewers and other utilities,

    (h) Building lines permissible,

    (i) Scale and north line,

    (j) Key plan.

29. Sanction with or without modification or refusal.

    (1) The Authority may either grant or refuse the approval in the plans or may approve them with such modifications as it may deem fit and thereupon shall communicate its decision to the person giving the notice within three months from the date of the notice.

(2) No person shall be allowed to construct a building on any plot of land, the subdivision of which has not been previously approved by the Authority.

30. Layout not according to plan: Should the Authority determine at any stage that the layout or the construction is not proceeding according to the sanctioned plan or is in violation of any provisions of this Act, it shall serve a notice on the applicant requiring him to stay further execution until correction has been effected in accordance with the approved plan.

30A. Power to stop development. *(May 1, 1985 insertion)*

(1) Where any development in any area has been commenced in contravention of the Master Plan or Development Scheme or without the permission, approval or sanction referred to in Section 29 or in contravention of any conditions subject to which such permission, approval or sanction has been granted, the Authority may, in addition to any prosecution that may be instituted under this Act, make and order requiring the development to be discontinued on and from the date of the service of the order and such order shall be complied with accordingly.

(2) Where such development is not discontinued in compliance with the order under sub-section (1). The Authority may require any Police Officer not below the rank of Sub-Inspector of Police to remove the person by whom the development has been commenced including all his assistants and workmen from the place of development within such time as may be specified in the requisition and such Police Officer shall comply with the requisition accordingly.

(3) After the requisition under sub-section (2) has been complied with, the Authority may depute by a written order a Police Officer or an officer or an employee or the Authority to keep a watch on the place to ensure that the development is not continued.

(4) The provisions of this Section shall be in addition to and not in derogation of any other provisions relating to stoppage of building operations contained in any other law for the time being in force.

30B. Power of demolition of building. *(May 1, 1985 insertion)*

(1) Where any development has been commenced or is being carried on or has been completer in contravention of the Master Plan or Development Scheme or with out the permission, approval or sanction referred to in Section 29 of this Act or in contravention of any conditions subject to which such permission, approval or sanction has been granted, the Authority may, in addition to any prosecution that may be instituted under this Act make an order directing that such development shall be removed

by demolition, filling or otherwise by the owner, occupier, manager or by any person at whose instance the development has been commenced or is being carried out or has been completed within such period not being less than five days and more than thirty days from the date on which a copy of the order of removal with brief statement of the reasons thereof has been delivered to the owner, occupier and manager or the person at whose instance the development has been commenced or is being carried out or has been completed as may be specified in the order and on his failure to comply with the order, the Authority may remove or cause to be removed the development and the expenses of such removal shall be recovered from the owner occupier, manager or any person at whose instance the development was commenced or was being carried out or was completed as arrears of land revenue provided that no such order shall be made unless the owner, occupier, manager or the person concerned has been given a reasonable opportunity to show cause why the order shall not be made.

(2) The provisions of this section shall be in addition to and not in derogation of any other provision relating to demolition of buildings contained in any other law for the time being in force.

(3) No compensation shall be claimed by any person for any damage which he may sustain in consequence of the removal of any development under this Section or the discontinuance of the development under Section 30A of this Act.

31. Penalty for violation: The Authority will have power to impose fine not exceeding Rs.250 on any person, firm or corporation who violates, disobeys, refuses to comply with, or who resists the enforcement of any of the provisions of this Act. Continuation of the violation shall constitute a separate offence for which a fine of Rs.50 per day may be imposed for the days after the first conviction. An appeal shall lie to the Appellate Authority constituted under this Act.

CHAPTER VI: ACQUISITION OF LAND

32. Power of State Government to acquire land: Where on the representation of the Authority it appears to the State Government that in order to enable it to execute the scheme the scheme it is necessary that land within, adjoining or surrounded by any such area should be acquired, the State Government may in consultation with the Council acquire the land by publishing in the Official Gazette a notice to the effect that the State Government has decided to acquire the land in pursuance of this section.

33. Proceeding for acquisition of land.
    (1) The provisions of the Land Acquisition Act, 1894 (Central Act No. 1 of 1894) shall be applicable for acquisition of land under this Act and the compensation shall be computed under the provisions of the same Act.
    (2) In computing compensation for land acquired, the value will be the market value as prevailed on the 1st of January, 1957.
    (3) The owner of the lands will also be entitled to the reasonable cost of development, if any, made during the period.
    (4) Twenty-five percent increase in value on the date of acquisition of the land.
34. Disposition of land: Subject to the rules made under this Act (- - - - - -)1, the Authority may retain, lease, exchange or otherwise, transfer any land acquired by it under this Act. Provided that in case of lease or transfer the owner will get first priority, if due to acquisition he becomes landless.
35. Provisions of private negotiation before compulsory acquisition.
    (1) The Authority may, in the first instance, make reasonable effort to purchase any land by private negotiation.
    (2) In case of failure to purchase the land by private negotiation within a specified time, the said land shall be compulsorily acquired.
    (3) Nothing in this section shall, however, debar the State Government or a local authority from compulsorily acquiring any land without prior private negotiation.
36. Payment to owner by adjustment: All payment due to be made to any person by the Authority under this act shall so far as possible, be made by an adjustment in respect of the plot concerned or of any other plot in which he has an interest and failing such adjustment shall be paid in cash or in such other way as may be agreed upon by the parties.

CHAPTER VII: COMPENSATION AND BETTERMENT

37. Right to compensation: Any person whose property is injuriously affected in value by the making of a scheme shall, if he makes a claim for the purpose within a period of three months after the date of publication of a notification sanctioning the scheme under Section 16, be entitled to obtain compensation in respect thereof from the Authority.
38. No right to compensation: A person shall not be entitled to obtain compensation under the foregoing section on account of any building erected on or contract made or other thing done with respect to any land within the area included in a scheme after the date of the notification of the scheme under Section 15.

Provided that this provision shall not apply to any building erected, contract made or other thing done in accordance with the permission granted under Section 13 and 17 of this Act.

39. Power of Government to exclude compensation in certain cases.

(1) No compensation shall be payable in respect of any property which may be injuriously affected by putting into operation of any provision of the scheme which:

(a) prescribes the space about buildings; or

(b) limits the number of buildings; or

(c) regulates the size, height, design or external appearance of buildings; or

(d) prohibits or restricts buildings operation permanently or temporarily or the ground that erection of buildings thereon will be likely to be injurious to the health of occupants or the neighbours or likely to cause excessive expenditure of public money in making provision for roads, sewer, water supply or other public services; or

(e) prohibits or restricts the use of land or a building for a purpose which may involve danger or injury to public hygiene or the health of the occupants or their neighbours or for a purpose which is against the public policy or public morals; or

(f) in the interests of safety, regulates the height and position of proposed walls, and building fences or hedges near the corner or bends of roads; or

(g) in the case of the erection of any building intended to be used for purposes of parking the vehicles.

(2) No compensation shall be payable for refusal of permission to make any alteration in any building which is not in conformity with the use specified in the Plan or in the scheme.

40. Right of owner to require Authority to acquire or purchase land.

(1) The owner of any land which is to be acquired for purpose of a scheme may, at any time, after the scheme by the Government, by a written notice to the authority in the prescribed manner, call upon it to acquire or purchase the land on so far as the land is to be acquired by the State Government or the Authority.

(2) If within six months of the service of the notice under sub-section (1) the land is not purchased or acquisition proceedings are not stated, the scheme, in so far as that land is concerned, shall be deemed to have been withdrawn and all notices and orders in that connection shall lapse.

41. Levy of betterment fee.

(1) Every property which has increased in value due to its inclusion within an area under a plan or a scheme or due to the execution of such schemes shall be charged a betterment fee. Provided that no such fee shall be levied on such public and or building as are used for charitable, religious and educational purposes or for places of non-professional entertainment and recreation.

(2) The betterment fee shall be an amount equal to twenty percent in case of residential holdings so long the original owners use for their residences and equal to fifty percent on case of non residential areas and will be realized in five equal instalments.

Explanation: The increase in value for the purpose of this section shall be the increase in the market prices in between the date on which a notification under sub-section (1) of Section 15 has been issued and the date on which the execution of the scheme has been substantially completed.

42. Appeal.

(1) Any person aggrieved by the decision of the Authority with respect to matters of compensation and betterment fee, may appeal to the Appellate Authority within thirty days of the award.

(2) If the owner of any property objects to the amount of betterment fee determined by the Authority on any ground, he shall also state the amount which, he contents would be correct and may within thirty days of the date on which the determination of his objection or appeal become becomes final by written notice, require the authority to acquire the property together with any building or other works that may exist thereon.

(3) The authority shall thereupon acquire the property.

CHAPTER VIII: APPEALS AND APPELLATE AUTHORITY

43. Appointment of Appellate Authority.

(1) Save as otherwise provided, the State Government shall appoint an Appellate Authority to hear all appeals arising out of the provisions of this Act. The decision of Appellate Authority shall be final.

(2) The person or persons appointed by the State Government as Appellate Authority shall have the qualification of a District Judge, or becoming a member of the Assam Board of Revenue constituted under the Assam Board of Revenue Act 1962, (Assam Act XXI of 1962). The appointment shall be on such terms and conditions as the State Government may decide.

44. Duties of the Appellate Authority.
    (1) The duties and power of the Appellate Authority shall be as follows:
        (a) to hear and decide appeals against the order of the Authority,
        (b) to decide and hear appeals in respect of such other matters and exercise such other powers as may be entrusted to and conferred upon it by the State Government in accordance with the provisions of this Act.
    (2) All appeals to the Appellate Authority shall be filed within a month from the date of the order appealed against. The time required for taking out copies of the order shall be excluded. The Appellate Authority may, however, in its discretion condone such delay in filing appeal for sufficient reasons.
45. Procedure of working of the Appellate Authority.
    (1) The Appellate Authority shall conduct its proceedings in the prescribed manner after giving the opposite party or any one interested in the order appealed against and opportunity of being heard.
    (2) The Appellate Authority may, at any time, call for any extract from any proceedings of the State Government or Authority and call for any return or statement or report concerning or connected with any matter with which the authority has been authorized to deal.
    (3) The Appellate Authority shall have all the power of a Civil Court for the purposes of taking evidence on oath of enforcing the attendance of witnesses including the parties interested or any of them and compelling the production of documents and material objection if considered necessary.
    (4) The Appellate Authority in its discretion may make any orders regarding the cost to be paid by any of the parties to the proceedings and the Appellate Authority shall have full power to determine by whom or out of what property and to what extent such costs are to be paid and the authority shall be bound to execute the orders of the Appellate Authority in accordance with the directions, if any, contained in the order and such costs or amounts awarded by the Appellate Authority shall be realized as arrears of land revenue.
46. Right to appear by recognized agent: Every party to any proceeding before the Appellate Authority shall be entitled to appear either in person or by his recognized agent.
47. Protection of action taken under this Act.

(1) No suit, prosecution or other legal proceedings shall lie against any person for anything which is in good faith done or intended to be done in pursuance of this Act or any order made thereunder.

(2) Save as otherwise expressly provided in this Act, no suit or other proceeding shall lie against the State Government for any damage caused or likely to be caused by anything in good faith done or intended to be in pursuance of this Act or any order made thereunder.

CHAPTER IX: FINANCE

48. Development fund: The receipt of Authority under this Act shall form a separate development fund and all expenditure under this Act or any development scheme thereunder, shall be defrayed out of such fund. No portion of the fund shall, except with the sanction of the Government, be expended for purposes not provided by this Act.

49. Power to borrow: Authority as defined in this Act shall be deemed to be a local authority as defined in the Local Authorities Loans Act, 1914 (Central Act, IX of 1914) for the purpose of borrowing money under that Act, and the making and execution of a plan and scheme shall be deemed to be a work which such local authority is legally authorized to carry out.

50. Grants, advance and loans: The Government may make such grants, advances, and loans to the Authority as the Government may deem necessary for the performance of functions of the Authority under this Act issued all grants.

50A. Levy of fees. *(May 1, 1985 insertion)*

(1) For the purpose of providing and maintaining any amenity, the Development Authority may levy such fees as it may consider necessary which shall be in addition to any fee for the time being Levi able under this Act or any other law in force, in respect of any site or building on the transferee or occupier thereof.

(2) Where any transferee or occupier makes any default in the payment of any fee levied under sub-section (1), the Authority may direct that in addition to the amount of the arrears, a sum not exceeding that amount shall be recovered from the transferee or occupier, as the case may be, by way of penalty.

(3) In case of any default in payment of an amount payable under this Act the outstanding amount in default together with any sum, if any, directed to be paid by way of penalty under sub-section (2) may be recovered from the transferee or occupier as the case may be, in the same manner as arrear of land revenue.

50B. Resumption of site or building. *(May 1, 1985 insertion)*
In case of non-payment of consideration money or any installments thereof on account of the transfer of any site or building or any rent due in respect of the lease of any such site or building or in case of the breach of any other condition or breach of any rules made under the Act, the Authority may if it thinks fit, resume the site or building so transferred and may further forfeit the whole or any part of the money, if any, paid in respect thereof.

50C. Audit of account of the Authority. *(May 1, 1985 insertion)*
The accounts of the Authority shall be subject to audit annually by the Accountant General, Assam. The accounts of the Authority along with the Audit Report shall be placed before the State Legislature.

CHAPTER X: LEGAL PROCEEDINGS

51. Penalty for breach of the provisions of the Master Plan or Scheme.
    (1) When a Master Plan or a scheme has been sanctioned under this Act any person who commits or knowingly permits a breach of any specified provisions of the Master Plan or of the scheme or who neglects or fails to comply with any such provisions shall be punishable under this section.
    (2) In case of any such breach or default the Authority shall send to any such person a notice calling on him to discontinue the breach or cause it to be discontinued or to comply with such provision of the Master Plan or the scheme within a time to be specified in the notice.
    (3) If after such time any such person under sub-section (1) continue to neglect or cause a breach of any specified provision, such persons shall be prosecuted and on conviction by a Magistrate be punishable by any or all of the following:
        (i) with fine which may extend to Rs.500 with or without simple imprisonment not exceeding a period of 2 months;
        (ii) if the breach, neglect or failure continues after such conviction with fine which may extend to Rs.30 for every day during which the breach, neglect or failure continues after such conviction.
52. Power to execute works on failure to comply with notice: If a notice has been given under this Act to a person requiring him to execute a work a work in respect of any property, movable or immovable, or to provide or do or refrain from doing anything within a time specified in the notice and if such person fails to comply with such notice, then the authority may cause such work to be executed or such thing to be provided or done, and may recover all expenses incurred by it on such account from the said person as an arrear of land revenue.

53. Right of occupier to execute works in default of owner: When default is made by the owner of a building or land in the execution of any work required under this Act to be executed by him, the occupier of such building or land may, with the prior approval of the Authority cause such works to be executed, and the expenses thereof shall, in the absence of any contract to the contrary, be paid to him by the owner, or the amount may be deducted out of the rent from time to time becoming due from him to such owner.
54. Procedure upon opposition to execution by occupier.
    (1) If after receiving information of the intention of the owner of any building or land to take any action in respect thereof on compliance with a notice issued under this Act, the occupier refuses to allow such owner to take action, the owner, may apply to a District Magistrate or Subdivisional Officer as the case may be.
    (2) The District Magistrate or Subdivisional Officer upon proof of such refusal may make an order in writing requiring the occupier to allow the owner to execute all such works, with respect to such building or land, as may be necessary for compliance with the notice, and may also, if he thinks fit, order the occupier to pay to the owner the costs relating to such application or order.
    (3) If after the expiry of eight days from the date of the Magistrate's order, the occupier continues to refuse to allow the owner to execute such work, the occupier shall be liable, upon conviction, to a fine which may extend to Rs.30 for every day during which he has so continued to refuse.
    (4) Every owner, during the continuance of such refusal shall be discharged from any liability on account of such breach or default.
55. Recovery of cost of work by the occupier: When the occupier of a building or land in compliance with a notice issued under this Act, executed a work for which the owner of such building or land is responsible, either in pursuance of the contract of tenancy or by law, he shall, in the absence of any contract to the contrary, be entitled to recover from the owner by deduction from the rent payable by him or otherwise the reasonable cost of such work.
56. Penalty for obstructing contractor or removing mark. If any person
    (a) obstructs or assaults any person with whom the authority has entered in to a contract for the performance or execution by such person of his duty or of anything which he is empowered or required to do under this Act; or
    (b) removes any mark set up for the purpose of indicating any level of direction necessary to the execution of works authorized under this Act, shall be punishable with fine which may extend to Rs.500 or with or without simple imprisonment for a term which may extend to two months.

57. Officers under the Act to be public servants: Every officer and servants of authority and every other officer employed by the State Government for the purpose of this Act, shall be deemed to be a public servant within the meaning of Section 21 of the Indian Penal Code (Central Act No. 15 of 1860).

58. Authority for prosecution: Unless otherwise expressly provided, no court shall take cognizance of any offence punishable under this Act, except on the complaint of, or upon information received from, the Authority or some person authorized by the Authority by order in this behalf.

59. Power of Authority to institute proceedings, etc., and to take legal advice: The Authority shall subject to rules framed under this Act have powers to

    (a) institute, defend or withdraw from legal proceedings under this Act;

    (b) compound any offence against this Act, before the matter is referred to the court;

    (c) admit compromise, or withdraw any claim made under this Act and

    (d) obtain such legal advice and assistance as it may from time to time think necessary or expedient to obtain for any of the purposes, referred to in the foregoing clauses of this section for securing the lawful exercise or discharge of any power or duty vested I or imposed upon the Authority or any officer or servant of the Authority.

59A. Power to recover dues as an arrear of land revenue: Any sum recoverable by the Authority under this Act, if not paid on demand, shall be recoverable as an arrear of land revenue.

60. Bar to suits and prosecutions in certain cases.

    (1) No suit, prosecution or other proceeding shall lie against and Authority or any officer or servant thereof or any person acting under their direction or any Government Officer or servant employed for the purposes of this Act for anything which is in good faith done in pursuance of this Act, or any rule thereunder.

    (2) No suit, prosecution or other proceedings shall lie against any officer or servant of the authority or any Government Officer or servant employed for the purposes of this Act for anything done under this Act,

        (a) unless the previous sanction of the State Government has been obtained; and

        (b) until the expiration of two months after notice in writing has been given to the person to be used, clearly stating the cause of action, and the nature of relief sought, etc.

61. Punishment for malicious abuse of powers: Any officer or servant of the Authority or of the Government who willfully or negligently abuse any power

conferred on him by or under this Act, shall be punishable with imprisonment which may extend to six months or with fine which may extend to Rs.500 or with both:

Provided that no prosecution shall be instituted under this section

(a) unless the previous sanction of the State Government has been obtained;

(b) until the expiry of two months notice in writing has been given too the person concerned clearly stating the cause of action and the nature of relief sought, etc.

62. Registration of documents plans, or maps in connection with scheme.

(1) Nothing in the Indian Registration Act, 1908 (Central Act No. 1908) shall be deemed to require the registration of any documents, plan or map prepared, made or sanctioned in connection with a scheme which has come into force.

(2) All such documents, plans and maps relating to the sanctioned scheme shall, for the purpose of Sections 48 and 49 of the Indian Registration Act, 1908 (Central Act of 1908) be deemed to have been and to be registered in accordance with the provisions of that Act:

Provided that documents, plans, and maps relating to the scheme shall be accessible to the public, free of charge in the manner prescribed.

63. Orders under the Act not to be questioned in any Court: No order made in exercise of any power conferred by or under this Act shall be called in question in any court except as provided in this Act.

64. Effect of orders inconsistent with other enactments: Any order made under this Act shall have effect notwithstanding anything inconsistent therewith contained in any enactment other than this Act or any instrument having effect by virtue of any enactment other than this Act.

CHAPTER XI: MISCELLANEOUS PROVISIONS

65. Service of notice: Every notice issued under this Act shall be served as prescribed by rules.

66. Method of giving public notice: Subject to the provisions of this Act, every public notice required under this Act shall be deemed to have been given if it is published in some local newspaper (if any) or a paper of general circulation in the area and posted upon a notice board to be exhibited for public information at the building in which the meetings of the Local Authority are ordinarily held or by publishing it in Official Gazette.

67. Formal defects in assessments and demands: No assessment list or other list, notice or other such document specifying, or purporting to specify with reference to any change, or fee, any person's property, or circumstances shall be invalid only by reason of a clerical or technical mistake in the name, residence, place of business or occupation of the person or in the description of property, thing or circumstances and it shall be sufficient if the person, property, thing or circumstances is described sufficiently for the purpose of identification, and it shall not be necessary to name the owner or occupier of any property liable in respect of the charge.
68. Power and duties of police in respect of offences and assistance to Authority: Every police officer, mauzadar or officer of the Local Authority shall give immediate information to the Authority of an offence to his knowledge which has been committed under this Act, or against any rule, made under this Act and shall be bound to assist all members, officers and servants of the Authority in the exercise of their lawful authority.
69. Decision of disputes between Authorities: Should a dispute arise between the Authority and any other Local Authority on any matter in which they are jointly interested, such dispute shall be referred to the State Government, whose decision shall be final.
70. Power to enter into land for inspection, etc: For the purpose of making or execution of any scheme, the Authority or persons appointed by the State Government, their subordinates and contractors may enter into or upon any land in order
    (a) to make any inspection, survey, measure valuation or enquiry;
    (b) to take levels;
    (c) to dig or bore into the sub-soil;
    (d) to set out boundaries and lines by for works;
    (e) to mark levels, boundaries and lines by marks and cutting trenches; or
    (f) to do any other thing, whenever it is necessary to do so, for any of the purposes of this Act or any rule made or scheme sanctioned hereunder or any scheme which the authority intends to frame hereunder:
    Provided as follows:
        (a) except when it is otherwise specially provided by a rule no such entry shall be made between sunset and sunrise;
        (b) except when it is otherwise specially provided by the rule, no building which is used as a human dwelling shall be so entered unless with the consent of the occupier thereof, without giving, the said occupier at

least 24 hours previous notice in writing of the intention to make such entry;

(c) due regard shall always be had, so far as may be compatible with the exigencies of the purpose for which the entry is made, to the social and religious usages of the occupants of the premises entered.

71. Mode of proof of the records of the Authority: A copy of receipts, application, plan, notice order, entry in a register, or other document in the possession of the Authority shall, if duly certified by the lawful keeper thereof or other person authorized by the Authority in this behalf be received as prima facie evidence of the entry or document and shall be admitted as evidence of the matters and transactions therein recorded in every case where, and to the same extent as, the original entry or document would, if produced, have been admissible to prove such matters.

72. Power of Authority to make agreements: The Authority shall be competent to make any agreement with any person in respect of any matters, which is to be provided for in a scheme and, unless it is otherwise expressly provided therein, such agreement shall take effect on and after the day on which the scheme comes into force.

73. Power of the State Government to make rules.

(1) The State Government may, after previous publication in the Official Gazette, make rule for carrying out the purposes of this Act.

(2) In particular and without prejudice to the generality of the foregoing power, the State Government shall have power to make rules in respect of the following matters:

(i) The manner of publication of the notification regarding scheme, their modifications, variations, revocations, submission and sanction by the State Government.

(ii) Powers that may be delegated to any Authority established under this Act or to any officer.

(iii) Procedure to be adopted for securing co-operation of various Government Departments, the owners or other persons or bodies interested in schemes.

(iv) All matters pertaining to land acquisition including procedure and making of award, compensation and the possession of land by Authority in ordinary and emergent cases.

(v) Calculation, assessment and payment of compensation in respect of property which is injuriously affected within the meaning assigned to it in Section 37 of this Act.

(vi) Calculation, assessment and collection of betterment contribution.

(vii) Procedure of filling, hearing and deciding objections and appeals under the Act and all matters connected therewith.

(viii) The delegation of power to and the duties that shall be discharged by the Director and the matters on which and the manner in which he shall be consulted.

(ix) Matters other than those referred to in foregoing clauses which are expressly or by implication requires or allowed by this Act to be prescribed by rules.

(x) Creation and administration of fund for the purpose of implementing the provisions of this Act.

(3) All rules made under this section shall be laid for not less than fourteen days before the Assam Legislative Assembly as soon as possible, after they are made and shall be subject to such modification as the Legislative Assembly may make during the session in which they are so laid or the session immediately following.

74. Power of the Authority to make bye-laws.

(1) The Authority shall have power to make bye-laws in respect of the matters enumerated under this section and not inconsistent with the rules made by the State Government

(i) land subdivision and lay out of public street,

(ii) width for different classes of public streets according to the nature of traffic to be carried thereon,

(iii) street lanes and setting back of buildings from the regular line of the street,

(iv) zoning regulations prescribing the type or description of building which may or may not be, and the purpose for which a building may or may not be created, in any prescribed area or areas,

(v) regulation and display of advertisement in the interest of amenity, aesthetic, or public safety,

(vi) regulations in any manner not specifically provided for in this Act, the erection of any enclosure, wall, fence, tent or other structure on any land within the limits of the authority.

(vii) time and place and transaction of business of the meeting of the Authority.

(2) The power to make bye-law under this Act shall be subject to the conditions of previous publication.

(3) No such bye-law shall come into force until it is approved by the State Government.

(4) The State Government may cancel their confirmation of any such bye-law and thereupon the bye-law shall cease to have effect.

75. Supersession of the Authority – If, at any time the State government is satisfied that the Authority constituted under Section 8B of this Act is not competent to perform or persistently makes default in the performance of the duties imposed on it by or under this Act or any other law or exceed or abuse its powers it may by notification, stating reasons declare the Authority to be superseded and on such supersession, the proviso to sub-section (1) of Section 8A of this Act shall apply.

Bibliography

American Planning Association, *Modernizing State Planning Statutes: The Growing Smart Working Papers, Volume I & II* (Chicago, American Planning Association, 1996)

American Planning Association, Meck, Stuart, General Editor, two volumes, *Growing Smart Legislative Guidebook: Model Statutes for Planning and the Management of Change* (Chicago, American Planning Association, 2002)

Bhargava, Gopal, *Development of India's Urban Rural & Regional Planning in 21st Century* (New Delhi, Gyan Publishing House, 2001)

Bureau of Indian Standards, *National Building Code of India 1983* (New Delhi, Bureau of Indian Standards, 2001)

Chapin, F, Stuart, Jr., *Urban Land Use Planning* (Urbana, Chicago, & London, University of Illinois Press, 1972)

Ehrlich, Doreen, *The Bauhaus* (New York, The Mallard Press, 1991)

Galantay, Ervin Y., *New Towns: Antiquity to the Present* (New York, George Braziller, 1975)

Gallion, Arthur B. & Eisner, Simon, *The Urban Pattern* (New York, Toronto, and London, D. Van Nostrand Company, Inc., 1963)

Goodman, William I. editor, *Principles and Practice of Urban Planning* (Washington D. C., International City Managers Association, 1968) Also see Butterworths Planning Law Service.

Greenwood, Brian edited, *Butterworths Planning Law Handbook*, Fifth edition (Butterworths, Edinburgh, New Delhi, and other countries, 2000)

Hart, Maureen, *Guide to Sustainable Community Indicators*, Second Edition (P. O. Box 361, North Andover, MA 01845, USA, Hart Environmental Data, 1999)

Hartshorn, Truman A., *Interpreting the City: An Urban Geography*, 2nd Edition (New York, John Wiley & Sons, 1992)

Hoch, Charles J. editor, *The Practice of Local Government Planning*, Third Edition (Washington D.C., International City/County Management Association, 2000)

International Code Council Inc., *2003 International Building Code* (Country Club Hills, IL, USA, 2002)

Isard, Walter, *Methods of Regional Analysis: An Introduction to Regional Science* (New York & London, The Technology Press of MIT, 1960)

Jagmohan, *Island of Truth* (Delhi, Vikas Publishing House Pvt. Ltd. 1978)

Kent, T. J. Jr., *The Urban General Plan* (San Francisco, Chandler Publishing Company, 1964)

Kushner, James A., *Comprehensive Urban Planning Law* (Durham, North Carolina, Carolina Academic Press, 2003)

McHarg, Ian L., *Design with Nature* (Garden City, New York, Doubleday & Company, Inc., 1971)

The McKinsey Quarterly, *Fulfilling India's Promise* (New York, N.Y., McKinsey & Company, 2005)

Quade, E.S., *Analysis for Public Decisions* (New York, American Elsevier Publishing Co., Inc., 1975)

Smith, Herbert H., *The Citizen's Guide to Planning* (Chicago, American Planning Association, 1979)

Soleri, Paolo, *The City in the Image of Man* (Cambridge, MIT Press, 1969)

Sonis, Michael, Bar-Ilan University, Israel, *Central Place Theory after Christaller and Losch: Some Further Explorations* (Paper presented at 45th Congress of the Regional Science Association, August 2005, Amsterdam)

Index